WETHERSFIELD INSTITUTE
Proceedings, 1988

NEWMAN TODAY

Newman Today

Papers Presented at a Conference on
JOHN HENRY CARDINAL NEWMAN

Sponsored by the Wethersfield Institute
New York City, October 14–15, 1988

EDITED, WITH AN INTRODUCTION BY
STANLEY L. JAKI

IGNATIUS PRESS   SAN FRANCISCO

Cover by Riz Boncan Marsella

With ecclesiastical approval
© 1989 Ignatius Press, San Francisco
All rights reserved
ISBN 0–89870–242–9
Library of Congress catalogue number 89–84012
Printed in the United States of America

CONTENTS

STANLEY L. JAKI

INTRODUCTION

Introductions, which are one's first encounter with an author's message, represent his final reflections on it. With first-rate writers the finality can come as a thumping note. Such is the phrase—To be deep in history is to cease to be a Protestant—in Newman's Introduction to his *Essay on the Development of Christian Doctrine*. Twenty years later, in the *Apologia*, Newman did not apologize for being blunt whenever the matter had to be put squarely: "There are but two alternatives, the way to Rome, and the way to Atheism." Nor did he shy away from spelling out plainly the implications for Anglicanism (Protestantism) and Liberalism, which were popular in Victorian England. He described each as a halfway house on one or the other of those ways.

A most important assurance for Newman for speaking time and again in uncompromising terms was the firm voice of the Catholic Church of his time. There were, of course, plenty of ecclesiastical intrigues and power plays. Newman was repeatedly their victim. Time and again the official supports offered to him from his new household of faith proved to be so many halfway houses. He was made to fail as a rector of a new Catholic University in Dublin; he was not made a bishop; he was not to regale English Catholics with a new translation of the Bible; he was forbidden to set up a house of studies in Oxford; he was labeled by some English Catholic careerists in Rome as the most dangerous Catholic in England; last but not least, an English cardinal almost succeeded in cheating him out of being created a cardinal.

Newman bore all these trials with equanimity. He took great

comfort from the fact that even his chief antagonists in the hierarchy were worthy to be called *hierarchoi*, that is, true leaders in all matters truly sacred. Not that Newman would be shaken in his Roman Catholic Faith by a rather different situation prevailing in not a few parts of the Church today. In fact, it was his lengthy contemplation of what he called the "Arian hurricane" that made him first perceive the unique strength of the See of Rome while so many bishops were compromising with theological "insights" as they bartered the patently sacred for the subtly secular. He would see another hurricane in the blaring choruses of uncertain trumpets or the equivocations of various national episcopal conferences about *Humanae vitae* and in their preaching an increasingly social Gospel.

In the eye of the hurricane Newman would see the See of Rome speaking with a consistently firm voice and unperturbed by the surrounding storm, a storm all the more dangerous because largely whipped up by some not so faithful in the household of faith. He would refer to Rome's firm voice as his sole ground if he were to repeat today his phrase that startled London and England in 1850. In that phrase, quoted in full in the essay by Ian T. Ker (p. 136), Newman held high the Catholic Church for holding a single venial sin a far greater calamity than the eventual collapse of the solar system or the possible starvation of many millions on this earth.

A dozen or so years later the Rev. Dr. Kingsley, the Queen's chaplain and literary cheerleader of a virulently chauvinistic establishment, found that phrase a greater threat than the insincerity with which, according to him, Dr. Newman advocated it. Not surprisingly, that phrase was part of Newman's lectures on *Difficulties of Anglicans*. Even Catholic Newmanists who should know better try to be apologetic about those lectures. They prefer to ignore that it was an Anglican, Richard H. Hutton, one present at most of those lectures and the first to come out with a monograph on Newman following his death, who spoke of those lectures as "the first book of Newman's generally read among Protestants in which the measure of his literary power could be adequately taken".

There was, of course, much more to those lectures than a display of literary prowess. Their gist was the remorseless logic whereby a national church is bound to degenerate into a church of secularism and condone sin rather than preach holiness. Such is, of course, a judgment that may seem to return as a boomerang in an age that has witnessed the sacrament of Confession become a near-extinct species in many parts of the Roman Catholic Church. There a legion of theological writers (they do not deserve to be called theologians) keep destroying awareness of the unqualifiedly sinful character of sundry immoral acts by trying to build up "personal" conscience. Newman would remind them of his warning in the *Apologia* about an "awful, never-dying duel" between Authority and Private Judgment. He would refer to the present Pontiff's firm voice as a ground for repeating from those lectures a statement of his that Dr. Kingsley, that great stalwart of a socially respectable "Creed" in which today all morality amounts to advocating liberation theology, singled out as supreme evidence that Dr. Newman was demented. For indeed, only a saint willing to espouse unreservedly the foolishness of the Cross would say, as Newman did:

> Take a mere beggar-woman, lazy, ragged, filthy, and not over-scrupulous of truth—but if she is chaste, and sober, and cheerful, and goes to her religious duties—she will, in the eyes of the Church, have a prospect of heaven, quite closed and refused to the State's pattern-man, the just, the upright, the generous, the honourable, the conscientious, if he be all this, not from a supernatural power—but mere natural virtue.

Whether this statement of Newman made its way into the *Oxford Dictionary of Quotations* for a motive similar to the one nurtured by the Rev. Dr. Kingsley may never be known. It should, however, be known sufficiently well that fashionable Catholic theologians would be the last to quote this and many similar statements of Newman, although they quote him profusely. Indeed, Newman has been turned by them into the chief theological authority for fomenting dissent from all-too-clear statements of the Magisterium.

Awareness of this situation prompted the decision that the Wethersfield Institute Conference of 1988 be devoted to the relevance of Newman and his thought to the prospects and problems of the Roman Catholic Church today. The conference was not to become another of those Newman jamborees that offer but a kaleidoscope of motley views on Newman's thought. His mind ranged, of course, far and wide, and, what is no less significant, he spoke his mind day in and day out. In addition to his many tracts, essays, sermons, and theological monographs, he kept writing letters at an astonishing rate. They are not all contained in the thirty or so large volumes that make him easily the most important epistolarian in English literature.

With such a vast output goes the hazard that Chesterton noted about history: its many data provide ample material for the apparent justification of any claim to be made about it. Newman would see in this a proof of his own remark in the *Essay on Development* that "history is not a creed or a catechism". But he would also warn that any historian merely introduces his own creed or catechism into his reading of history if he is not willing to accept history as a fact "that gives lessons rather than rules". To accept lessons has never been the quality of proud minds, who, on seeing their interpretations of history destroyed by towering facts, are apt to reply with some equivalent of Hegel's defiance of facts: "Then so much the worse for history."

Under no circumstance would Newman, who saw everything in its historical reality, have countenanced historical relativism. The latter is nowadays the support of a theological pluralism in which only fleeting references are made to what is universally valid truth all across history and in respect to the plurality of churches. In this age of often misguided ecumenism, which saw Paul VI decry some Catholic theologians for their resolve to introduce Protestantism into the Church, there is an eerie relevance in Newman's reflection on doctrinal history:

> No one can mistake its general teaching in this matter, whether he accept it or stumble at it. Bold outlines and broad masses of colour rise out of the records of the past. They may be dim, they may be incomplete; but they are definite. And this one thing at least is certain; whatever history teaches, whatever it omits, whatever it exaggerates, whatever it says and unsays, at least the Christianity of history is not Protestantism. If ever there were a safe truth, it is this.

The safety of that truth largely rested in Newman's eyes on the towering facts of Church history that are the saints. As an Anglican, he had eyes for the weight carried by the holiness of Anthony, *the* saint of Arian days, in favor of orthodoxy. Newman's conversion to Catholicism would not loom ever larger had it not been a principal act of his unremitting quest for holiness. For him the true Church's purpose was to generate saints and saintliness. He saw the Roman Catholic Church rise above the flatlands of human history because saints were continually rising within that Church.

It is in this light that one should read these essays. The selection of their topics was made by the advisory board of Wethersfield Institute. While only such Newmanists were invited as speakers who had not previously made a sport of setting up Newman as a *peritus* in theological relativism (be it in the guise of pluralism), they were given full freedom to work out the topics suggested to them. The result proved that diversity of scholarship, taste, and background can be very productive of an instinctive unity of vision and ethos. The Conference had hardly progressed beyond the reading of the first papers when the large audience began to sense a basic message coming through. For each paper contained some rarely quoted statements of Newman that could but have an illuminating and electrifying effect.

Such was the case when Fr. Ford emphasized the all-important difference between modern historians of doctrine and Newman, the historian of doctrinal development. Since the former look at history from below, whereas Newman looked at it from above, they find it impossible to share his view of "the facts of history as ordered by the overarching guidance of Providence at work in both the Church and the world" (p. 35). The view from above alone permits a focusing on the sacred, which in Fr. Chavasse's paper on Newman and the laity comes into prominence through his pointing out that Newman took the sacramental system of the Church for an unfailing means whereby lay Christians grow in holiness: "This picture of the lay Christian in, but not of, the world must have touched and inspired many of Newman's audience and influenced them for good for many years to come" (p. 53).

Next came a relatively short paper, but one rich in data relating to the many facets of the antiliberalism of Newman. A very conservative man with some startlingly liberal views, Newman fought all his life the kind of liberalism for which no religion was essentially better than any other. This pivotal point was certainly in focus as Fr. O'Connell recalled at length a sermon of Newman that contains the phrase acceptable only when holiness is the supreme standard: "[The Pope's] yoke is the yoke of Christ; *he* has the responsibility of his own acts, not we; and to his *Lord* must he render account, not to us" (p. 83). Newman's antiliberalism was indeed a relentless effort on his part to hold secure the high ground of true holiness from where he could see, to recall Fr. O'Connell's concluding quotation, in the spuriously sacred offered by pantheism "the great deceit which awaits the age to come" (p. 91). Here too Newman proved to be a frighteningly accurate prophet. Pantheism sets the tone of a flood of recent books on the universe. Their authors use, or rather abuse, the modern science of cosmology as a pretext for setting up the universe as its own creator and as the supreme object with which man has to develop a mystical symbiosis if he is to have any salvation at all. Pantheism is indeed the subtlest form of the desecration of the sacred.

The desecration is most effectively taking place in terms of what is being thought and acted out in modern university campuses. To compound the tragedy, many Catholic colleges and universities seem to have charted in the 1960s a course that, as argued with vibrant wit by Fr. Rutler, leads in a direction very different from the one that Newman set up as the chief guideline for a truly Catholic university. Newman's vast views on what a Catholic university has to be have as their unifying force his unreserved commitment to the sacred insofar as it is enjoined by the Vicar of Christ. It was that Vicar's command that sustained Newman in a colossal task whenever he felt crushed under its burden. Newman knew "that the idea of a university was not his but the sagacity of an apostle. He was no slave to that authority because he had been freed by it" (p. 116).

The educator Newman was in reality the theologian Newman, who in turn was ultimately a shepherd of souls. But as Fr. Ker's analysis of the manifold aspects of Newman's theology shows, its pastoral orientation has little in common with much of post-Vatican II theology steeped in pastoral concerns. While the latter all too often does not transcend purely natural psychology and sociology, the proper worship of a transcendental God is invariably the overriding concern of Newman the theologian. Indeed, Newman, still an Anglican, voiced suspicion "of any religion that is a people's religion, or an age's religion" (p. 137). In the recent decline of the popularity of the "people of God" as the center of ecclesiology, Newman would undoubtedly see a much-needed reorientation toward ideas with more substance.

That substance is, of course, inseparable in Newman's view from the truly objective foundation of man's holiness or the nature of Justification by faith. No single theological topic was treated by Newman so systematically as this, and he considered the *Lectures on the Doctrine of Justification* his best book. It tells

something of the insensitivity of his times to the truly supernatural that the publication of the *Lectures* hardly created a
stir. That in our times it has been carefully avoided by those
who, in the wake of Vatican II, loudly claim Newman for
themselves tells something of their unease with its principal
thesis. Their claim of doing full justice to human nature is, as
Fr. Morales shows, a far cry from the truly human, and
therefore genuinely divine, perspective in which Newman
treated man's Justification. For him man's real gain in the
process was most realistically supernatural: "It is the very
triumph of God's grace that He enters the heart of man, and
persuades it, and prevails with it, while He changes it. He
violates in nothing that original constitution of mind which
He gave to man: He treats him as man; He leaves him the
liberty of acting this way or that" (p. 161). In that book too
Newman offered a final view that has the impact of a thumping
end note: "Luther found Christians in bondage to their works
and observances; he released them by his doctrine of faith; and
he left them in bondage to their feelings."

When a great intellect turns instinctively to the reality of the
supernaturally sacred in so many different areas of reflection
and action, he clearly must be led by a principle which is
more than merely intellectual. The existential plus in that
intellectuality was emphasized in Fr. Bouyer's reflection on his
studies of Newman. The ultimate nature of that principle is of
course Newman's lifelong quest for holiness. As one close to
the preliminary steps dealing with Newman's canonization,
Fr. Michael Sharkey casts a much-needed light on what may be
the most promising aspect of Newman's life as a witness to
holiness. He was no wonder worker, not even an ascetic. Nor
have significant cures so far been obtained through his intercession. Yet at least one such cure must be registered for his
eventual beatification. At any rate, much will be made by the
promoter of Newman's cause of his relentless emphasis on
holiness as the great aim of all acts of a Christian.

In Newman's case a principal part of that activity was his

apostolate through writing. All his publications reveal a sustained attention to the pursuit of holiness. As the present writer tried to show in the concluding lecture, that pursuit served Newman as a guiding star even in his coming to grip with basic problems of philosophy. Time and again Newman could have run aground as he tried to chart a new course for apologetics in the *Grammar of Assent*. He came repeatedly close to the fateful rocks of empiricism as he emphasized the unique persuasiveness of facts, especially of facts registered by the eye. In a very plain sense too he was a "visionary". He could at times appear a grim nominalist as he poured scorn on universals taken for reified notions. Last but not least, he often struck a phenomenologist note that could seem to amount to a rejection of metaphysics.

Yet there was a force working within him that pulled him back from the edges of an intellectual abyss and secured credibility to his endorsements of universally valid objective truths. The force was Newman's saintly sensitivity to the reality of God's message speaking through the voice of his conscience. His emphasis was always on the objective content of the message carried by that voice and never on his subjective receptivity to it. This is why he could justifiably claim that in spite of his cavalier handling of the universals—the touchstone of truth in all philosophy—he was sincere in upholding the idea of universal truth. This alone should show how far he was from the subjectivism that inevitably sets the tone of relativistic and pluralistic trends in modern Catholic theology.

So much by way of introduction to a set of lectures that have as their aim the showing of what Newman's work and life mean today. Editorial work has been limited to giving essential uniformity to the style of notes. Contributors were free to quote any edition of Newman's works. Throughout the notes *Letters and Diaries* stands for the thirty-one-volume edition of *The Letters and Diaries of John Henry Newman* published under various editors between 1961 and 1984 by Clarendon Press, Oxford, and Thomas Nelson and Sons, London. On perusing the rich material and wealth of incisive reflections offered in this book, its readers should feel grateful to the generosity of Mr. Chauncey Stillman, President of Wethersfield Institute, but above all to his deep commitment to Catholic orthodoxy. All those who were privileged to enjoy his amiability during the previous Wethersfield Institute Conferences felt keen disappointment over his inability to be present. (This turned into a deep sadness when he passed away on January 22, 1989.) Mr. Stillman and the officers and advisory board members of Wethersfield Institute ardently hope that readers of this book become convinced about an all-important point that may paraphrase the first statement of Newman quoted in this Introduction: To be deep in Newman is to cease to be a neo-modernist.

JOHN T. FORD

FAITHFULNESS TO TYPE IN NEWMAN'S "ESSAY ON DEVELOPMENT"

Ours is a time of change. Contrary to our penchant for permanence, change appears to be the rule, while stability seems to be the exception. One, of course, expects such fluidity in the world of fashion, where last year's styles have been discarded and this year's designs will soon be passé. Likewise, one may be resigned to the rapidity of change in the world of technology, where a computer tends to be obsolete before its operator has learned how to use it. In fact, it is hard to think of any area of modern life where change is not a frequent, formidable, and sometimes frustrating experience.

Not even the world of religion, where fidelity and commitment are customarily considered virtues, has escaped the pervasive phenomenon of change. But how do people cope with such changes? Some imitate the world of fashion and change their theology and practice each season. Others abandon their efforts to keep pace with change, like the frustrated computer trainee who turns off the machine and looks for another occupation. But some attempt to find a balance between change and continuity; many of the latter have been fortunate enough to discover a mentor to guide them in their religious pilgrimage: John Henry Newman.

"Change and continuity" were a leitmotiv in Newman's life. His *Apologia pro Vita Sua*, for example, portrays the "history of his religious opinions" as a series of stages:[1] the conventional piety of a middle-class English family where the Bible was read but where religious enthusiasm was suspect;

17

the evangelical fervor prompted by an adolescent conversion experience;[2] the theological inquiry characteristic of an academic environment devoted to the intellectual pursuit of truth; the determined search for an ecclesial community that would afford doctrinal certainty amidst the changing course of history.[3] As he passed through these different stages, Newman's "religious opinions" gradually changed as they were incorporated into a theological vision of the Church's continuity through history.[4] Newman, then, was speaking from his own experience when he wrote in *An Essay on the Development of Christian Doctrine*: "In a higher world it is otherwise, but here below to live is to change, and to be perfect is to have changed often" [I.1.7].[5]

Newman's *Essay on Development* is not only the culmination of the religious journey described in his *Apologia* (though the latter was actually written nearly two decades after the former); the *Essay on Development* is also sort of an *apologia pro ecclesia sua*, which interprets the historical development of the Church's "religious opinions". Moreover, just as change and continuity were a reappearing tension in Newman's personal pilgrimage, change and continuity have been a recurring dialectic throughout the Church's history. In his personal journey, Newman came to differentiate between genuine doctrines and their deceptive counterfeits; by the time he wrote the *Essay on Development*, his lengthy series of separate questions about the legitimacy of specific changes within the Church had been reduced to one central issue: Where does one find the Church of the Apostles today?

Thus, Newman's *Essay* was not intended to be a systematic treatment of the problem of doctrinal development, such as those elaborated in theological monographs in the twentieth century.[6] Rather, Newman's purpose in writing his *Essay* was much more personal and apologetic, the culmination of a decade of inquiry that began with the Oxford Movement in 1833.[7] Newman's questions were historical rather than theoretical: Has the Church of the Apostles continued down to the present? And if so, which Church is that continuation?[8]

In other words, Newman's concern was "not so much that Roman Catholic doctrine corresponded most closely to the teaching of the apostolic Church, but rather that the complex concrete reality of the Roman Catholic Church . . . corresponded more closely than any other claimant to the concrete reality of the Church of the Fathers".[9] Consequently, Newman's *Essay* is not so much a study in comparative dogmatics as an "identity test". As Newman remarked about his *Essay* in a letter to Henry Wilberforce: "If that book is asked, why does its author join the Catholic Church? The answer is, because it is the Church of St. Athanasius and St. Ambrose."[10] Thus, by the time that Newman wrote his *Essay*, his ecclesiological concerns were personal, concrete, and apologetic: Can the contemporary Roman Catholic Church be identified as the continuation of the Church of the Apostles?[11]

To give more than an arbitrary answer to this question, indeed to give an intellectually satisfying response, Newman obviously needed a set of criteria. Instead of using those of other ecclesiologists, Newman devised his own "notes"—seven in number—for distinguishing between authentic doctrinal developments and doctrinal corruptions.[12] While this procedure may seem comparatively routine in our age, which takes doctrinal development for granted, such was not the case in Newman's day. His *Essay* broke new ground in a number of innovative ways.

First of all, Newman's *Essay* was an unexpected *Apologia* in favor of Roman Catholicism in an environment that had long been hostile to Rome—a hostility that Newman himself had previously voiced.[13]

Second, Newman's attitude toward doctrine was different from that of many of his contemporaries: in contrast to those theologians who considered "religion a mere sentiment", Newman acknowledged that "dogma has been the fundamental principle of my religion"; in contrast to those religious leaders who considered the Church primarily as a spiritual reality, Newman insisted that "there was a visible Church, with

sacraments and rites which are the channels of invisible grace";
and in contrast to those ecclesiastics who considered the structures of the Church a matter of political convenience, Newman
defended both the "Episcopal system" and "the authority of
Bishops".[14]

Third, Newman's *Essay* presented a significantly original
approach to the problem of doctrinal development. In contrast
to those theologians who discounted the doctrinal differences
between churches as merely semantic variations or cultural
modifications, Newman was convinced that what was at stake
was the Truth of the Gospel. Yet, while Newman took
seriously both doctrines and their development, he also recognized that doctrinal developments have not been uniform, but
of different "kinds":

> Taking the Incarnation as its central doctrine, the Episcopate, as
> taught by St. Ignatius, will be an instance of political develop-
> ment, the *Theotokos* of logical, the determination of the date of
> our Lord's birth of historical, the Holy Eucharist of moral, and
> the Athanasian Creed of metaphysical [I.2.10].

Insofar as Newman's use of these different "kinds" of
development was innovative, he needed to elaborate new
criteria for distinguishing between authentic and spurious
developments. Consequently, in contrast to previous theologians, who derived their "notes" from biblical texts or
creedal statements, Newman's "notes" were original not only
in themselves but also in their derivation from categories
discernible in the world about us.[15]

While it is unclear how Newman arrived at these "notes" or
how these seven notes are to be aligned with the five "kinds"
of development,[16] it is clear that these "notes" collectively
constitute an "identity test": they are intended to show that the
Roman Catholic Church can be identified as the continuation
of the Church of the early Christians, the continuation of the
Church of the Patristic age, the continuation of the Church of
the Councils. Such a purpose is unequivocally clear in the case

of the note to which Newman gave the most prominent treatment, the note to whose application he devoted almost as much space as that given to the application of the other six notes combined: "preservation of type".

Preservation of Type

Newman's *Essay* discusses the "preservation of type" in two different places: the first is a brief description of the note itself (Chapter V); the second is a lengthy discussion of the note's application (Chapter VI).

Newman initiates his general description by pointing out that this note "is readily suggested by the analogy of physical growth" [V.1.1]. "Preservation of type", however, is found not only among growing organisms but also within institutions, where "every calling or office has its own type, which those who fill it are bound to maintain"; such a type is clearly discernible insofar as deviation "from the type in any material point is to relinquish the calling", as in the case of unfaithful priests and corrupt magistrates [V.1.2]. Such examples suggest that a "type" may be easiest to identify from its deviations.

Newman in fact explicitly warns that external appearances can be deceptive; for example, a

> popular leader may go through a variety of professions, he may court parties and break with them, he may contradict himself in words, and undo his own measures, yet there may be a steady fulfilment of certain objects, or adherence to certain plain doctrines, which gives a unity to his career, and impresses on beholders an image of directness and large consistency which shows a fidelity to his type from first to last [V.1.3].

Accordingly, Newman insists that while "this unity of type" is "characteristic . . . of faithful developments", nonetheless, it "must not be pressed to the extent of denying all variation, nay considerable alteration of proportion and relation, as time goes on, in the parts or aspects of an idea". Thus, for Newman, "preservation of type" is compatible with "great changes in outward appearance" [V.1.4].

Such "great changes" are obvious in the two organic examples that Newman mentions in this paragraph: the change from an egg to a "fledged bird" and from a grub to a butterfly [V.1.4]. "More subtle still and mysterious are the variations which are consistent or not inconsistent with identity in political and religious developments" [V.1.5]. The historical instances that Newman cites not only corroborate his contention that variations are subtle and mysterious; they also (though perhaps unintentionally) suggest that sometimes there is only a fine line differentiating development and corruption.

For example, after observing that "the political doctrines of the modern Tory resemble those of the primitive Whig", Newman concludes that "few will deny that the Whig and Tory characters have each a discriminating type" [V.1.5]. While it is comparatively easy to think of other examples where the liberal positions of one generation are accepted by the next generation's conservatives, what is not so clear is whether these conservatives have simply liberalized their platform or whether they have really changed their type.

Equally puzzling is Newman's contention that "Calvinism has changed into Unitarianism: yet this need not be called a corruption, even if it be not, strictly speaking, a development" [V.1.5]. Historically, however, Calvinism was originally Trinitarian; Unitarianism would thus seem to be a corruption of authentic Calvinism.[17] One wonders, in this example, whether Newman's antipathy toward the continental reformers may have gotten the best of him;[18] at least in this instance, one is left wondering how "preservation of type" can be utilized as an evaluative note.

Newman is more successful in showing that "ideas may remain, when the expression of them is indefinitely varied"; nonetheless, there appears to be a gap between the seminal form of a "type" and its later manifestations. For example, after observing that "it must have been an extreme shock to St. Peter to be told he must slay and eat beasts, unclean as well as clean", Newman notes that "such a command was implied already in that faith which he [Peter] held and taught" (Acts 10:10–17). At first sight, such an observation seems more a credit to Peter's faith than beneficial to understanding how such "an extreme shock" is an instance of "preservation of type" [V.1.7]. Just as the type of bird may not be clear unless and until it hatches from the egg, so it may not be clear in the initial stage of development what the "type" is.

This difficulty in understanding Newman's general description of the "preservation of type" is compounded by his observation that "real perversions and corruptions are often not so unlike externally to the doctrine from which they come as are the changes which are consistent with it and true developments" [V.1.8]. Newman feels that this was the case when "Rome changed from a republic to an empire; it was a real alteration of polity, or what may be called a corruption; yet in appearance the change was small", since the external offices and functions were retained; or as Gibbon commented, the empire was "an absolute monarchy disguised by the forms of a commonwealth" [V.1.8].

Readers who expect this example to serve as an argument in favor of retaining external forms as a way of preserving the latent type will be caught short, for Newman points out that "one cause of corruption in religion is the refusal to follow the course of doctrine as it moves on, and an obstinacy in the notions of the past". Then, as if to remove any doubt about the need to accept developments, Newman reminds his readers that "our Lord found His people precisians in their obedience to the letter; He condemned them for not being led on to its spirit, that is, to its developments" [V.1.8].

Newman ends his introductory description of the "first note of a genuine development" with his readers undoubtedly convinced that an idea "does not always bear about it the same external image"; however, readers may be puzzled by Newman's claim that "*unity of type* becomes so much the surer guarantee of the healthiness and soundness of developments, when it is persistently preserved in spite of their number or importance" [V.1.9]. How can one tell which developments really do preserve the original type?

Application of the First Note

To answer such questions, a reader looks with expectation to Newman's lengthy discussion of the "application of the first note of a true development" [Chapter VI]. After observing that "all great ideas are found, as time goes on, to involve much which was not seen at first to belong to them" [VI.0],[19] Newman raises three questions: "How does this apply to Christianity? What is its original type? Has that type been preserved in the developments commonly called Catholic?" [VI.0].

Since it would be impractical to attempt to trace the "original type" through each generation of the Church's history, Newman opts to compare Christianity "as the world once viewed it in its youth" with the way that "the world now views it in its age" [VI.0]. As the point of departure for this comparison, Newman describes early Christianity as it presumably appeared to its pagan contemporaries:

> There is a religious communion claiming a divine commission, and holding all other religious bodies around it heretical or infidel; it is a well-organized, well-disciplined body; it is a sort of secret society, binding together its members by influences and by engagements which it is difficult for strangers to ascertain. It is spread over the known world; it may be weak or insignificant locally, but it is strong on the whole from its continuity; it may be smaller than all other religious bodies together, but is larger than each separately. It is a natural enemy to governments external to itself; it is intolerant and engrossing, and tends to a new modelling of society; it breaks laws, it divides families. It is a gross superstition; it is charged with the foulest crimes; it is

despised by the intellect of the day; it is frightful to the imagination of the many. And there is but one communion such [VI.o].

This rhetorical description is double edged; it represents not only the way that pagans presumably regarded the early Christians but also the way that many of Newman's Anglican contemporaries regarded the Roman Catholic Church.[20]

Newman builds on this description by considering the views of Tacitus, Suetonius, Pliny, and other pagan writers. Aside from demonstrating his familiarity with ancient history, both classical and Christian,[21] this inordinately lengthy treatment provides Newman with a framework for interpretive comments,[22] one of which seems to reflect his experience in the Oxford Movement: "Changes in society are, by a providential appointment, commonly preceded and facilitated by the setting in, of a certain current in men's thoughts and feelings in that direction towards which a change is to be made" [VI.1.3]. Just as he had earlier hoped that the Oxford Movement would aid the Church of England in rediscovering its Catholic roots—an endeavor that was widely rejected by the Anglicans of his day[23]—Newman seems to hint what his new "direction" will be.[24] Accordingly, his intention in evaluating "preservation of type" seems apologetical as well as historical.

Newman next uses a lengthy and rather tedious survey of pagan and Gnostic rites—perhaps as a rhetorical parallel for what Victorians usually considered the superstitious practices of Roman Catholicism?—to point out that "even mistakes carry information; for they are cognate to the truth, . . . Often what seems like a mistake is merely the mode in which the informant conveys his testimony, or the impression which a fact makes on him" [VI.1.14]. Such a line of argument, however, seems puzzling. Certainly it is an indication of the author's integrity, yet from both an apologetical and theological viewpoint, it is at best ambivalent, particularly insofar as "there is a certain general correspondence between magic and miracle, obstinacy and faith, insubordination and zeal for religion, sophistry and argumentative talent" [VI.1.14].[25] One is left wondering what criteriological grounds there are for distinguishing between genuine developments and counter-feit facsimiles.

Newman does give a preliminary but subtle hint at how the process of discernment proceeds: "Public men care very little for books; the finest sentiments, the most luminous philo-sophy, the deepest theology, inspiration itself move them but little; they look at facts, and care only for facts" [VI.1.19]. Such a preference for the factual may be the reason why this chapter of the *Essay* is so heavily historical. This orientation to the factual is exemplified in Newman's subsequent reference to "jesting Pilate", whose rhetorical question—"What is Truth?"— expected and received no answer; what was important was "the sure instinct which taught him to dread Christianity" [VI.1.19]. Is this a hint that people make decisions not solely on the basis of logical arguments but through inferential judgments about facts?[26]

For the present, however, Newman chooses to pursue an-other theme—what today might be called the civil disobedience of the early Christians. Newman justifies the practice of a "vagrant and proselytizing" religion:

> The justification of such disobedience lies simply in the necessity of obeying the higher authority of some divine law; but if Christianity were in its essence only private and personal, as so many now think, there was no necessity of their meeting together at all [VI.1.22].

This assessment is effectively a two-pronged attack: on the one hand, it enables Newman to reject that species of Victorian individualism that considers each individual the final arbiter of religious belief; on the other hand, it suggests a further parallel between the early Christians and British Roman Catholics.

The situation of the first Christians being forced by a higher law to disobey imperial edicts parallels the situation of Roman Catholic recusants in evading the "penal laws":[27] "But, like other laws which are founded upon tyranny, and are at variance with the first principles of justice, it is probable that this law about corporate property was evaded" [VI.1.23]. This parallel has an ironic twist: if the early Christians and British Roman Catholics could be accused of disobeying civil laws, their persecutors, respectively pagan and Anglican, were disregarding divine justice.

In any case, appeals to a higher order were lost on both civil authorities and law-abiding citizens; Christians were regarded as misguided at best: " 'A good man Caius Seius, only he is a Christian.' So another, 'I marvel that that wise man Lucius Titius hath suddenly become a Christian' " [VI.1.24]. Newman's rhetorical dialogue proved to be prophetic: similar comments were made when he decided to become a Roman Catholic.[28]

Newman concluded his commentary on "the Church of the First Centuries" with a rhetorical flourish that turned the pagan accusations against the early Church into an apologetical argument suggesting the identity of its present-day continuation:

> If there is a form of Christianity now in the world which is accused of gross superstition, of borrowing its rites and customs from the heathen, and of ascribing to forms and ceremonies an occult virtue; a religion which is considered to burden and enslave the mind by its requisitions, to address itself to the weak-minded and ignorant, to be supported by sophistry and imposture, and to contradict reason and exalt mere irrational faith; . . . if there be such a religion now in the world, it is not unlike Christianity as that same world viewed it, when first it came forth from its Divine Author [VI.1.30].

The Church of the Fourth Century

While the choice between paganism and Christianity seems clear-cut, how does one choose among rival forms of Christianity? Newman looked to "the Church of the Fourth Century" to identify the Church that continued the Church of the Apostles.

In the fourth century, prospective Christians had to choose

among a variety of rival ecclesiastical claimants: Donatists, Priscillians, Manicheans, Novatianists, Luciferians, to name but a few. For people of that time, the choice was a matter not of historical study but of personal decision: "How was the man to guide his course who wished to join himself to the doctrine and fellowship of the Apostles in the times of St. Athanasius, St. Basil, and St. Augustine?" [VI.2.2].

The correct choice was far from obvious: "St. Augustine was nine years a Manichee; St. Basil for a time was in admiration of the Semi-Arians" [VI.2.4]. If even saints were attracted to aberrant Christian groups, "how was an individual inquirer to find, or a private Christian to keep the Truth, amid so many rival teachers?" [VI.2.4].[29] Newman's response provides a test for distinguishing the true Church from fraudulent facsimiles: "The Church is everywhere, but it is one; sects are everywhere, but they are many, independent and discordant. Catholicity is the attribute of the Church, independency of sectaries" [VI.2.4].

While the presence of unity is an indication of the true Church, heresies, in contrast, seem to be characterized by their hatred of the Catholic Church. Indeed, the very title "Catholic" is usually "a confirmatory proof and symbol of what is even otherwise so plain", that the Church "was everywhere one, while the sects of the day were nowhere one, but everywhere divided" [VI.2.10]; "the Church was that body which was spread over the *orbis terrarum*, and sects were those bodies which were local or transitory" [VI.2.11].

Newman next considered the claim that "this universality which the Fathers ascribe to the Catholic Church lay in its Apostolical descent, or again in its Episcopacy" [VI.2.13]. Newman, however, found such claims deficient: "As a kingdom admits of the possibility of rebels, so does such a Church involve sectaries and schismatics, but not independent portions" [VI.2.14]. Like any kingdom, the Catholic Church needs authoritative leadership: "Above all the See of Rome itself is the centre of teaching as well as of action, is visited by Fathers and heretics as a tribunal in controversy, and by ancient

custom sends her alms to the poor Christians of all Churches"
[VI.2.14].

Newman concludes his treatment of the Church in the
fourth century with another rhetorical flourish that envisions
the Church of that era as the prototype for the present age:

> If there be a form of Christianity at this day distinguished
> for its careful organization, and its consequent power; if it
> is conspicuous for zealous maintenance of its own creed; if it is
> intolerant towards what it considers error; if it is engaged in
> ceaseless war with all other bodies called Christian; if it, and it
> alone, is called "Catholic" by the world, . . . such a religious
> community is not unlike historical Christianity as it comes
> before us at the Nicene Era [VI.2.17].

The Church of the Fifth and Sixth Centuries

In the fourth century, the Catholic Church found itself "lying
in the midst of sects, all enemies to it" [VI.3.1.10]; thus, the
challenge was to decide which of the competing churches was
the true claimant; during the fifth and sixth centuries, the
competition changed:

> Heresy is no longer a domestic enemy intermingled with the
> Church, but it occupies its own ground and is extended over
> against her, even though on the same territory, and is more or
> less organized, and cannot be so promptly refuted by the simple
> test of Catholicity [VI.3.1.10].

Accordingly, Newman feels it necessary to defend a double
assumption: "To call Arianism, Nestorianism, and Eutychianism
heresies" and "to identify the contemporary Catholic Church
with Christianity" [VI.3.0].

In the case of the various tribes converted to Arianism,
although "it cannot be supposed that these northern warriors
had attained to any high degree of mental cultivation", still "they
understood their own religion enough to hate the Catholics"

[VI.3.2]. Such Arian animosity posed a considerable threat to Catholic Christianity, insofar as its barbarian sponsors achieved military and political supremacy; nonetheless,

> the duration of this ascendency of error had not the faintest tendency to deprive the ancient Church of the West of the title of Catholic. . . . The Arians seem never to have claimed the Catholic name. It is more remarkable that the Catholics during this period were denoted by the additional title of "Romans" [VI.3.5].

This association of Catholicism with Rome was also in evidence in the Nestorian and Monophysite controversies.[30] Among the many Patristic writers who testified to the doctrinal hegemony of Rome was Theodoret:

> That all-holy See has the office heading the whole world's Churches for many reasons; and above all others, because it has remained free of the communion of heretical taint, and no one of heterodox sentiments hath sat in it, but it hath preserved the Apostolic grace unsullied [VI.3.10].

Thus, by listening to Rome, the Nestorians and Monophysites could have avoided not only endless theological disputes but also their lapse into heresy; "their refusal to obey the voice of the Church was a token of real error in their faith" [VI.3.17].

Newman concludes his application of the "preservation of type" with a rhetorical comparison similar to those he had used previously:

> If then there is now a form of Christianity such that it extends throughout the world, though with varying measures of prominence or prosperity in separate places; . . . that it has lost whole Churches by schism, and is now opposed by powerful communions once part of itself; that it has been altogether or almost driven from some countries; that in others its line of teachers is overlaid, its flocks oppressed, its Churches occupied, its property held by what may be called a duplicate succession; . . . and that amid its disorders and its fears there is but one voice for whose decisions the peoples wait with trust,

one Name and one See to which they look with hope, and that name Peter, and that see Rome, such a religion is not unlike the Christianity of the fifth and sixth centuries [VI.3.23].

In effect, Newman's historical investigation of the "preservation of type" not only led him to Roman Catholicism; in the process, his historical comparisons also enabled him to confront and reject three contemporary rivals: first, in parallel with ancient paganism was the challenge of a utilitarian religiosity; second, paralleling the rivalry of the heretical sects of the fourth century was the competition of a variety of denominations; and third, in contrast to the officially sponsored but heretical churches of the fifth and sixth centuries, were the established churches, particularly the Church of England.

Such historical comparisons had tremendous influence on Newman's decision to become a Roman Catholic; as he graphically described his experience in his *Apologia*: "I saw my face in that mirror, and I was a Monophysite. The Church of the *Via Media* was in the position of the Oriental communion, Rome was, where she now is; and the Protestants were the Eutychians."[31]

Critique

The comparative implications of Newman's historical investigations eventually convinced him that the Roman Catholic Church had preserved the "type" of the Apostolic Church; in other words, he came to see the Roman Catholic Church as the present-day embodiment of the Church of the Apostles; the other six notes thus appear anticlimactic, simply providing additional confirmation for a conclusion of which he was already convinced.

The historical evidence for the identification of the Roman Catholic Church with the Apostolic Church was certainly convincing to Newman, but how persuasive is such evidence for others? Even raising such a question may seem presumptuous, yet not to raise it would be a disservice. Just as one expects Thomists not only to read and reflect upon Aquinas but also critically to examine his thought, the same ought to be expected of Newmanists. And, just as Thomists frequently begin their appraisals of Aquinas with an acknowledgment of the perennial value of his *Summa Theologiae*, it seems appropriate to recognize that Newman's *Essay on Development* is "the almost inevitable starting point for an investigation of development of doctrine"[32]—a theological classic.

There is a danger in describing any work as a classic, for all too often classics are volumes with elegant bindings that are placed in decorative bookcases but never read, much less critiqued. Fortunately, such has not yet been Newman's fate. Judging from the continued republication of his writings in popular editions, Newman is still read, though perhaps not as analytically as he should be.

The lack of analysis is partially circumstantial. At the time of its first publication, the *Essay on Development* was severely criticized by many Anglicans,[33] while Roman Catholics experienced ambivalent feelings:

> His person they welcomed with warmth and sympathy, his thought perplexed and sometimes frightened them. "The Roman theologians", wrote Father Ignatius Ryder later, saw Newman to be "a formidable engine of war on their side, but they were distinctly aware that they did not thoroughly understand the machinery. And so they came to think, some of them, that it might perhaps one day go off of itself or in the wrong direction."[34]

This combination of suspicion and lack of understanding seems to have had the side effect of preempting serious criteriological dialogue among Roman Catholics about Newman's view of development.

A similar by-product is evident in the "adoption" of Newman by two subsequent but quite dissimilar groups. First were the Roman Catholic "modernists" who adapted Newman's idea of development to their own purposes; as a result, his writings were suspect in some circles while uncritically defended in others.[35] Second were the Roman Catholic dogmatists who rejected the modernists' interpretations of Newman but like them distorted his view of development by fitting it in procrustean fashion to a neoscholastic matrix. Only comparatively recently have systematic theologians analyzed Newman more critically.[36]

Three questions are crucial for present purposes: What contribution does the *Essay* make to ecclesiology? How persuasive are the notes as ecclesiological criteria? And what is the specific contribution of the first note, "preservation of type"? In answering such questions, one needs to look at the limitations of, respectively, the *Essay* as a whole, the notes in general, and the "preservation of type" in particular. An awareness of these limitations should afford a greater appreciation of the genuine strengths of the *Essay on Development*.

Limitations

Some of the limitations of the *Essay* have only become evident with the passage of time. For example, when Newman wrote his *Essay*, "theological development" was a novel idea; it is not surprising, then, that Newman treated "development" as "an hypothesis to account for a difficulty".[37] In contrast, development is now considered a fact of life rather than a hypothetical explanation. Thus, were Newman to write his *Essay* today, he presumably would adopt a fundamentally different perspective regarding development itself.

Insofar as Newman's view of development is hypothetical, present-day readers of the *Essay* may need to revise their expectations. If readers approach the *Essay* anticipating a systematically developed "theory" of development, not only will their expectations go unfulfilled, but also they may miss the genuine accomplishments of the *Essay*. What the *Essay* offers is an *apologia pro ecclesia sua*, an ecclesiological apologetic based not on biblical exegesis or on theological systematization but on the concrete reality of the Church, as "a great and perpetual motive for belief as well as an indisputable testimony of its divine mission".[38]

Such an ecclesiological approach may seem strange to those accustomed to regard the Church more as an institution than as a sacramental reality.[39] Yet Newman's focus in the *Essay* is not so much on the institutional Church as such but on the Church as a living reality that began with the Apostles and has continued down to the present. It is within such a vital ecclesiology that Newman's repeated recourse to organic images (such as the child growing to an adult) both makes sense and has rhetorical force. By the same token, outside such an ecclesiology, organic images easily become theoretically meaningless and apologetically ineffective.

Newman's ecclesiology was linked to an equally sacramental view of Christian history as "an outward visible sign of an inward spiritual grace".[40] Such a view of history was also an apologetic stance, insofar as it contrasted sharply with the historicism and utilitarianism of his day. On the one hand, Newman's view of history had the merit of recapturing the Platonic legacy of the ancient Church; on the other, it set him apart from other contemporary Church historians such as Döllinger, whose desire to see dogma proved by facts led him to accuse Newman of using dogma to align the facts.[41]

Newman's view of history, however, was not only at odds with that of Döllinger in particular and nineteenth-century historicism in general; it is also foreign to many twentieth-century historians, whose understanding of history tends to be pragmatic and secularistic. Even if current historiography has in some measure retreated from the historicism and utilitarianism that Newman battled, contemporary historians are usually unwilling to discuss the history of the Church in Newman's organic terminology, much less within his sacramental ecclesiology.

Thus, where Newman was prepared to view the facts of

history as ordered by the overarching guidance of Providence at work in both the Church and the world,[42] modern historians are more likely to see history as a series of discrete events, whose interpretive linkage is an artful, yet ultimately arbitrary, juxtaposition of well-selected vignettes. Newman looked at history "from above", contemporary historians "from below". Accordingly, if contemporary historians would have to choose, most would probably be more comfortable with nineteenth-century historicism than with Newman's historical vision.

What seems needed today for an appreciation of the *Essay* is the theological equivalent of bilingualism. To understand the *Essay*, one must learn its vocabulary; one must accept its grammatical rules. But also, like the student of a foreign language, one must appreciate its *idiosincrasia*; one must acquire a *Sprachgefühl*. Otherwise, one will not be able to savor the meaning of the *Essay on Development*.[43]

The Notes as Criteria

Granting that the *Essay* must be read in light of Newman's purpose in writing it, how persuasive are the notes as ecclesiological criteria? Some commentators have seen the notes as unquestionably demonstrating Roman Catholic claims; others, in contrast, have categorically denied any value to the notes: "No one ever believed in the operation of these seven tests. No one believed in them when the book first came out and no one has believed in them since."[44] Neither of these positions is acceptable: an unquestioning acceptance exaggerates by overstatement, while a peremptory rejection cavalierly refuses even to consider whether or not there is a legitimate but limited use of the notes. Just as a yardstick is useful for measuring a football field but not intergalactic distances or molecular interstices, Newman's notes, like any set of criteria, are useful when properly applied but tend to become useless when utilized for purposes for which they are not intended.

Newman designed the notes to be an "identity test" in

answer to the question: Is there a present embodiment of the Church of the Apostles? In the course of writing the *Essay*, Newman gradually became convinced that the answer was the Roman Catholic Church. This "identity test" convinced not only Newman but also others, among them Edward Caswall, a former Anglican clergyman and future Oratorian, "who was received into the Church in Rome after reading through the *Essay* four times".[45]

Newman's identification of the contemporary Church with the early Church was as persuasive as his extraordinary rhetorical abilities could make it. Nonetheless, it is comparatively easy to overextend the implications of his "identity test"; for example, Newman felt that the historical evidence in his *Essay* showed that "the existing doctrine and practice of the Roman Catholic Church is not necessarily a 'corruption' "; however, it would be a gratuitous aggrandizement of the results of this generic identification to claim that "the papacy of Pius IX represents the ideal form of Church government".[46] Thus, to say that the notes indicate the identity of the Roman Catholic Church with the Apostolic Church is one thing; to claim that the Roman Catholic Church has achieved its ideal identity at a particular stage of its history works against the very idea of development and in any case would require a different set of "tests" than the ones that Newman proposed.

In a similar vein, it is questionable whether the notes can legitimately be used as criteria for evaluating specific proposals for changes within the present-day Church. For example, when ecclesiastical changes are proposed today, often the question is implicitly or explicitly raised: Is such a proposal an opportunity for genuine development or a potential case of fundamental corruption? While such questions must be asked, it seems exaggerated to expect Newman's notes to furnish a definitive, much less an automatic, answer. Insofar as Newman's notes were originally intended to test the identity of the Roman Catholic Church with the Apostolic Church, they are both *generic* and *ecclesial* in their application. Applying this test to *specific* proposals for *ecclesiastical* change certainly goes beyond Newman's application, and so such proposals must be validated on the basis of other criteria, not by a superficial appeal to Newman's notes.

Another misapplication of Newman's notes is sometimes found in the area of ecumenism. It is undeniable that the *Essay on Development* was the work that convinced Newman that he should join the Roman Catholic Church; the *Essay* was simultaneously his invitation to other members of the Oxford Movement to follow suit. In the preecumenical climate of mid-nineteenth-century Britain, it is not surprising that Newman's "conversion" was interpreted as a "betrayal" by many of his former colleagues and as a "victory" by his new coreligionists. It is then comparatively easy for Roman Catholics with a triumphalistic bent to apply Newman's notes in an unecumenical way, for example, by denying any validity to the Anglican communion in particular, and to other non-Roman communions in general.

Such a conclusion, however, ignores two important aspects, one of Newman's life and the other of his *Essay*: first, while Newman undoubtedly hoped that his Anglican friends and acquaintances would become Roman Catholics, he still (at least after the first, and somewhat enthusiastic, years following his "conversion") consistently paid respect to his Anglican origins: "Catholics did not make us Catholics; Oxford made us Catholics."[47]

Second, from a theological point of view, it is important to emphasize that the notes were intended to show the *ecclesial* identity of the Roman Catholic Church with the early Church. For Newman, the notes were effective in answering the question: Which is the Church? However, this question is not identical with another important question: What ecclesial elements are found in other churches? Thus, while the notes may lead to the conviction that the Roman Catholic Church is identifiable with the Church of the Apostles, such a judgment certainly does not preclude the possibility either of recognizing genuine ecclesial elements in other churches or of allowing some type of mutual recognition among churches.[48]

Finally, insofar as a measurement is only as reliable as the one doing the measuring, one must be concerned not only about the range of applicability of the notes but also about the reliability of the person making those applications. The use of Newman's notes is neither routine nor automatic, not like entering data into a computer that will then process the material and provide a printout of the findings. Nor is the use of the notes arbitrary and subjective, allowing as many opinions as the number of those using the notes. The application of the notes is a matter neither of computer-style logic nor of personal whim.

The notes are comparable to the tests that a detective might use in examining evidence discovered at the scene of a crime. While the evidence is essential, it is inconclusive by itself; what is crucial is the detective's skill in using the evidence to reconstruct the crime and to identify the criminal. Clues do not make sense by themselves; they are the raw material for a solution to the crime, and such a solution comes only when someone has the skill to assemble the disparate and sometimes divergent clues into a coherent picture.

A comparable situation exists in regard to the use of the notes. A person seeking the modern actualization of the Apostolic Church may use the notes to test the claims of various churches. Like the clues available to a detective, the notes do not automatically verify the identity of any church claiming to be Apostolic; rather, the notes, sometimes singly (like a key piece of evidence), sometimes cumulatively (like the force of interlocking bits of evidence), point toward the one Church that seems best to actualize the Church of the Apostles in the present day.

The notes, then, do not possess the logical force necessary to compel a person's assent; nonetheless, the notes are not simply arbitrary criteria that one may employ or discard at will. The notes are ecclesiological tests for evaluating the various historical clues that identify the present actualization of the Apostolic Church. Just as any technique is useless without a reliable technician, so the notes presuppose a person willing to use them for the purpose for which they were intended. And just as a technician must take responsibility for the findings that result from conducting tests, so too a believer must take responsibility for deciding what action to take regarding the Church. The notes do not make decisions for anyone; however, the notes can be an important aid to a person who sincerely wants to identify the Apostolic Church today.[49]

Preservation and Organism

Among the notes, "preservation of type" occupies pride of place not only because it is the first note discussed and the one to which Newman gave the most extensive treatment but also because it clearly underscores the identity of the Roman Catholic Church under the headship of the Bishop of Rome with the Church of the Apostles under the leadership of Peter. "Preservation of type" also conveys a sense of corporate identity and ecclesial community between the Church of the present and the Church as it has continued through the ages. "Preservation of type", then, is a note that is rhetorically appealing and apologetically persuasive.

Part of this persuasiveness is linked to the various organic images that Newman used in speaking of "preservation of type" in particular and of development in general. Organic images, such as the bird emerging from the egg and the caterpillar from the grub, furnish an imaginative comparison for understanding how the contemporary Church developed from the Apostolic Church [V.1.4]. Such images, particularly the more familiar ones of an acorn growing into an oak and an infant developing into an adult, are subtly persuasive: even though an oak does not look like an acorn, such was its origin; correspondingly, even though externally the highly structured

Roman Catholic Church of the present may not look like the primitive Church of the Apostles, such was its beginning. Given the clarity of such comparisons, it is hardly surprising that these images have become popular ways of describing the development of Christian doctrine.

Implicit in such an employment of organic images, however, is a crucial ecclesiological assumption: the theological legitimacy of describing the Church in biological terms. In its favor, such an approach has the best of precedents, insofar as the New Testament frequently describes the Church by using organic images.[50] In other respects, however, while such images of the Church may be highly attractive and thought provoking, they unfortunately do not and cannot provide the categories necessary for systematically specifying and analyzing the structures of the Church.

There is, of course, an indisputable need for both types of description: organic imagery is more useful for apologetical and pastoral purposes; systematic terminology is necessary for more analytic and academic purposes. And since Newman's purposes were more often the former than the latter, it is not surprising that in writing about the Church, he frequently employed organic imagery rather than scholastic terminology.[51]

Newman's use of organic imagery was not only congenial, even instinctive (as far as his personality was concerned); his use of organic imagery seems more appropriate and effective for the presentation of a hypothesis, whereas systematic terminology would be mandatory for the rigorous proof of a thesis. In line with their aims, seminal thinkers may need to talk in images, while systematic theologians must speak in analytic terms.

Yet, however necessary or effective the use of organic imagery may be, it leaves readers on their own in attempting to translate organic images into systematic terminology; for example, it is practically impossible to apply organic images, and the corresponding notes, with criteriological rigor. Thus, those who use Newman's notes need to be modest in their theoretical expectations. For example, one hazard encountered in the application of "preservation of type" is the difficulty of comparing the earliest stages when developments are only beginning to unfold and the later stages when the process is far along; this difficulty is similar to that of attempting to recognize a person from his baby picture.

Another problem is the applicability of "preservation of type" in the embryonic stage of development, where the "type" is still not apparent and its "preservation" problematic. By way of comparison, until an acorn has germinated into an oak seedling, or until an egg has hatched into a nestling, the "type" to be preserved may be difficult to identify; thus, it is hard to predict in advance what path authentic development should take in order to preserve the original "type". For example, if one considers the Judaism contemporary with Jesus, it would have been hard to predict the emergence of Christianity as a world religion. Thus, "preservation of type", while useful as a criterion in retrospect over the course of centuries, is difficult, if not impossible, to apply in the initial stages when the main path of development has yet to take place.[52]

Conclusion

It is an anomaly that the *Essay on Development* has often been treated as a work of systematic theology presenting a history of development, when Newman frequently denied that he was a theologian at all.[53]

Insofar as the *Essay* is not a treatise in systematic theology but an attempt—thus, truly an "essay"—at exploring a concrete ecclesiological question, then Newman might well be described as a theological pioneer, an ecclesiological explorer. Insofar as the nineteenth century expected theological methodology to be deductive, then Newman was right in considering himself an apologist and in denying that he was a theologian. And at least in the English-reading world of the nineteenth century, Newman was more successful as an apologist for Catholic theology than any theologian of his day.

What continues to be anomalous is that Newman, unlike most apologists of the nineteenth century, continues to be read and revered. It now seems fortunate, indeed providential, that Newman turned out to be a theological pioneer, because in that role he could explore questions that the theological professionals of his day had difficulty even in seeing, much less in solving. The role of pioneer allowed Newman to raise questions, to formulate hypotheses, and to share ideas in ways that his theological contemporaries simply did not, and possibly could not, do. It seems ironic that it is precisely because of his questions, hypotheses, and ideas that Newman is still widely read today, while the writings of other once highly regarded theologians are gathering dust on library shelves.

Newman, of course, had the great gift of being a seminal thinker, a person who perceived issues that others only vaguely sensed. This gift is what makes it worthwhile to read Newman today: his probing questions have become our pressing concerns; his tentative hypotheses have become the bases for our theories; his ideas have become our ideals. Like his own contemporaries, readers of Newman still have the uncanny feeling that he knew in advance the questions that were troubling them, the principles that they were seeking, and the insights for which they were searching. The fact that Newman seems to have recognized our concerns in advance of our expressing them is why it is still so helpful to look to him for guidance.

The greatest compliment that can be paid to the *Essay on Development* is that it is still read today; yet Newman would probably consider it an even greater compliment if his *Essay* were not simply read, but critically discussed and analyzed; if so, the *Essay on Development* will truly preserve its "type" as a theological classic.

NOTES

¹ The *Apologia pro Vita Sua* was originally published as eight separate pamphlets that were later collected in book form (London: Longman, Roberts, and Green, 1864); the printing of 1873 carried the subtitle *Being a History of His Religious Opinions*; among the many subsequent reprintings, one of the most useful for its explanatory notes and supplemental essays is that edited by David J. DeLaura (New York: W. W. Norton & Company, 1968). For information about the publication history of Newman's works, see Vincent Ferrer Blehl, *John Henry Newman: A Bibliographical Catalogue of His Writings* (Charlottesville: University Press of Virginia, 1978).

² Cf. C. S. Dessain, "Newman's First Conversion, 'A Great Change of Thought', August 1st till December 21st 1816", *Studies* 46 (1957), pp. 44–59; also in *Newman Studien* 3 (1957), pp. 37–53.

³ Among the many biographies of Newman, of particular value for his Anglican years are Meriol Trevor, *Newman: The Pillar of the Cloud* (Garden City, N.Y.: Doubleday, 1962), and Maisie Ward, *Young Mr. Newman* (New York: Sheed & Ward, 1948).

⁴ Charles Frederick Harrold, *John Henry Newman: An Expository and Critical Study of His Mind, Thought and Art* (London, New York, and Toronto: Longman, Green, 1945; reprinted, Hamden, Conn.: Archon, 1966), pp. 6–22, describes Newman's passage from Evangelicalism, through liberalism, to High Church Anglicanism and his indebtedness to all three movements.

⁵ *An Essay on the Development of Christian Doctrine* was first published in 1845 with a second edition correcting errors in 1846 (London: James Toovey; both editions); a new and completely revised edition was published in 1878 (London: Basil Montagu Pickering) and is the edition most widely available today; since pagination differs in various reprintings, references to the 1878 edition will be given in brackets in the text; thus, the sentence cited [I.1.7] is found in Chapter I, Section I, subsection 7; variants of this system will be explained on first appearance.

⁶ For example, Jan Walgrave, *Unfolding Revelation: The Nature of Doctrinal Development* (Philadelphia: Westminster; London: Hutchinson, 1972).

⁷ Cf. Richard Greene, *John Henry Newman's Theology of Doctrinal Development in Reference to the Oxford Movement, 1833–1843* (unpublished dissertation, The Catholic University of America, 1975, abstracted in *Dissertation Abstracts International* 36/7 [1976], p. 4580 A).

⁸ William Bonner, *A Thematic Comparison of the Apologetic Writings of John Milner and the Anglican Writings of John Henry Newman* (unpublished dissertation, The Catholic University of America, 1984, abstracted in *Dissertation Abstracts*

International 46/2, 451A), pp. 460–63, points out that this argument, which was derived from Cyril of Jerusalem, was also used by John Milner in *End of Religious Controversy* (1818).

⁹ Nicholas Lash, *Newman on Development: The Search for an Explanation in History* (Shepherdstown, W.V.: Patmos, 1975), p. 9.

¹⁰ Newman to Wilberforce (March 7, 1849), *Letters and Diaries*, vol. XIII, p. 78.

¹¹ This ecclesiological concern was already evident in *Tract XC* (1841), in which Newman attempted to show that the official teaching of the church of England as presented in the Thirty-nine Articles was not doctrinally opposed to the teaching of the Council of Trent; the rejection of this interpretation by the Anglican hierarchy was one of several incidents that turned Newman toward Roman Catholicism: "From the end of 1841, I was on my death-bed, as regards my membership with the Anglican Church, though at the time I became aware of it only by degrees" (*Apologia*, ed. DeLaura, p. 121).

¹² The number of notes proposed by ecclesiologists has varied over the centuries; the reason why Newman settled on seven is unclear; cf. Lash, op. cit., p. 179, n. 55.

¹³ Cf. Paul Misner, "Newman and the Tradition Concerning the Papal Anti-Christ", *Church History* 42 (1973), pp. 377–95.

¹⁴ *Apologia*, ed. DeLaura, pp. 51–53.

¹⁵ As T. J. Mashburn, "The Categories of Development: An Overlooked Aspect of Newman's Theory of Doctrinal Development", *Heythrop Journal* 29 (1988), pp. 33–43, indicates, there has been little systematic discussion of Newman's categories; nor has the relationship of the categories and the notes been sufficiently explored.

¹⁶ Cf. Lash, op. cit., pp. 71; 179, n. 55. Of these five different "kinds" of development that Newman found operative in the area of doctrine, some appear to be more "organic" (political, ethical, historical), others more "logical" (logical, metaphysical); a similar difference appears among the notes: the first (preservation of type), third (power of assimilation), and seventh (chronic vigor) are more "organic", while the second (continuity of its principles) and fourth (logical sequence) appear more "logical"; the fifth (anticipation of its future) and sixth (conservative action upon its past) seem to admit both "organic" and "logical" aspects. This is another aspect of the "notes" that deserves more attention.

¹⁷ Cf. Calvin's treatment of the Trinity in his *Institutes of the Christian Religion*, trans. Henry Beveridge (Grand Rapids, Mich.: W. B. Eerdmans, 1975); for example, p. 124: "What, then, is our Saviour's meaning in commanding baptism to be administered in the name of the Father, and the Son, and the Holy Spirit, if it be not that we are to believe with one faith in the name of the Father, and the Son, and the Holy Spirit?" [I.13.16]; as for the spiritual

descendants of Calvin, John Leith, *An Introduction to the Reformed Tradition: A Way of Being the Christian Community* (Atlanta: John Knox, 1977), p. 96, insists that "Reformed theology acknowledges the Triune God".

18 In his *Apologia* (ed. DeLaura, p. 33), Newman mentions that it was Hurrell Froude who "taught me to look with admiration towards the Church of Rome, and in the same degree to dislike the Reformation"; cf. Piers Brendon, *Hurrell Froude and the Oxford Movement* (London: Paul Elek, 1974), pp. 87–123.

19 [VI.o] refers to the preliminary paragraphs preceding [VI.1] in the 1878 edition. It may be helpful to note that the 1845 edition of the *Essay* treated "fidelity in development" in chaps. IV and V, while the 1878 edition treats "preservation of type" in chap. VI; the treatments are comparable but not identical in every respect.

20 Similar descriptions are repeated in the rest of this section, for example, [VI.1.26] and [VI.1.30]; in a similar vein, Newman presented what has become a classic description of recusant Roman Catholicism in his sermon "The Second Spring", *Sermons Preached on Various Occasions* (London, New York, and Bombay: Longman, Green, 1898), pp. 171–73.

21 Cf. Thomas Bokenkotter, *Cardinal Newman as an Historian* (Louvain: Publications Universitaires de Louvain, 1959).

22 Newman used a similar approach in 1859 in writing *On Consulting the Faithful in Matters of Doctrine*, ed. John Coulson (New York: Sheed & Ward, 1961), where his thesis is corroborated, if not overwhelmed, by the catena of historical examples.

23 See the ecumenical reassessment of Newman's "conversion" to Roman Catholicism by A. M. Allchin, "The *Via Media*—An Anglican Reevaluation", in *Newman: A Portrait Restored*, ed. A. M. Allchin and John Coulson (London, Melbourne, and New York: Sheed & Ward, 1965), pp. 62–111.

24 While Newman's *Essay* represents the cumulative set of arguments that convinced him to become a Roman Catholic, it was not until the book was at the printers that he finally made that decision (cf. the "Postscript" to the "Advertisement to the First Edition").

25 The ambivalence is heightened by Newman's presentation of "a vivid picture of Plutarch's idea of the essence of superstition" [VI.1.17]; concealed behind this purportedly pagan description of the early Christians is the popular Victorian antagonism toward Roman Catholicism. Here again, a masterful rhetorical flourish is simultaneously combined with a criteriological conundrum: How does one determine whether the apparently superstitious is authentically religious?

26 This section [VI.1.19] seems to anticipate two important positions that Newman later elaborated in *An Essay in Aid of a Grammar of Assent* (London: Burns & Oates, 1870): first, the need to begin intellectual inquiry with an

analysis of facts (as in chap. 1); secondly, the crucial role of what Newman calls here a "sure instinct" in arriving at assents (cf. his description of the "illative sense" in chap. 9).

[27] On the survival of Roman Catholicism under the "penal laws", see Philip Hughes, *The Catholic Question, 1688–1829: A Study in Political History* (London: Sheed & Ward, 1929); M. D. R. Leys, *Catholics in England, 1559–1829: A Social History* (New York: Sheed & Ward, 1961); David Mathew, *Catholicism in England, 1535–1935, Portrait of a Minority: Its Culture and Tradition* (London: Catholic Book Club, 1938); Bernard and Margaret Pawley, *Rome and Canterbury through Four Centuries: A Study of the Relations between the Church of Rome and the Anglican Churches, 1530–1981* (London and Oxford: Mowbray, 1981); E. I. Watkin, *Roman Catholicism in England from the Reformation to 1950* (London, New York, and Toronto: Oxford University Press, 1957).

[28] On the contemporary reactions to Newman's "conversion" to Roman Catholicism, cf. Ward, op. cit., pp. 449–59, and R. W. Church, *The Oxford Movement, Twelve Years, 1833–1845*, ed. Geoffrey Best (Chicago and London: University of Chicago Press, 1970), pp. 264–72.

[29] Such a question was also applicable to Victorian England, as is evident in Newman's novel *Loss and Gain: The Story of a Convert* (published three years after the *Essay*), where he parodied the variety of esoteric sects in Victorian England (chaps. VIII and IX).

[30] Newman's attention to historical detail was already evident in his first book, *The Arians of the Fourth Century* (London: J. G. & F. Rivington, 1833).

[31] *Apologia*, ed. DeLaura, p. 96.

[32] Jaroslav Pelikan, *Development of Christian Doctrine: Some Historical Prolegomena* (New Haven and London: Yale University, 1969), p. 3.

[33] Cf. C. G. Brown, "Newman's Minor Critics", *Downside Review* 89/294 (1971), pp. 13–21; David Nichols, "Gladstone and the Anglican Critics of Newman", in *Newman and Gladstone: Centennial Essays*, ed. James D. Bastable (Dublin: Veritas, 1978), pp. 121–44.

[34] Cf. Owen Chadwick, *From Bossuet to Newman: The Idea of Doctrinal Development* (Cambridge: University Press, 1957), pp. 169–70; this lack of understanding on the part of Roman theologians plagued Newman from the time of his studies in Rome (1846–47) until the bestowal of the cardinalate by Leo XIII in 1879.

[35] Cf. *Newman and the Modernists*, ed. Mary Jo Weaver (Lanham, New York, and London: University Press of America, 1985).

[36] For a useful survey of recent critiques, see Ian Ker, "Newman's Theory: Development or Continuing Revelation?" in *Newman and Gladstone*, ed. Bastable, pp. 145–59.

[37] Lash, op. cit., pp. 17–19.

[38] The phrase is translated from *Dei Filius*, chap. 3, of the First Vatican

Council: *"Magnum quoddam et perpetuum est motivum credibilitatis et divinae suae legationis testimonium irrefragabile"* (H. Denzinger, A. Schönmetzer, *Enchiridion Symbolorum* [1967], 3013 = 1794 in earlier editions); the phrase was due to Victor Dechamps, not to Newman; cf. Roger Aubert, *Le problème de l'acte de foi* (Louvain: E. Warny, 1945), pp. 142–45, 191–200.

[39] The difference in approaches has been clearly and concisely drawn by Avery Dulles, *Models of the Church* (Garden City, N.Y.: Doubleday, 1974).

[40] Lash, op. cit., p. 28.

[41] Cf. Wolfgang Klausnitzer, *Päpstliche Unfehlbarkeit bei Newman und Döllinger: ein historisch-systematischer Vergleich* (Innsbruck, Vienna, and Munich: Tyrolia, 1980).

[42] "Providence" is a topic that looms large in Newman, though it is most often treated not in relation to his view of history but as a leitmotiv of his spirituality; cf. C. S. Dessain, *Newman's Spiritual Themes* (Dublin: Veritas, 1977); Hilda Graef, *God and Myself: The Spirituality of John Henry Newman* (London: Peter Davies, 1967).

[43] For a helpful discussion of the personal dimension necessary for reading the *Essay*, cf. William Kelly, "The Development of Doctrine: Another Look at the Underlying Image", in *Newman and Gladstone*, ed. Bastable, pp. 89–119.

[44] Owen Chadwick, *Newman* (Oxford and New York: Oxford University, 1983), p. 47.

[45] Chadwick, *From Bossuet to Newman*, p. 178.

[46] Lash, op. cit., p. 40.

[47] Newman to E. E. Estcourt (June 2, 1860), *Letters and Diaries*, vol. XIX, p. 352; cf. Charles S. Dessain, "Cardinal Newman and Ecumenism", *The Clergy Review* 50 (1965), pp. 119–37, 189–206; John Tracy Ellis, "John Henry Newman, A Bridge for Men of Good Will", *Catholic Historical Review* 56 (1970), pp. 1–24; Edward Jeremy Miller, *John Henry Newman on the Idea of Church* (Shepherdstown, W.V.: Patmos, 1987), pp. 55–57.

[48] Cf. the "Toronto statement" of the World Council of Churches (in *A Documentary History of the Faith and Order Movement 1927–1963*, ed. Lukas Vischer [St. Louis, Mo.: Bethany, 1963], p. 174): "The member Churches of the World Council recognize in other Churches elements of the true Church."

[49] Thus, the appropriate use of the notes seems to depend on what Newman described in his *Grammar of Assent* (1870) as the functioning of the illative sense.

[50] Cf. the study by Paul Minear, *Images of the Church in the New Testament* (Philadelphia: Westminster, 1960).

[51] Newman did use scholastic terminology in some of his Roman Catholic works; his *Letter Addressed to His Grace the Duke of Norfolk* (1875), for example, uses a number of scholastic sources and arguments, but those sections seem much less readable than his historical and descriptive sections.

[52] Newman seems to have sensed this difficulty; in any case, his fifth note, "anticipation of the future", complements "preservation of type"; the relationship between these two notes needs to be explored.

[53] Cf. Nicholas Lash, "Was Newman a Theologian?" *Heythrop Journal* 17 (1976), pp. 322–25.

PAUL CHAVASSE

NEWMAN AND THE LAITY

The emergence of the Catholic Church in England from the shadows that had engulfed it at the time of the Reformation was a process both long and difficult. Gathering speed as the end of the eighteenth century approached and continuing to accelerate in the first half of the nineteenth century, the movement for the emancipation of Catholics meant that many and varied attempts resulted as the quiet and retiring followers of the "old religion" reaccustomed themselves to long-forgotten privileges in society at large. What concerns us here is the part played by John Henry Newman in the process of "reemergence" and in a particular way the contribution his thought and writings made to the establishment of the place or role of the laity in the newly emancipated English Church.

Architecture is often as good a guide as any to the state of a civilization and its cultural life, and the Church cannot be an exception to that rule. After Catholic Emancipation in 1829 and the impetus this gave to an ordered growth of ecclesiastical architecture, a hotly disputed argument arose between, on the one hand, the supporters of Augustus W. N. Pugin and the Gothic Revival and, on the other, those, like Newman and the Oratorians, who adopted another, more classical, style, which was condemned by Pugin as "pagan and non-Christian". For the supporters of the Gothic their churches, with dark and mysterious interiors, with the rood screen separating the sanctuary from the rest of the building, were an eloquent witness to the way they wished to perceive the Church as a living reality: the rood screen was as much a real as a symbolic separation of the laity from that holier province occupied by the clergy. For Newman, with his preference for open, classical buildings, where all could see and more effectively share in what was happening at the altar, this, too, reflected a view of the Church, one that has more of an idea of "totality", of clergy and laity together, all part and parcel, so to speak, of that one overarching reality of the Catholic Church, the Mystical Body of Christ.

When the name of John Henry Newman is linked to the laity, more often than not it is "On Consulting the Faithful in Matters of Doctrine", his famous article in the *Rambler*, that springs to mind. One needs to remember, however, that this justly important article is but one item in a much larger corpus of writings on the laity and their vocation within the Church. In order to perceive the significance of the laity for Newman, one needs to examine much more of his output.

Throughout his long life, from its beginnings in the Church of England and the influence he exerted there, particularly in Oxford, to its close as a cardinal of the Roman Church, it is possible to see in Newman's thought on the laity a continuing, harmonious pattern. In Newman, wherever we look, we see a concern to create of the laity an active force that would be at work both in the Church and in the world at large. For this task the laity needed to be properly educated and equipped, and Newman saw this work of education as one to which he was particularly called: "From first to last education, in the large sense of the word, has been my line."[1] After 1845, when Newman became a Catholic, this call to educate the laity inspired a whole host of his undertakings; more than ever he felt called to take up arms in order to awaken in the Catholic Church the slumbering significance of the laity. An educated laity could capture and transform the public mind and in so doing make it that much more receptive to Catholic truth. As Newman said in 1851:

What I desiderate in Catholics is the gift of bringing out what their religion is. . . . I want a laity, not arrogant, not rash in speech, not disputatious, but men who know their religion, who enter into it, who know just where they stand, who know what they hold and what they do not, who know their creed so well that they can give an account of it, who know so much of history that they can defend it. I want an intelligent, well-instructed laity. . . . I wish you to enlarge your knowledge, to cultivate your reason, to get an insight into the relation of truth to truth, to learn to view things as they are, to understand how faith and reason stand to each other, what are the bases and principles of Catholicism and where lies the main inconsistencies and absurdities of the Protestant theory. I have no apprehension you will be the worse Catholics for familiarity with these subjects, provided you cherish a vivid sense of God above and keep in mind that you have souls to be judged and saved. In all times the laity have been the measure of the Catholic spirit; they saved the Irish Church three centuries ago and they betrayed the Church in England. You ought to be able to bring out what you feel and what you mean, as well as to feel and mean it; to expose to the comprehension of others the fictions and fallacies of your opponents; to explain the charges brought against the Church, to the satisfaction, not, indeed, of bigots, but of men of sense, of whatever cast of opinion.[2]

This most justifiably famous address to the Brothers of the Little Oratory in Birmingham[3] is important as a focus for many of the ideas, hopes, and aspirations that Newman held on the laity, their education, and their irreplaceable contribution to the Church's apostolic activity. That Newman's hopes were realized in his own day only in part and even in our own not in any way completely only serves to underscore the magnificence of his vision that address reveals and the depths of the tragedy its lack of implementation has caused.

Newman was always deeply conscious, as the above address shows, of the importance of history in the Church and of how it was ever a determining factor for both its present and its future. Looking back over the centuries, Newman noted the importance the laity had had in either furthering or halting the work of the Reformation, and his earlier studies of the Arian crisis and St. Athanasius had already planted firmly in his mind the indisputable fact that the laity not only *might* be but actually *had been* the champions and preservers of the orthodox Faith in the dark days of the fourth century when Arianism was apparently set to triumph. As he wrote:

> In the earliest age it was simply the *living spirit* of the myriads of the faithful, none of them known to fame, who received from the disciples of the Lord, and husbanded so well and circulated so widely and transmitted so faithfully, generation after generation, the once-delivered apostolic faith; who held it with such sharpness of outline and explicitness of detail, as enabled even the unlearned *instinctively* to discriminate between truth and error, spontaneously to reject the very shadow of heresy and to be proof against the fascination of the most brilliant intellects, when they would lead them out of the narrow way.[4]

If in the fourth, why not in the nineteenth century? An educated laity and a faithful laity—these above all Newman desired; as he put it in "On Consulting the Faithful", a laity "well-catechised and faithful to their baptismal promises".[5] Education is something taught and assimilated according to a man's intelligence and capabilities; faith is a gift that all, of whatever quality and degree, are capable of receiving as bestowed by God and "transmitted" through Baptism. The linking of the laity, education, and Baptism in one train of thought brings us to the very core and origin of the place the laity occupy as a right, a right Newman had ascertained early in his life as an Anglican minister. The importance of the laity and their inherent capability to be defenders of the Faith are rooted in the principle of sacramentality and acquired through the Divine Indwelling received at Baptism, which makes of the baptized visible "signs and instruments" of the Holy Spirit. This fact of the Divine Indwelling and what it implied for each member of the Church in terms of both rights and responsibilities is something that exercised Newman very much from his first experience of apostolic work, and this can be seen clearly from the plentiful references found in his Anglican sermons and in his *Lectures on Justification*.[6] The presence of the Holy Spirit within the hearts and minds of believers means that "the laity receive certain truths of revelation directly from God"[7] and that they therefore possess a definite charism of their own that cannot be neglected and that enables them to bear witness to the Faith that is in them by their word and example—as they did to such a high degree in the Arian crisis.

These ideas were developed by Newman in *Sermons Bearing on Subjects of the Day*, where he reflects on the idea of the Christian's vocation: "Raise the level of religion in your own heart and it will automatically rise in the world. The Christian, then, who prays and is devout is in contact both with Christ and all other Christians."[8] Again, in the sermon entitled "The Apostolical Christian", preached in February 1843, Newman deduces his famous portrait outlining the characteristics of the devout Christian: that he lives according to the Bible, that he looks to Christ and not for the trappings of this world, that he is a man of prayer, that he lacks worldly ties and has a true eschatological attitude, and that joy fills his heart because he knows he lives in the presence of Christ.[9] This picture of the lay Christian in, but not of, the world must have touched and inspired many of Newman's audience and influenced them for good for many years to come.

The Divine Indwelling meant, for Newman, even more than the fact that the faithful rejoice in Christ's presence; it meant that the faithful reproduce him in their lives, and in particular in his threefold office of King, Priest, and Prophet. That is, they reproduce Christ as King in their working and in their endurance, because for the Christian the true royalty is that produced by work that gives dominion over the earth; as priest through the practice of prayer and striving after true sanctity; and as prophet (important for this consideration) by witnessing to the teaching of Christ and similarly teaching to others that witness, passing on from "generation to generation" the truths they have received. "Thus the heart of every Christian ought to represent in miniature the Catholic Church, since the Spirit makes both the whole Church and every member of it to be His Temple."[10]

The meditation and reflection upon divine truth that this doctrine implies help the laity to make explicit their faith and similarly should help to establish that inner sense of what is true and what is false, and from this we can perceive how Newman thought the laity could actually participate in the development of doctrine through the quality of their faith and its lived expression. The discerning between the true and the false is one of the ways in which the "illative sense" is at work in the faithful, both as individuals and as a body. That illative sense is that moral conscience, that striving for conformity between the moral order and the light of revelation, that is felt in some way by all men and that assists the faithful in believing with assurance that which is not clearly seen. This is particularly the case in the areas of worship and devotion, which Newman saw as peculiarly the province of the laity.[11]

A further development in Newman's thought regarding the laity as participators in the prophetical office of Christ and all that that meant for their place in the Church arose when Newman, still an Anglican, had his attention drawn to the many popular devotions held in such esteem by Catholicism. He found it difficult to discern in any sure way what was revealed doctrine and what was only an opinion or a tolerated exercise of piety or ultimately a pious legend. Newman had striven to find a middle way whereby faith was not limited solely to the Scriptures, on the one hand, while on the other it was not extended to include all the things he then regarded as the corruptions of devotion. Newman came to the conclusion that it was necessary to distinguish a twofold Tradition. One can be termed the "episcopal Tradition", comprising the Creed and the Church's solemn rites and ceremonies, all handed down from bishop to bishop, witnessing to belief in the objects of which they are the signs. The second can be called the "prophetic Tradition", which is at work in those who "interpret" revelation. They develop and define its mysteries, clarify its documents, harmonize its content, and apply its promises. The teaching of the prophetic Tradition cannot be easily summarized because of its profusion. The prophetic Tradition is (as Newman wrote in *Via Media*), "the thought and principle that breathes in the Church, her accustomed and unconscious way of viewing things, the body of her received notions and practices, rather than any definite and systematic collection of dogmas elaborated by the intellect". Sometimes it will coincide with the episcopal Tradition; at other times it dissolves in "fable and legend". It is partly written, partly oral, partly a supplement to Scripture; sometimes expressed, sometimes hidden, contained in liturgies, controversies, prejudices, and customs. It is the "thought of the Spirit" or "the breath of the Church". It pertains par excellence to the laity because it is lived, not formulated, and is susceptible to corruption if the Church is not vigilant of it.[12] But it is a rich source of witness to the Faith and what it implies both implicitly and explicitly. Newman, in recognizing this particular way in which the laity share in the prophetic Tradition of the Church, was also led to see how good and how appropriate it is to "consult" those who hold such a richness in their spiritual lives.

These two strains of Tradition never exist in isolation of each other, but they serve to illuminate the fact that the laity's experience of Christianity, lived out in the world as well as in the Church, is indeed for them something unique, which gives a particular insight or preserves a particular truth in a different fashion. It is a reflection of how Newman saw the Church at work: as a totality of both hierarchy and laity together, differing, complementary expressions of the same truth.[13]

The ideas that Newman had pondered and developed for over twenty years (aided, it must be said, by others, such as the Roman theologian Perrone)[14] reached a synthesis—and a controversial one at that—in 1859, when he came to write his renowned article for the magazine *Rambler*. The significance of

the *Rambler* came from the fact that it was carried on by
laymen; its articles were of a high standard, equal to those in
the great reviews; and it presented a Catholic interpretation of
the questions of the day that was appreciated by Catholics and
non-Catholics alike. The object of the magazine was much in
line with Newman's own, for it wished above all to create a
body of thought against the false intellectualism of the age
and to give to Catholicism suitable defenders and defenses,
much in the same way as Lacordaire or Montalembert on the
Continent. Unfortunately, the magazine had managed to offend the bishops because of its often daring theology and
seeming disrespect to Cardinal Wiseman and the system of
seminary education. Its articles were seen as increasingly
carping and provocative, and matters came to a head in
January 1859, when an article (unsigned, but written by Scott
Nasmyth Stokes, a leading Catholic lay authority) criticized
the English bishops for their handling of the current question
of state support for Catholic schools. Stokes was accused of
disloyalty, and at a meeting in London the bishops decided
that unless the editor, Richard Simpson, retired and the spirit
of the magazine changed, they would be forced to censure it.
To avoid a public scandal Newman was approached, as acceptable to both sides, to convince Simpson to go and, as it
turned out, to succeed him as editor. Unwillingly, and after
much prayer, Newman agreed and became editor, seeing in
his new task a means of serving the educated laity and helping
to preserve a magazine that was vital to that particular work of
education in the Church.

In May 1859 the first issue with Newman as editor was
published. The magazine's attitude was changed, and Newman
published an apology for the previous criticism of the bishops
but suggested that "their Lordships really desire to know the
opinion of the laity on subjects in which the laity are especially
concerned". He added that if even in the preparation of a
dogmatic definition, such as recently on that of the Immaculate
Conception, the laity were consulted, how much more they

should be in a practical matter that concerned them closely, such as education. A row developed, as some theologians, principally John Gillow of Ushaw College, Durham, thought Newman's language had implied too much to the role of the laity; and Dr. Ullathorne, Newman's bishop in Birmingham, asked him to give up the newly acquired editorship. Newman had one issue still in hand, that of July 1859, and he regarded it as his last remaining opportunity to explain both himself and the true place of the laity within the Church. He worked hard, his letters almost ceased, and in July there duly appeared "On Consulting the Faithful in Matters of Doctrine". What Newman taught in that article was to be taught in a more solemn manner some one hundred years later in the decrees of the Second Vatican Council. But in the Church of 1859 the reception to his words was very different, and eventually he was secretly delated to Rome for heresy by Bishop Brown of Newport. Early in 1860 Dr. Ullathorne informed Newman of this, and he at once offered to explain his writings in a Catholic sense. Due to a series of misunderstandings between Newman, Wiseman, and Manning, Rome gained the impression that Newman had refused to comply with the request. Much whispering against Newman in both Rome and London for years to come meant that his influence was both suspect and curtailed heavily. As John Coulson put it:

> His publication of this essay was an act of political suicide from which his career in the Church was never fully to recover; at one stroke he, whose reputation as the one honest broker between the extremes of English Catholic opinion had hitherto stood untarnished, gained the Pope's personal displeasure, the reputation in Rome of being the most dangerous man in England, and a formal accusation of heresy proffered against him.[15]

The source of this terrible tragedy lay in a deep-rooted misunderstanding of what Newman meant by the word "consult". In order to grasp Newman's entire thought on the laity, it is essential to be clear on this vital point. We have seen how Newman had come to regard the laity as one of the places in which the Holy Spirit dwelt, how he was active in preserving and stimulating the Faith, and that the richness contained in the lay "prophetical Tradition" and the consensus it gave to Catholic truth enabled it to be seen as one of the areas where the infallible voice of the Church could be heard, as Tradition manifested itself sometimes through bishops and doctors, people, liturgies, rites, and history, any one of them being able to make up for a deficiency in another.[16] However, Newman's eager critics could and did interpret his words as saying that this consultation of the laity was a right they possessed that enabled them, along with the successors of the Apostles, to make the law, as if the laity were also the foundation of the Church. It looked as if they could *demand* to be consulted, as if there was an obligation on the part of the bishops to seek the laity's point of view. Of course this democratic view of Church life and procedure is not at all what Newman meant. We have already noted that Newman was concerned with seeing the Church as a whole, as a totality, and did not wish any division to exist between the rulers of the Church and the laity. Instead a *"conspiratio"* (literally, a "breathing together") should exist: "The two, the Church teaching and the Church taught, are put together as one twofold testimony, illustrating each other, and never to be divided."[17] In his article Newman explains quite clearly: first, what he means by "consult": that it is to establish the *fact* of the laity's belief, just as one might consult a barometer about the weather or a watch about the time of day, not so as to solicit an opinion but to establish a fact. Similarly, in the preparation of a dogmatic definition the faithful are consulted: "Doubtless their advice, their opinion, their judgement on the question of definition is not asked; but the matter of fact, viz. their belief, is sought for, as a testimony to that apostolical tradition, on which alone any doctrine whatsoever can be defined."[18]

That Newman's clarity remained obscurity for some became painfully evident very soon after the article's publication, and even ten years after the *Rambler* crisis, Newman had to pen a brief but authoritative interpretation of what he had meant by "consult" and, therefore, what the status of the laity was in the infallible Church. Just two weeks after the First Vatican Council had defined papal infallibility, Newman referred in a letter (concerned with the acceptance of the dogma) to what is known as the consensus of the Universal Church (using the phrase "*securus judicat orbis terrarum*") "as the ultimate guarantee of revealed truth", but he hastened to add

> that, according to my recollection, my paper in the *Rambler* is not in point. I think the paper was on the *sensus*, not the *consensus* fidelium—their voice was considered as a witness, not as an authority or a judgement—I compared consulting it to consulting a barometer viz. for a fact. Thus it was a *fact* that the fideles in Arian times were for Our Lord's divinity *against* their Bishops— but in the article, I think, I expressly reserved the "Magisterium" for the authorities of the Church.

It was the Magisterium alone that had the ultimate judging, discerning voice.[19] Newman's critics had quite misunderstood the point at issue.

The second major point of the article in the *Rambler* sees Newman address the question of why the laity are consulted.

> And the answer is plain, viz. because the body of the faithful is one of the witnesses to the fact of the tradition of revealed doctrine, and because their *consensus* through Christendom is the voice of the Catholic Church.
>
> I think I am right in saying that the tradition of the Apostles, committed to the whole Church in its various constituents and functions *per modum unius*, manifests itself variously at various times: sometimes by the mouth of the episcopacy, sometimes by the doctors, sometimes by the people, sometimes by liturgies, rites and ceremonies and customs, by events, disputes, movements, and all those other phenomena which are comprised under the name of history. It follows that none of these channels of tradition may be treated with disrespect; granting at the same time fully, that the gift of discerning, discriminating, defining,

promulgating and enforcing any portion of that tradition resides solely in the Ecclesia docens.[20]

And this also covers the doubts Newman had had years before about deficiencies in the Patristical testimony in behalf of various points of Catholic dogma: the *consensus fidelium* supplied such deficiencies, because it too operated as a work of the Holy Spirit—it is "distinct (not separate) from the teaching of their pastors".[21]

In the third major section of the article Newman goes on to show the different ways in which the consent of the faithful is to be regarded: "(1) As a testimony of the fact of apostolical dogma; (2) as a sort of instinct or φρόνημα deep in the bosom of the Mystical Body of Christ; (3) as a direction of the Holy Ghost; (4) as an answer to its prayer; (5) as a jealousy of error, which it at once feels as a scandal".[22] As a practical example of what he means, Newman returned to that era of Church history that had been his special study for his first book, *The Arians of the Fourth Century*, and he shows by a very large number of examples from that era

that in that time of immense confusion the divine dogma of Our Lord's divinity was proclaimed, enforced, maintained and (humanly speaking) preserved, far more by the Ecclesia docta than by the Ecclesia docens; that the body of the episcopate was unfaithful to its commission, while the body of the laity was faithful to its baptism.[23]

Newman quoted at great length the various ancient authorities to show that what he maintained was in fact the case—that during the greater part of the fourth century the dogma of Nicaea was preserved "(1) not by the unswerving firmness of the Holy See, Councils or Bishops, but (2) by the consensus fidelium".[24] Of course Newman was all too well aware that there were enormous differences between the fourth and the nineteenth centuries and that there was not much likelihood that the bishops or the Holy See of his own day would fail in their defense of the orthodox Faith, but nevertheless "each constituent portion of the Church has its proper functions, and no portion can safely be neglected. Though the laity be but the reflection or echo of the clergy in matters of faith, yet there is something in the 'pastorum et fidelium conspiratio' which is not in the pastors alone."[25] This point about the importance of each section of the Church in relation to the whole is emphasized by the remark Newman made that "a person may consult his glass and in that way know things about himself which he can learn in no other way".[26] It is possible, therefore, that the faithful laity can give a greater and more eloquent witness to their Faith, can have an apprehension of it or give an account of it that can serve to illumine it in a way hitherto unattainable. Once again Newman is at pains to emphasize what he sees as the fullness, the totality of Catholic life and practice—that Catholic idea that forms the "secret life of millions of faithful souls",[27] which includes clergy and laity together, possessed of a resiliency and durability in matters of faith that enabled them to survive the great crisis of Arianism.

> It was fitting that those mixed, unlettered multitudes, who for three centuries had suffered and triumphed by virtue of the inward vision of their Divine Lord, should be selected, as we know they were, in the fourth, to be the special champions of His Divinity and the victorious foes of its impugners, at a time when the civil power, which had found them too strong for its arms, attempted, by means of a portentous heresy in the high places of the Church, to rob them of that Truth which had all along been the principle of their strength.[28]

That this grasp of the essentials of the Faith was not something confined to ages long past, but that it continued in his own day, Newman recounted in a letter that also appeared in the *Rambler* for July 1859.[29] This letter is a reply to his own letter that had appeared in the May issue, entitled "Tradition of History in the Schools", and is concerned with "Lay Students in Theology".[30] Newman writes:

> I recollect some twenty-five years ago three friends of my own, as they then were, clergymen of the Establishment, making a tour through Ireland. In the West or South they had occasion to

become pedestrians for the day; and they took a boy of thirteen
to be their guide. They amused themselves with putting questions to him on the subject of his religion; and one of them
confessed to me on his return that that poor child put them all
to silence. How? Not of course by any train of argument or
refined theological disquisition, but merely by knowing and
understanding the answers in his catechism.[31]

That example surely illustrates the basic, bottom-line defense
that Newman hoped *all* the laity could provide—all of them
well catechized and faithful to the promises of their Baptism.

That letter, and so very much else with which Newman
concerned himself on the laity's behalf, was to do with building
up a well-catechized laity and turning some of it into a well-
educated laity that could take its place in the world and in
that world be able to debate intelligently with, and answer
accurately the questions of, the Protestant majority. It would
not be enough for the layman to say, "I leave it to theologians",
or, "I will ask my priest"—he must, as Newman put it, be able
there and then to lay down the law. The need Newman
perceived for the laity to have clear convictions about revealed
doctrines as well as expertise in worldly affairs and intellectual
disciplines led Newman to see that the Church had a definite
obligation to support superior higher education for its laity,
and this education, he saw, must be suited to the lay life as
such; it was not enough for it to be a watered-down type of
seminary. All his hard work and many labors at the Catholic
University in Dublin were concerned with setting up precisely
this sort of establishment and atmosphere in which the Catholic
layman could learn and develop. The many intense frustrations
of the Dublin years, caused by a deep-rooted mistrust and
misunderstanding on the part of the Irish bishops, caused
Newman much personal anguish because he realized what was
at stake and the supreme folly of throwing over the oppor-
tunities provided. He saw in Ireland that the ecclesiastical
powers were in fact jealous of the laity and, what is more,
fearful of them, if their knowledge and education grew too

great.[32] For the bishops their control had to be absolute, and Newman could not tolerate this. Again, in England the failure to allow English Catholics to attend the universities of Oxford and Cambridge filled him with foreboding. If university life were to be prohibited and nothing provided in its place, then Catholicism would never exert an influential voice in secular affairs because there would be no one who held Catholicism dear capable of rising in society. "Are Catholics to be worse educated than all other gentlemen in the country?" Newman asked.[33] "I am inclined to think that the Archbishop considers only an ignorant laity to be manageable."[34] Newman could not understand this attitude of mind:

> On both sides of the Channel the deep difficulty is the jealousy and fear which is entertained in high quarters of the laity . . . nothing great or living can be done except where men are self-governed and independent: this is quite consistent with a full maintenance of ecclesiastical supremacy.[35]

But Newman could and did understand the grave dangers the attitude brought in its train. Newman wrote to George Fottrell:

> As far as I can see there are ecclesiastics all over Europe whose policy is to keep the laity at arms-length; and hence the laity have been disgusted and become infidel and only two parties exist, both ultras in opposite directions. I came away from Ireland with the distressing fear that in that Catholic country, in like manner, there was to be an antagonism, as time went on, between the hierarchy and the educated classes. You will be doing the greatest possible benefit to the Catholic cause all over the world, if you succeed in making the University a middle station at which clergy and laity can meet, so as to learn to understand and to yield to each other—and from which, as from a common ground, they may act in unison upon an age which is running headlong into infidelity.[36]

A thwarted laity would turn anticlerical, if not worse. However, with education they would be transformed into the main-stay of the Church: "I am sure they may be made in this day the strength of the Church"[37]—giving and receiving responsibility, support, and trust. Without this degree of involvement, which education would stimulate, the Church would be greatly impoverished and many people would turn from her in frustration, or, if they stayed, they would be reduced to having only an "implicit faith" in the Church's teachings, "which in the educated classes will terminate in indifference and in the poorer in superstition".[38] The mere imposition of doctrines on the faithful without any attempt at education in the reasons why, or their being asked to deal with subjects that seem far removed from what is apprehended by them as their "real" belief, runs the danger of a growing sense of alienation setting in among the laity—on the one hand indifference, if not outright rejection; on the other hand the growth of a quasi-magical or superstitious religiosity, having no root in the fundamental tenets of the Christian Faith. A wise approach to the teaching and handing on of the Faith, and that alone, was the safest way in which to build up a faithful, intelligent body of believers. Thwarted in Ireland and in his hopes at Oxford, Newman had greater success nearer home, in the establishment of a school for boys at the Birmingham Oratory, in which his principles could be put to work, and, of course, in the Oratory itself as a community of priests working in a city in order to serve the laity there, after the example of the Oratory's founder, St. Philip Neri himself. Many were the works the Fathers undertook in often difficult circumstances in Birmingham in order to raise the level of Catholicism there and influence, in that winning, personal way, so favored by St. Philip, the non-Catholic world around them.

> He [Philip] preferred to yield to the stream and direct the current, which he could not stop, of science, literature, art and fashion, and to sweeten and sanctify what God had made very good and man had spoilt. . . . Whether or not I can do anything at all in St. Philip's way, at least I can do nothing in any other.[39]

All of these many works and enterprises find an echo in a famous sermon that Newman preached in Dublin:

Some persons will say that I am thinking of confining, distorting, and stunting the growth of the intellect by ecclesiastical supervision. I have no such thought. Nor have I any thought of a compromise, as if religion must give up something and science something. I wish the intellect to range with the utmost freedom, and religion to enjoy an equal freedom; but what I am stipulating for is this, that they should be found in one and the same place and exemplified in the same persons. . . . Devotion is not a sort of finish given to the sciences, nor is science a sort of feather in the cap, if I may so express myself, an ornament and set-off to devotion. I want the intellectual layman to be religious, and the devout ecclesiastic to be intellectual.[40]

The amount of time and energy Newman put into his educational affairs, the intensity with which he felt the need for the laity's baptismal prerogatives to be respected, acted upon and developed for the greater good of the whole Church, lead us on to ask the simple question "Why?" What was the underlying concern that gave rise to all this activity? Was it solely that the Church might be seen in all its glorious fullness, or was there something further, perhaps more immediate? The answer is, of course, that there was an immediate reason for Newman's concern for the preparedness of the laity, and what has already been said has given some insight into the reasons why.

Newman had early on recognized the prophetical Tradition at work in the Church and had learned the value of that Tradition in preserving the Faith in a time of crisis. Newman, to use "prophetical" in a more everyday sense, was much concerned with, and worried about, the future of the Church and the preparations that had to be made in order to meet the challenge of the future in an appropriate fashion. From his earliest days in Oxford, Newman had perceived that an intellectual movement was growing up that would sap the foundations of revealed religion. As a result of this movement, and as its ideas percolated through society and became part of society's received and accepted wisdom, Newman could see that the future Church would enter a period in which she would be confronted by an atheism both learned and cultured and in which she would need competent and trained defenders, who would have to come in large part from the laity. Newman could see so clearly a future world, gathered around "two conflicting poles", that of the conscious atheists and that of the convinced Catholics, with the intermediary positions having ceased to exercise any worthwhile influence. The philosophy of Newman's day, as well as much of its literature, and the growing power and influence of science and technology were all in the process of destroying or abandoning their Christian roots and were therefore destined to clash, sooner or later, with religion. It was the role of the educated, committed laity to evangelize this nascent secularist society and witness in the best way they could to their living Faith and its power. The layman was now being called to become the "apostle of the latter times", and he must be equipped for his task.

One of Newman's most famous analyses of the forces at work in his day and what they portended for the future is found in the *biglietto* speech of May 1879, given in Rome when Newman was there to receive his cardinal's "red hat" from Pope Leo XIII. During the course of his speech, Newman said:

> And I rejoice to say, to one great mischief I have from the first opposed myself. For thirty, forty, fifty years I have resisted to the best of my powers the spirit of liberalism in religion. Never did Holy Church need champions against it more sorely than now, when, alas! it is an error overspreading, as a snare, the whole earth. Liberalism in religion is the doctrine that there is no positive truth in religion, but that one creed is as good as another . . . it is inconsistent with any recognition of any religion as true . . . revealed religion is not a truth but a sentiment and a taste; not an objective fact, not miraculous, and it is the right of each individual to make it say just what strikes his fancy.

He regretted the fact that the old dictum that "Christianity is the law of the land" had been replaced, "nearly forgotten", and that "instead of the Church's authority and teaching, they would substitute, first of all, a universal and a thoroughly secular education". He was saddened by it all "because I see that it may be the ruin of many souls".[41]

Some six years before this speech, in 1873, Newman had preached at the opening of St. Bernard's Seminary, Olton, and having entitled his sermon "The Infidelity of the Future", he told his hearers:

> I think that the trials which lie before us are such as would appall and make dizzy even such courageous hearts as St. Athanasius, St. Gregory I or St. Gregory VII. And they would confess that, dark as the prospect of their own day was to them severally, ours has a darkness different in kind from any that has been before it. . . . Christianity has never yet had experience of a world simply irreligious. The ancient world of Greece and Rome was full of superstition but not of infidelity, for they believed in the moral governance of the world and their first principles were the same as ours. Similarly the northern barbarians . . . believed in an unknown providence and in the moral law. But we are now coming to a time when the world does not acknowledge our first principles.[42]

If that is how Newman could look back over his long life and see in his opposition to liberalism and the defense of dogma and revealed religion the thread that linked his work together, and if looking to the future he could see the emergence of an age darker than any hitherto experienced because for all practical purposes without God and his Law, we can perhaps the better understand the urgency and concern that marked his work for the laity. It was a matter of survival that dictated his ultimate agenda, not a desire to foment rebellion in the ranks or to unsettle the bishops, which is how many evaluated him; always the need to train and equip the troops necessary to be a defense against the new world and its secularist heresy—that was what counted above all else. That so much of what Newman tried to do for the laity was misunderstood and quite deliberately thwarted can now be seen, in the light of his prophetic remarks, as the terrible tragedy it was for the future of the Church. "Here was the one man who could perhaps

have stemmed the tide of unbelief, and his ecclesiastical
superiors sedulously kept him from the intellectual centre of
England."[43]

Some one hundred years after Newman's death, what can
we say about his thoughts on the laity and their vital role in the
life of the Church? Seen positively, many of Newman's deepest
insights have been taken up and have become an accepted part
of modern ecclesiological thinking. This is undoubtedly because
Newman's research and thought were so soundly based on
Scripture and the Fathers; his own "methodology" sprang
from a true understanding of the Church's Tradition. Any true
renewal has to begin in this manner: a true growth based on
what has gone before, seen in the needs that the present and
future make apparent. The breadth of vision and understanding
that Newman presents in his writings was such as to make him
the "unseen guide" in so many of the deliberations of the
Second Vatican Council and in its teachings on the laity in the
Church. It will be profitable to see this in practice, by quoting
one or two passages from the conciliar documents. For instance,
the constitution *Lumen Gentium* contains the following reflection
on how the faithful share in Christ's prophetic message:

> The holy People of God shares also in Christ's prophetic office:
> it spreads abroad a living witness to him, especially by a life of
> faith and love and by offering to God a sacrifice of praise, the
> fruit of lips praising his name (cf. Heb 13:15). The whole body
> of the faithful who have an anointing that comes from the holy
> one (cf. 1 Jn 2:20 and 27) cannot err in matters of belief. This
> characteristic is shown in the supernatural appreciation of the
> faith (*sensus fidei*) of the whole people, when, "from the bishops
> to the last of the faithful" they manifest a universal consent in
> matters of faith and morals. By this appreciation of the faith,
> aroused and sustained by the Spirit of truth, the People of God,
> guided by the sacred teaching authority (magisterium) and
> obeying it, receives not the mere word of men, but truly the
> word of God (cf. 1 Th 2:13), the faith once for all delivered to the

saints (cf. Jude 3). The People unfailingly adheres to this faith, penetrates it more deeply with right judgment, and applies it more fully in daily life.[44]

This paragraph had originally been intended to form part of Chapter IV, on the laity, but was brought forward into the chapter on the People of God in order to mark the unity that exists between the laity and the hierarchy, which together form the People of God, who cannot err in matters of belief when they show that *"universalis consensus"* in matters of faith and morals. Objections and amendments to the text, which had wanted to highlight the role of the hierarchy more prominently, were not admitted, because the Council Fathers wanted to show that the *sensus fidei* was not to be considered as a particular prerogative of the hierarchy but as a power of the whole Church. There is a unity in bearing witness to the Faith that belongs to the totality of the Body of Christ. This concern of the Council Fathers is a most eloquent echo of the *"pastorum et fidelium conspiratio"* that Newman believed in and advocated so strongly.

Newman's explanation of the importance of the consensus of the faithful and how that assists the Church is also to be found in the Council documents. Some of the bishops wished to say that the faithful are infallible because they *reflect* the teaching of the infallible Magisterium, but this was objected to as being an inadequate notion. Investigating Tradition, as Newman had done, it was obvious that the process of doctrinal development sometimes begins with the people: their consensus activates the infallible teaching authority of the Magisterium, which must discern and judge what has happened. The laity do not just reflect the teaching of the Magisterium, but they possess an active exercise of their prerogative that comes from their being constituted as the people of God. This is so made up of all the baptized because, irrespective of their hierarchical status or lack of it, they are the recipients of those motions or inspirations of the Holy Spirit that form the "dynamic element" in the Church, over against the "static element", which is the hierarchy as such.

> It is not only through the sacraments and the ministrations of the Church that the Holy Spirit makes holy the People, leads them and enriches them with his virtues. Allotting his gifts according as he wills (cf. 1 Cor 12:11), he also distributes special graces among the faithful of every rank. By these gifts he makes them fit and ready to undertake various tasks and offices for the renewal and building up of the Church, as it is written, "the manifestation of the Spirit is given to everyone for profit" (1 Cor 12:7). Whether these charisms be very remarkable or more simple and widely diffused, they are to be received with thanksgiving and consolation since they are fitting and useful for the needs of the Church.[45]

This teaching on the gifts of the Holy Spirit being given to and for the good of the whole Church is also identical to that which Newman believed and proclaimed to be the case. His own criterion, which established the fact that the laity ought to be consulted, is precisely that they are open to and led by the workings of the Holy Spirit—the Divine Indwelling. This enables them, as devout believers, to appreciate ever more readily the Church's Traditions and beliefs and, as we have already noted, guided by the same Holy Spirit, the laity has the gift of knowing the meaning of the Creed and the Deposit of Faith and in such a way that they can resist heresy and cling unswervingly to the truth.

Newman's analysis of the role of the laity was, of course, intended to provide a theological foundation for a greater degree of cooperation between the laity and the hierarchy of the Church. Similarly, in the Second Vatican Council we find manifested a like desire. The laity are urged to respond to the injunction that they should "disclose their needs and desires with that liberty and confidence which befit children of God and brothers of Christ".[46] Again, "an individual layman, by reason of the knowledge, competence, or outstanding ability which he may enjoy, is permitted and sometimes even obliged to express his opinion on things which concern the good of the Church",[47] which is complemented by words in the constitution *Gaudium et Spes* on the Church in the modern world, "All the faithful, clerical and lay, possess a lawful freedom of enquiry and of thought, and the freedom to express their minds humbly and courageously about those matters in which they enjoy competence."[48] These ideas reach their fullest formation in the decree *Apostolicam Actuositatem*, on the apostolate of the laity, which complements the other decrees and highlights once again that cooperation, *conspiratio*, so much desired by Newman. *Apostolicam Actuositatem* sees the laity as having a "special and indispensable" position in the Church's mission. Especially important in view of what Newman taught is the following passage:

> For the exercise of the apostolate [the Holy Spirit] gives the faithful special gifts . . . so that each and all, putting at the service of others the grace received, may be "as good stewards of God's varied gifts" (1 Pet 4:10). . . . From the reception of these charisms, even the most ordinary ones, there arise for each of the faithful the right and duty of exercising them in the Church and in the world for the good of men and the development of the Church.[49]

That "right and duty" Newman had perceived at work when the laity helped save the Church from the Arian heresy. In a later age, he hoped it would be developed and used again to defend the Church from outside attacks, and, within, to prevent the Church from becoming too clericalized and turned in upon itself, and he hoped that a well-deployed, educated, and faithful laity would be able to do more good in those many areas of secular life where even an army of priests could not penetrate so effectively.

These decrees of the Second Vatican Council represent, in a wonderful way, that restoration of a balanced ecclesiological outlook, a return to that view of the totality of the Church

that inspired Newman. However, even though so many of
Newman's fondest hopes found their realization in the Council,
they did so at the same time as some of his worst fears for the
future Church were also in the process of becoming realities.
That the final acceptance of so much of Newman's thought on
the laity should have coincided with a crisis of authority, of
faith, and of morals within the Church has led to a degree of
confusion almost without parallel, which has affected those
very laymen Newman wished to help. Very many have been
the comments and analyses of the present crisis, some more
accurate than others.[50] The present Holy Father, Pope John
Paul II, offered this reflection:

> [We] must not forget that there are difficulties in living the Faith.
> They are not only due to constraints by men, laws, or regimes.
> They can also come from customs and ways of thinking which
> are contrary to evangelical principles and which have a powerful
> influence on society. Again it could be the influence of materialism
> and of religious indifference which kills spiritual aspirations; or
> the false and individualistic notion of freedom which confuses
> the possibility of choosing whatever gratifies one's passions
> with the concern for fully developing one's human callings,
> spiritual destiny, and the common good. It is not this kind of
> freedom which forms the basis of human dignity and encourages
> Christian faith. Believers who are surrounded by such influences
> need great courage to remain sane and faithful and to exercise
> their freedom properly.[51]

In many quarters now there is great confusion about what
the laity might or might not be able to do, even in the highest
sacramental activities, time and again debates or agreements
hinge on the question of whether the Church has truly advanced
in the light of the Council or whether the freedoms and new
impetus of the 1960s have already been dissipated and lost. In
the years immediately after the close of the Second Vatican
Council, the conciliar texts quoted above, all of them un-
impeachable when seen as according to the mind of the
Church, were eagerly seized upon to justify what was falsely

announced as "the age of the laity", which had now dawned upon the Church. In truth, what the Council had tried to make clear was not that the laity were now to be the guiding lights of the Church but rather the exact point that Newman had tried to make in 1859—that they have an indispensable role in the life and mission of the Church; in short, that they cannot be ignored. What the Council hoped for was not "the age of the laity" but a truly renewed Church, drawing new life from her sources, from Scripture, Tradition, and the Fathers. The concept of the "infallible laity", as so often encountered in these days, is not one that would have sat easily on the shoulders of Newman, for so often, as was pointed out in a recent issue of *Faith and Reason*,[52] behind the desire to boost the laity is lurking "the glorification of private judgment", which, as we have seen, was part of that liberalism that Newman resisted so strongly. He would have no patience with that judgment even when presented as the sacredness of conscience. Nothing was more sacred to him than that inner voice about morally good and morally evil which, in his most considered judgment, is the most direct evidence of God. But he had no use for the culturally sanctioned meaning of conscience which he branded publicly as a "miserable counterfeit" in his Letter to the Duke of Norfolk:

> [It is] the right of thinking, speaking, writing and acting, according to their judgement or their humour, without any thought of God at all. They do not even pretend to go by any moral rule, but they demand, what they think is an Englishman's prerogative, to be his own master in all things, and to profess what he pleases, asking no-one's leave, and accounting priest or preacher, speaker or writer, unutterably impertinent, who dares to say a word against his going to perdition, if he like it, in his own way. Conscience has rights because it has duties; but in this age, with a large portion of the public, it is the very right and freedom of conscience to dispense with conscience, to ignore a Lawgiver and Judge, to be independent of unseen obligations. It becomes a license to take up any or no religion, to take up this or that and

let it go again, to go to Church, to go to Chapel, to boast of being above all religions and to be impartial critic of each of them. Conscience is a stern monitor, but in this century it has been superseded by a counterfeit, which the eighteen centuries prior to it never heard of, and could not have mistaken for it, if they had. It is the right of self-will.

He had respect only for a conscience which was the very opposite to a "longsided selfishness" and a "desire to be consistent with oneself".[53]

Those who seek to use Newman as the apostle of the age of the laity would do well to pay close attention to his words before they hold him up as someone who, for example, would maintain that *Humanae vitae* is a dead letter because it has failed to receive that "ecclesial reception" from the laity, which would surely have marked it if it had been an authentic exercise of the teaching authority of the Church.[54] The man who held that sort of a view could not have written, for example: "Everyone in the Church, ignorant or learned, must absolutely submit his mind with an inward assent to the Church as the teacher of the whole Faith."[55] Or again: "It is no trouble to believe, when the Church has spoken; the real trouble is when a number of little Popes start up, laymen often, and preach against Bishops and Priests, and make their own opinions the faith, and frighten simple-minded devout people and drive back inquirers."[56]

Newman nowadays is often held up as the theologian of evolution, and many things are claimed for him that he would have repudiated in his lifetime. His ideas on the laity in the Church surely reveal him to have been much rather the upholder of identity, searching always to discover that "unity of type", that fundamental and abiding identity that adheres to the Church of Christ in all its totality that when found is a sure sign that the searcher is on the right path. On Newman's memorial in the cloisters of the Oratory in Birmingham are carved the words he himself chose with such care: *"Ex umbris et imaginibus in veritatem"* and *"Cor ad cor loquitur"*—these can be taken as summing up what he himself regarded as the meaning of his long life and many labors for the Church of Christ and for Christ's Truth, his own brief summary of a life lived for others in that Church, a life lived in union with God. His work was surely that of striving to bring not just a part but the whole Church, clergy and laity, into the Truth of Christ, in a fuller, more explicit fashion; establishing that *conspiratio* that should exist between all the members of the one Mystical Body.

Newman's work for the laity was undertaken so that the graces they had received in Baptism might develop and flower —so that they might grow in holiness through a deeper love of prayer, Scripture, and the sacraments; so that through their education, although not on the level of theologians, nevertheless, they might still live out to a high degree their faith and in so doing raise the level of religion in both themselves and the world; so that through the quality of their faith they might be signposts, pointing out the true meaning of Christianity in the modern world and doing it with a sense of freedom and responsibility in loyal and loving union with the Magisterium and all that that implies.

It was Newman's desire that the whole Church "might go on in her own proper duties in confidence and peace" and in so doing, "to stand still and see the salvation of God".[57]

Where this "confidence and peace", stemming from the unity of priests and people around Christ their Head, have been established (and they can be found in the Church today), they are at their best, "that realization of the insights into the nature and membership of the Church [which were] made clear by the Council [and] which owe[s] much to the vision and courage of John Henry Newman".[58]

NOTES

[1] *Autobiographical Writings*, ed. H. Tristram (London: Sheed & Ward, 1956).

[2] *The Present Position of Catholics in England*, ed. D. O'Connell, S.J. (New York: America Press, 1942), pp. 299–300.

[3] The Little Oratory is the association or brotherhood of laymen, young and old, served by the Fathers of the Oratory, and dedicated, in a quiet way, to prayer and good works. Newman sees their influence as possibly very far-reaching!

[4] *Historical Sketches* (Westminster, Md.: Christian Classics, 1970), vol. I, pp. 209–10.

[5] *On Consulting the Faithful in Matters of Doctrine*, ed. with an introduction by J. Coulson (London: Collins, 1961), reissued with a foreword by Derek Worlock, Archbishop of Liverpool (London: Collins, 1986), p. 76.

[6] For instance, many of the sermons in *Parochial and Plain Sermons* (San Francisco: Ignatius Press, 1987), vol. I, such as no. 6, "The Spiritual Mind" (pp. 50–56), or no. 14, "Religious Emotion" (pp. 113–20), or from vol. V, no. 2, "Reverence, a Belief in God's Presence" (pp. 959–68).

[7] See *The Idea of a University Defined and Illustrated*, ed. I. T. Ker (Oxford: Clarendon Press, 1976), pp. 379 and 441.

[8] *Sermons Bearing on Subjects of the Day* (Westminster, Md.: Christian Classics, 1970), pp. 133–34.

[9] Ibid., pp. 275–92.

[10] See *Idea of a University*, pp. 235 and 238.

[11] In 1865 Newman wrote: "The people have a special right to interfere in questions of devotion." See J. Derek Holmes, ed., *The Theological Papers of John Henry Newman on Biblical Inspiration and Infallibility* (Oxford: Oxford University Press, 1979), p. 104.

[12] *Via Media*, vol. I, p. 251. But he warned, "What has power to stir holy and refined souls is potent also with the multitude; and the religion of the multitude is ever vulgar and abnormal; it will ever be tinctured with fanaticism and superstition, while men are what they are. A people's religion is ever a corrupt religion, in spite of the provisions of Holy Church." *Certain Difficulties Felt by Anglicans in Catholic Teaching* (Westminster, Md.: Christian Classics, 1969), vol. II, p. 80.

[13] For a masterly synthesis of this line of thought in Newman, see J. Guitton, *The Church and the Laity* (New York: Alba House, 1965), pp. 43–47.

[14] The Newman-Perrone paper has the Latin title "*De Catholici dogmatis evolutione*", published as "The Newman-Perrone Paper on Development", *Gregorianum* 16 (1935), pp. 404–44.

[15] Coulson, op. cit., p. 2.

[16] *On Consulting the Faithful*, pp. 64–70.

[17] Ibid., p. 71.

[18] Ibid., pp. 54–55.

[19] Letter of Aug. 3, 1870, to F. Rymer, *Letters and Diaries*, vol. XXV, p. 172. This passage of capital importance was called to my attention by Fr. Jaki during his visit in Birmingham Oratory in Aug. 1988. See also his article quoted in n. 52 below.

[20] *On Consulting the Faithful*, p. 63.

[21] Ibid., p. 66.

[22] Ibid., p. 73.

[23] Ibid., p. 76. In the 1871 edition of *The Arians of the Fourth Century*, Newman added the following:

> The Catholic people, in the length and breadth of Christendom, were the obstinate champions of Christian truth, and the bishops were not. . . . And again, in speaking of the laity, I speak inclusively of their parish priests (so to call them), at least in many places; but, on the whole, taking a wide view of history, we are obliged to say that the governing body came short and the governed were preeminent in faith, zeal, courage and constancy. This is a remarkable fact; but there is a moral in it. Perhaps it was permitted in order to impress upon the Church . . . the great evangelical lesson that, not the wise and powerful, but the obscure, the unlearned and the weak constitute her real strength. It was mainly by the faithful people that paganism was overthrown; it was by the faithful people, under the lead of Athanasius and the Egyptian bishops, and in some places supported by their bishops and priests, that the worst of heresies was withstood.

Quoted by Coulson, op. cit., pp. 109–10.

[24] Ibid., p. 77.

[25] Ibid., pp. 103–4. See also Newman writing in 1842: "The Church has authority only while all members conspire together." In *Letters and Correspondence of John Henry Newman during His Life in the English Church*, ed. Anne Mozley (London: Longman, 1891), vol. II, p. 400.

[26] Ibid., p. 72.

[27] *Fifteen Sermons Preached before the University of Oxford* (Westminster, Md.: Christian Classics, 1966), pp. 313 and 323.

[28] *An Essay in Aid of a Grammar of Assent*, ed. I. T. Ker (Oxford: Clarendon Press, 1985), p. 312.

[29] *The Rambler* (July 1859), pp. 238–41.

[30] The full text is given in *Letters and Diaries*, vol. XIX, pp. 543–47.

[31] For the actual event, see Mozley, op. cit., vol. I, p. 211.

[32] See, for example, letters to Ormsby (*Letters and Diaries*, vol. XX, p. 241) and to Allies (vol. XXI, pp. 326–27, and vol. XXIV, p. 46).

[33] *Letters and Diaries*, vol. XXI, pp. 384–85.

[34] *Letters and Diaries*, vol. XXVI, p. 66.

[35] *Letters and Diaries*, vol. XXI, p. 331.

[36] *Letters and Diaries*, vol. XXVI, pp. 393–94. Fottrell was president of the Literary and Historical Society at the Catholic University of Ireland, Dublin.

[37] *Letters and Diaries*, vol. XIV, p. 252.

[38] *On Consulting the Faithful*, p. 106.

[39] *Sermons Preached on Various Occasions* (London: Longman, 1870; Westminster, Md.: Christian Classics, 1968), pp. 236–37.

[40] Ibid., p. 13.

[41] *Addresses to Cardinal Newman and His Replies, 1879–1881*, ed. W. Neville (London: Longman, 1905), pp. 61–71.

[42] *Catholic Sermons of Cardinal Newman* (London: Burns & Oates, 1957), pp. 121 and 123.

[43] Anthony Hanson writing in *The Irish Times*, July 31, 1971, reviewing vol. XXI of *Letters and Diaries*.

[44] *Lumen Gentium*, no. 12, in *Vatican II: The Conciliar and Postconciliar Documents*, ed. A. Flannery (Dublin: Dominican Publications, 1975), p. 363.

[45] Ibid.

[46] *Lumen Gentium*, no. 37, in Flannery, op. cit., p. 394.

[47] Ibid.

[48] *Gaudium et Spes*, no. 62, in Flannery, op. cit., p. 968.

[49] *Apostolicam Actuositatem*, no. 3, in Flannery, op. cit., p. 769.

[50] One of the most interesting in recent years is that of Anne Roche Muggeridge, *The Desolate City* (Toronto: McClelland & Stewart, 1986).

[51] Pope John Paul II speaking in Lourdes, Aug. 14, 1983.

[52] Stanley L. Jaki, "Newman's Logic and the Logic of the Papacy", in *Faith and Reason* 3 (1987), pp. 241–65.

[53] The quotation is from Newman's *Letter to the Duke of Norfolk*, p. 58.

[54] See *John Henry Newman on the Idea of the Church*, ed. Jeremy Miller (Shepherdstown, W.V.: Patmos Press, 1987), p. 152.

[55] *Letters and Diaries*, vol. XXIII, p. 100.

[56] Ibid., vol. XXIII, p. 272.

[57] *Addresses to Cardinal Newman*, pp. 69–70.

[58] Archbishop Derek Worlock, in his foreword to *On Consulting the Faithful*, p. vii.

Marvin R. O'Connell

NEWMAN AND LIBERALISM

> I often think it's comical
> How nature always does contrive
> That every boy and every gal
> That's born into the world alive
> Is either a little Liberal
> Or else a little Conservative.[1]
>
> W. S. Gilbert

This bit of doggerel from the second act of Gilbert and Sullivan's *Iolanthe* expresses the homely truth that some categories of thought, once peripheral accretions have been stripped away from them, are reducible to fundamental and intelligible alternatives. Thus it may not be an exaggeration to say that the Western philosophical tradition established a permanent dichotomy as early as the fourth century before Christ, in Athens, where Aristotle, so to speak, confronted Plato, and that ever since that time differing explanations of the causes of things have given evidence, in one way or another, of the perduring contest between realism and idealism.

> Every baby weaned, I wist,
> Is an Aristotelian or a Platonist.

Similarly, the terms "liberal" and "conservative" represent an ultimate choice, the kind of rock-bottom difference of view that, W. S. Gilbert seemed to imply in his libretto, divides the human family from infancy onward. Not, of course, "liberal" and "conservative" in any partisan sense. Indeed, the use of these terms as labels for political parties or factions has become so diffuse that all meaning has been drained from them. Thus Mr. Gorbachev and his allies in the Kremlin are dubbed "liberals", and their opponents "conservatives". Thus Mr. Peres leads the "liberal" faction within Israel's coalition government, and Mr. Shamir the "conservative". Thus the "liberals" at this summer's Democratic convention in Atlanta insisted that the health and even the survival of the republic depend upon Senator Bentsen of Texas being a single heartbeat from the presidency. Much the same irrelevance has fallen upon those other warhorses of journalistic jargon, "left" and "right", which have been relentlessly misapplied ever since the French Revolution—so much so that a recent issue of the London *Economist* opined, not altogether with tongue in cheek, that the demise of socialism being admitted now, even within the Soviet Union itself, pundits who want to continue to employ the categories "left" and "right" will have to confine themselves to describing various attitudes toward the environment or scientific research.[2]

But despite this chronic carelessness in usage, there remains a sense in which "liberal" and "conservative" can still offer a measure of illumination. The distinction may indeed be too bland and general to satisfy really acute thinkers, but perhaps for us lesser mortals it may serve a turn. A liberal is somebody who wants to change what is wrong. A conservative is somebody who wants to preserve what is right. And since a condition of life in this valley of tears, in this imperfect universe, is that everything displays an admixture of wrong and right, it follows that both the liberal and the conservative positions are radically defensible. In fact, one would be hard pressed to find a concrete situation in which the individual human actors did not manifest in their behavior a combination of the two.

Be that as it may, one must proceed warily in attempting to determine Newman's relationship to liberalism, not because Newman failed to give precision to his own understanding of the term but because "liberalism", if it has virtually no meaning today, meant, during the nineteenth century, a great variety of things.[3] The pious Gladstone was a liberal, and so was the apostate priest Lamennais, and so were Cavour, Garibaldi, and Mazzini. Napoleon III's regime—which was anathema to the liberal Montalembert—was nevertheless called a "liberal" empire.[4] "I die", said Father Lacordaire, the great preacher of Notre Dame de Paris and the restorer of the Dominican order in France, "I die a penitent Catholic and an impenitent liberal." Newman held Gladstone's person in high regard, though he disliked the Grand Old Man's politics.[5] Lamennais, whom he never met, seemed to him a tragic figure rather than an intellectually significant one.[6] As for Montalembert and Lacordaire, "I do not believe", Newman wrote in the *Apologia*, "that it is possible for me to differ in any important matter from two men whom I so highly admire. In their general line of thought and conduct I enthusiastically concur, and consider them to be before their age."[7]

There is no doubt that Newman's reluctance to condemn in strong enough terms the brand of liberalism represented by Cavour and Garibaldi moved some of his English coreligionists to suspect him of being a "liberal Catholic", to brand him, indeed, as one of them did, "the most dangerous man in England".[8] It is not easy to recapture over this distance of time the sense of outrage among Catholics a hundred years ago at the assault launched against the Holy See by the forces of the Italian *risorgimento*. Denunciation of the aggressive designs of the King of Piedmont and his minions upon the Papal States became for many Catholics, in England and elsewhere, the litmus test of true religion. Not that Newman harbored any sympathy for those who aimed to despoil the Pope of the dominions he and his predecessors had ruled for a thousand years. "Sacrilegious robbers", he called them in a sermon preached in 1866.[9] But neither was he prepared to overestimate the importance of the Temporal Power or to allow loyalty to the Pope as Vicar of Christ and supreme teacher of the Church to be confused with the position of the Pope as a temporal sovereign, however venerable that sovereignty may have been. Newman recalled from his youth "Lord Palmerston's words that, as Dr. Sumner made an excellent Archbishop [of

Canterbury], yet it did not follow that he would succeed as Prime Minister". Perhaps "the Holy Father had far too much on his hands as Pastor of the Catholic Flock to acquit himself well as the Temporal Ruler of a territory over and above his *ecclesiastical* training". [10]

This last remark Newman made in private. In public he expressed himself on the Temporal Power with that precision of language that often led irritated opponents to accuse him of excessive subtlety. As one of them put it in a different context, "[Newman] simply twists [people] round his little finger, and bamboozles [them] with his carefully selected words and plays so subtly with his logic that [their] simplicity is taken in." [11] Zealots are indeed seldom patient with "carefully selected words", and many Catholic zealots of the 1860s and 1870s —including persons in very high places—were determined— incredible as it may seem to us—to resist the guns of the Piedmontese by securing a formal definition of the Pope's Temporal Power as an Article of Faith. [12] "What I especially was anxious about", Newman noted later, "was that there should be no attempt to make the Temporal Power a doctrine *de fide*, and that for two reasons. First, perhaps it was in God's Providence to cease to be. Second, it was not right to frighten, worry, irritate Catholics by forcing on them as *de fide* what was not." [13]

In the late summer of 1866 Ullathorne, Newman's bishop, decreed that throughout the diocese of Birmingham the feast of the Rosary, October 7, be celebrated with particular solemnity and that "in the Sermon at the Mass of the Festival . . . the preacher should instruct the faithful on their obligations to the Holy See, and on the duty especially incumbent on us at this time of praying for the Pope". No one could fail to understand why Pius IX needed prayer "at this time", in the Bishop's words: the Piedmontese had already occupied Romagna and the Marches, and only the presence in Rome of a French garrison prevented them from seizing *la città* itself. Newman, ever reverential toward episcopal authority, readily complied with the directive and, at the same time, took advantage of the opportunity to draw for his parishioners—and for that larger public, friendly or unfriendly, which, since the publication of the *Apologia* two years before, listened carefully to his every word—to draw those distinctions so necessary to a genuine appreciation of the spiritual primacy of the Pope. The sermon was an exercise not in subtlety but in clarity.

Indeed, clarity is too weak a word. Newman constructed his argument with the meticulous care of one who realized he spoke not only to those who actually heard him that October day in the Oratory church on the Hagley Road in Birmingham, not only to his legion of admirers all over England, Ireland, and America, but also to those potentates and opinion makers —many of them, like Manning and W. G. Ward, Oxford converts—who had once been his disciples and who now, like the pharisees of old, were anxious to catch him in his speech. He therefore punctiliously followed Bishop Ullathorne's instruction and dealt with his subject in terms of "obligations to the Holy See" and "the duty of praying for the Pope". The obligation was clear enough, he began, from the very words of Scripture that proclaim the Petrine office as a special mercy of God to his people, an office exercised

> by the popes, one after another, as years have rolled on, one dying and another coming, down to this day, when we see Pius the Ninth sustaining the weight of the glorious apostolate, and that for twenty years past—a tremendous weight, a ministry involving momentous duties, innumerable anxieties, and immense responsibilities. . . . There are kings of the earth who have despotic authority, which their subjects obey indeed, but disown in their hearts; but we must never murmur at that absolute rule which the Sovereign Pontiff has over us, because it is given to him by Christ, and, in obeying him, we are obeying the Lord. . . . His yoke is the yoke of Christ; *he* has the responsibility of his own acts, not we; and to his *Lord* must he render account, not to us.

And there was obligation also, Newman contended, in another, narrower sense.

Wc in this country owe our highest blessings to the See of St. Peter—to the succession of Bishops who have filled his Apostolic chair. For first it was a Pope who sent missionaries to this island in the first age of the Church, when the island was as yet in pagan darkness. Then again, when our barbarous ancestors, the Saxons, crossed over from the Continent and overran the country, who but a Pope, St. Gregory the First, sent over St. Augustine and his companions to convert them to Christianity?

As for the present Pontiff, who reestablished the English hierarchy in 1850,

I would have you recollect, my Brethren, that it is he . . . who has redressed a misfortune of nearly three hundred years standing. Twenty years ago we were a mere collection of individuals; but Pope Pius has brought us together, has given us Bishops, and created out of us a body politic, which (please God), as time goes on, will play an important part in Christendom with a character, an intellect, and a power of its own, with schools of its own, with a definite influence in the counsels of the Holy Church Catholic, as England had of old time.

But there were even more personal grounds for gratitude to Pius IX:

His great act towards us here, towards me. One of his first acts after he was Pope was, in his great condescension, to call me to Rome; then, when I got there, he bade me send for my friends to be with me; and he formed us into an Oratory. And thus it came to pass that, on my return to England, . . . did we establish our own Oratory here.

Newman may not have measured his loyalty to the Pope as did W. G. Ward, who would have liked a papal bull to read each morning at breakfast along with the *Times*. But no one entertained a warmer affection than Newman did for the grand, courtly, flamboyant, pious, narrow-minded, sweet-tempered Pius IX:

He is one whom to see is to love, one who overcomes even strangers, even enemies, by his very look and voice; whose presence subdues, whose memory haunts even the sturdy, resolute mind of the English Protestant. . . . Such is he; and, great as he is in office, and in his beneficent acts and virtuous life, as great is he in the severity of his trials, . . . and in the gravity of his perils.

And so, since "the crisis of the long-protracted troubles of [this] pontificate . . . seems close at hand", Newman turned to "the second point to which I have to direct your attention, my Brethren—the duty of praying for the Holy Father".

We are to pray for Rome as the seat, not only of [the Pope's] spiritual government, but of his temporal. We are to pray that he may continue king of Rome; that his subjects may come to a better mind; that, instead of threatening him and assailing him, or being too cowardly to withstand those who do, they may defend and obey him; that instead of being the heartless tormentors of an old and venerable man, . . . instead of needing to be kept down year after year by troops from afar, . . . they may pay a willing homage to the Apostle of God.

Well enough, then, to pray that the Temporal Power, whatever its political faults—and Newman did not deny them—to pray that the Temporal Power be sustained in some form.[14] But prayer, he reminded his congregation, has its own rules.

We do not absolutely know God's will in this matter; we know indeed it is His will that we should ask. . . . If we were quite sure what God intended to do, whether to continue the temporal power of the Pope or to end it, we should not pray. . . . We hope indeed to gain our prayer if we pray enough; but, since it is ever uncertain what *is* enough, it is ever uncertain what will be the event.

Of the two possible outcomes, Newman thought the Pope's success to be, humanly speaking, "highly probable. . . . It is cheering to begin our prayers with . . . signs of God's providence in our favour." But in suggesting what those signs might have been, he gave small comfort to those who wanted to lend to a political struggle a romanticized or spiritualized aura. "I think the Romans will not be able to do without [the Pope]—it is only a minority even now which is against him; the majority of his subjects is not wicked, so much as cowardly and incapable." And, based upon a long historical record, fickle.

> Even if they renounce him now for a while, they will change their minds and wish for him again. They will find out that he is their real greatness. Their city is a place of ruins, except so far as it is a place of holy shrines. It is the tomb and charnel-house of pagan impiety, except so far as it is sanctified and quickened by the blood of martyrs and the relics of saints. To inhabit it would be a penance, were it not for the presence of religion. Babylon is gone, Memphis is gone, Persepolis is gone; Rome would go, if the Pope went.

But what if, indeed, the Pope did go?

> Let us suppose that the Pope loses his temporal power, and returns to the condition of St. Sylvester, St. Julius, St. Innocent, and other great Popes of early times? Are we therefore to suppose that he and the Church will come to nought? God forbid! To say that the Church can fail, or the See of St. Peter can fail, is to deny the faithfulness of Almighty God to His word. "Thou art Peter and upon this rock will I build My Church, and the gates of hell shall not prevail against it." . . . The Church is not the creature of times and places, of secular politics or popular caprice. Our Lord maintains her by means of this world, but these means are necessary to her only while He gives them; when He takes them away they are no longer necessary. He works by means, but He is not bound to means. He has a thousand ways of maintaining her; He can support her life, not by bread only, but by every word that proceedeth out of His mouth. If He takes away one defence, He will give another instead. We know nothing of the future: our duty is to direct our course according to our day; not to give up of our own act the means which God has given us to maintain His Church withal, but not lament over their loss, when He has taken them away. Temporal power has been the means of the Church's independence

for a very long period; but, as her Bishops have lost it a long
while, and are not less Bishops still, so would it be as regards her
Head, if he also lost his. The Eternal God is her refuge, and as He
has delivered her out of so many perils hitherto, so will He
deliver her still.[15]

Sixteen years later, when he was an old man past eighty,
Newman wrote a note apropos of this sermon, which, in its
published form, he had titled "The Pope and the Revolution".
"What I . . . said [then] I hold now. I have no reason to
suppose that in so holding I have not the sanction of the Pope's
opinion, but," he added with the refinement so characteristic
of him, "being now a Cardinal, whatever might be my personal
opinion, I should submit to him and act with him, should the
question of the Temporal Power come into discussion."[16] By
that time, of course, the Temporal Power had indeed come to
an end, and the Pope was the self-proclaimed "Prisoner of the
Vatican", a status destined to continue until the Lateran Treaties
of 1929. And the very fact that Newman was now a member of
the sacred college had put to rest, as he expressed it, "all the
stories which have gone about of my being a half Catholic, a
Liberal Catholic,[17] not to be trusted".[18] When the news arrived in Birmingham that Leo XIII had determined to bestow
upon him a red hat, Newman said exultantly to his Oratorian
brethren, "The cloud is lifted from me forever."[19]

"*Il mio cardinale*", Pope Leo called Newman, "my cardinal".
There was much resistance to the appointment. "It was not
easy", the Pope recalled later, "It was not easy. They said he
was too liberal."[20] When he went to Rome for his formal
installation into the college, Newman, old and frail but as
unshakably principled as ever, took the occasion to answer
that unspecified "they" to whom the Pope referred. There is in
the famous *biglietto* speech a reminder of another great English
Catholic, St. Thomas More, who chose silence over rebellion,
until, the victim of perjury and condemned to death, he spoke

his full mind about the transgressions of his King. The analogy is by no means perfect, but Newman, too, had often remained silent in the midst of controversy, lest he be misinterpreted, as he so frequently had been, and thereby scandalize the faithful. But now he was a cardinal, a prince of the Church, and amid the glitter of a crowded Roman salon, he would draw once more those distinctions the Mannings and Wards of this world were so reluctant to hear.

"It must be borne in mind", he said in the voice that was still music to the ear,

> that there is much in the liberalistic theory which is good and true; . . . the precepts of justice, truthfulness, sobriety, self-command, benevolence . . . are among its avowed principles. . . . It is not till we find that this array of principles is intended to supersede, to block out, religion, that we pronounce it to be evil.

Here, in this substitution lies the "one great mischief I have from the first opposed myself. For thirty, forty, fifty years I have resisted to the best of my powers the spirit of Liberalism in religion. . . . Liberalism in religion is the doctrine"—note the word—

> that there is no positive truth in religion, but that one creed is as good as another. . . . It is inconsistent with any recognition of any religion as *true*. It teaches that all are to be tolerated, for all are matters of opinion. Revealed religion is not a truth, but a sentiment and a taste; not an objective fact, not miraculous; and it is the right of each individual to make it say whatever strikes his fancy. Devotion is not necessarily founded on faith. Men may go to Protestant Churches and to Catholic, may get good from both and belong to neither. They may fraternise together in spiritual thoughts and feelings, without any views at all of doctrines in common, or seeing the need of them. Since, then, religion is so personal a peculiarity and so private a possession,

we must of necessity ignore it in the intercourse of man with man. If a man puts on a new religion every morning, what is that to you? It is as impertinent to think about a man's religion as about his sources of income or his management of his family. Religion is in no sense the bond of society.[21]

Here was the mortal enemy thrown up by the modern world, "this great *apostasia*", he labeled it, "one and the same everywhere", compared to which the absorption of the old Papal States into the new kingdom of Italy was merely a species of trivia. Newman might have preferred—as indeed he did—that the Pope retain his civil princedom, just as he would have preferred, a little later, that his friend the Liberal Prime Minister Gladstone should have sent a British army to rescue General Gordon at Khartoum. He was disappointed in both these hopes, but such disappointment seemed to him hardly more threatening than so many other inevitable slings and arrows that bruised the Christian soul on its way toward "the blessed vision of peace". "Liberalism in religion" was another matter altogether.

He battled it, he claimed in the *biglietto* speech, as Anglican and Catholic, "for thirty, forty, fifty years", and the evidence amply bears him out.[22] He used whatever weapon came to his fine hand, ridicule among them. In the novel *Loss and Gain*, written in 1848, Newman introduced to the world Dr. Brownside, Dean of Nottingham, "a little, prim, smirking, bespectacled man, bald in front with curly black hair behind, somewhat pompous in his manner", for whom revelation,

instead of being the abyss of God's counsels, with its dim outlines and broad shadows, was a flat sunny plain, laid out with straight macadamized roads. . . . He maintained that in Revelation all that was mysterious had been left out, and nothing given us but what was practical and directly concerned us. . . . He said . . . that in fact there was no truth or falsehood in received dogmas of theology; that they were modes, neither good nor bad in themselves, but personal, national, or periodic, in which

the intellect reasoned upon the great truths of religion; that the
fault lay, not in holding them, but in insisting on them, which
was like insisting on a Hindoo dressing like a [Westerner], or a
regiment of dragoons using the boomerang.

Then there was Mr. Batts, "a pale-faced man of about thirty-
five, who, when he spoke, arched his eyebrows, and had a
peculiar smile". Mr. Batts was the director of the Truth
Society, among whose patrons were Abelard, Benjamin
Franklin, and Julian the Apostate and whose guiding principles were "first, it is uncertain whether truth exists, and,
second, it is certain that it cannot be found".[23]

But of course Newman never thought that the blight of
liberalism-in-religion was at all a laughing matter, and his
ordinary mood in talking or writing about it was somber. It
may be that a speaker at a conference such as this should try to
conclude his remarks upon a high and optimistic note. If so, I
am afraid that, in order to be faithful to my subject and to the
theme of this conference, I must, for once, defy the con-
ventions. "Newman Today" is what has brought us together,
and Newman yesterday—exactly a century and a half ago, in
1838, at the height of the Oxford Movement—left us a melancholy prophecy—much of which, alas, has sadly come true—
about the deleterious effects of liberalism-in-religion.

The view henceforth is to be, that Christianity does not exist in
documents, any more than in institutions; in other words, the
Bible will be given up as well as the Church. It will be said that
the benefit which Christianity has done to the world, and which
its Divine Author meant it should do, was to give an impulse to
society, to infuse a spirit, to direct, control, purify, enlighten the
mass of human thought and action, but not to be a separate and
definite something, whether doctrine or association, existing
objectively, integral, and with an identity, and forever, and with
a claim upon our homage and obedience. And all this fearfully
coincides with the symptoms in other directions of the spread of

a Pantheistic spirit, that is, the religion of beauty, imagination, and philosophy, without constraint, moral or intellectual, a religion speculative and self-indulgent. Pantheism, indeed, is the great deceit which awaits the age to come.[24]

NOTES

[1] "Iolanthe, or, The Peer and the Peri", in ed. Frederick Hobbs, *Authentic Libretti of the Gilbert and Sullivan Operas* (New York: Crown, 1939), p. 62. Private Willis, on sentry duty outside Westminster Palace. "Then let's rejoice with loud Fal, lal, la, la! / That Nature always does contrive—Fal, lal, la, la! Etc. till a final Fal, lal, la."

[2] *The Economist* 308, no. 7562 (Aug. 6–12, 1988), pp. 8–9.

[3] See the standard work Guido de Ruggiero, *The History of European Liberalism*, trans. R. G. Collingwood (Boston: Beacon Press, 1959), esp. pp. 347–69.

[4] See Marvin R. O'Connell, "Montalembert at Mechlin: a Reprise of 1830", *Journal of Church and State* 26 (1984), p. 533.

[5] See, for example, Newman to Blachford, Jan. 26, Apr. 23, May 19, May 23, and Dec. 28, 1885, vol. XXXI, pp. 19, 55, 67, 69, and 106.

[6] "The Fall of de Lamennais", in *Essays Critical and Historical* (London: Longman, 1890), vol. I, pp. 138–72. Originally published as "Affairs of Rome", *British Critic* 22 (Oct. 1837), pp. 261–83.

[7] *Apologia pro Vita Sua* (London: Longman, 1921), p. 285.

[8] Talbot to Manning, Apr. 25, 1867, quoted in Edmund S. Purcell, *Life of Cardinal Manning* (London: Macmillan, 1896), vol. II, p. 318.

[9] "The Pope and the Revolution", in *Sermons Preached on Various Occasions* (London: Longman, 1921), p. 307. There is an irony in the fact that the first edition of this volume (1857) was dedicated to Manning, whose extreme views in favor of the Temporal Power Newman opposed as much as he did the machinations of the Piedmontese. This sermon was added to the collection in the third edition (1870), and the dedication remained as before.

[10] "Memorandum", May 22, 1882, *Letters and Diaries*, vol. XIX, pp. 561–62, and vol. XXX, pp. 89–90.

[11] Ullathorne's account of his last conversation with Manning, quoted in E. C. Butler, *The Life and Times of Bishop Ullathorne* (London: Longman, 1926), vol. II, p. 159.

[12] See, for example, the treatment in Purcell, *Manning*, vol. II, pp. 151–69, on the Temporal Power as an Article of Faith.

[13] See n. 10 above.

[14] "I had no thought of making [the Pope] a *subject* to any secular power. I thought he might have Rome and a slice of territory to the sea, or at least an honorary sovereignty." See n. 10 above.

[15] "The Pope and the Revolution", pp. 282–313.

[16] See n. 10 above.

[17] Despite Newman's own repudiation of the term "liberal Catholic" as applied to himself, modern scholars perversely insist upon categorizing him so. See for one among many possible examples James Tunstead Burtchaell, *Catholic Theories of Biblical Inspiration since 1810* (Cambridge: Cambridge University Press, 1969), p. 65.

[18] Newman to Church, Mar. 11, 1879, *Letters and Diaries*, vol. XXIX, p. 72.

[19] Wilfrid Ward, *The Life of John Henry Cardinal Newman*, 2 vols. (London: Longman, 1913), vol. II, p. 438.

[20] See Marvin R. O'Connell, "Newman: the Victorian Intellectual as Pastor", *Theological Studies* 46 (1985), pp. 329–33.

[21] Ward, *Newman*, vol. II, pp. 460–62.

[22] Among many possible examples perhaps the most familiar—and a kind of summing up—can be found in the *Apologia*, pp. 14, 203–4, 214, 261–64, 285–97.

[23] *Loss and Gain. The Story of a Convert* (London: Longman, 1906), pp. 67–70, 405.

[24] "Holy Scripture and Its Relation to the Catholic Creed", in *Discussions and Arguments on Various Subjects* (London: Longman, 1907), p. 233. Originally published as Tract Eighty-five (Sept. 1838), "Lecture on the Scripture Proof of the Doctrines of the Church".

George W. Rutler

NEWMAN'S IDEA OF A
CATHOLIC UNIVERSITY

We feel assured that the plan for the higher education and the
system of University government which you initiated and organized, will, centuries hence, be studied by all who may have
to legislate for Catholic education, as among the most precious
of the documents which they shall possess to inform and guide
them (address from the Rector and Senate of the Catholic
University of Ireland, October 28, 1879).

A Rational Obedience

It remains paradoxical that some of those who would be
Newman's friends have so offended his memory. I speak
particularly of the self-appointed spokesmen who have tried to
remake Newman in their own image. The Abbé Bremond
helped to start this line, which while diffuse has one common
assumption: that when Newman says to be alive is to change,
he means to be alive is to be confused. Newman only changed
his opinions when he was not confused. He was a singularly
consistent man, as is seen in the slight revision of his writings
that he undertook from about 1871 to 1874.

In all phases of his intellectual and spiritual development, he
was certain of this: truth is sovereign and it is objective, as both
reason and will are ordered correctly only when they are
subject to it. Newman's enterprise, even when he did not say
so categorically, was to salvage learning from the Kantian
legacy of divorce between reason and will, a contrived trauma
that had hypnotized the intelligentsia of his generation and that

by now has put educators into an epistemological coma. Newman knew it as liberalism when it was young and fresh; it is known by many names today even when it will not speak its true name because it has grown old and bitter. Newman maintained what liberalism came into being by denying: the duty never to sin against the light, a claim prior to all other moral attentions. In silent witness in his austere room in the Birmingham Oratory, there still hangs his Oxford M.A. hood. The redder robes of a cardinal did not replace it; they vindicated it. The lifelong commitment had been to mastering the art of knowledge. Knowledge is a thing sacred in itself, and valid only when it does not conjure a competition against holiness. So when brought to the test, he chose to leave Oxford for a higher learning; and when he accepted the rectorship of the Catholic University of Ireland, it was with the understanding that he was a priest of the Oratory functioning as the head of a university, and not the head of a university functioning as a priest of the Oratory.

This is a thing to remember when now, as in the instance of Father Corcoran guided by a different prejudice some sixty years ago, it is suggested that Newman diminished the Catholic identity of the university when he spoke of knowledge as an end in itself.[1] To refute any such misuse of this "Philosophy of Severance" between learning and piety, Newman penned an Introduction to the second collected edition of the original Dublin discourses, in which he observed

(1) That he is treating here of the Object of a University in the *abstract* and in its *idea*; (2) that, as such, its object is *knowledge*, as such; (3) but that a *Catholic* university will, in all its regulations and appointments, and in its routine, distinctly recognize Catholicism; and (4) that, for its *integrity*, though not for its essence, it ought to be invested with a *coercive* power, enforcing order, discipline, and religious and moral behaviour on its subjects.[2]

At the heart of much current confusion about the definition of Catholic education is this economy of essence and integrity.

The burden of his sixth discourse in the original Dublin lectures is to show that the university functions to teach the mind how to think, while its Catholic identity rests upon its purpose to manifest how right thought leads to the truth of the Faith. His listeners were reminded of the scholastic distinction between immediate and ultimate ends. The current debate is muddled when the Principle of Severance is made a Principle of Contradiction, as when one president of a Catholic university allows, "We have never said that a student coming here is going to be indoctrinated. Just as a Catholic hospital is, first of all, a hospital, a Catholic university is, first of all, a university."[3]

Newman would not permit such clumsiness. Of course he disdained any attempt to make his university a place of rote learning, but he did think that it should be a place of right learning. The misuse of propaganda does not destroy the right to propagate, nor does the preachiness of some cancel the commission to preach, and neither then does the sad history of false indoctrination make the Catholic university any less a place of honest indoctrination. It all depends on how we respect Newman's thesis in the *Idea of a University*, which is consistent with the case he makes in the *Essay on the Development of Christian Doctrine*. For as he made a benign distinction between a natural knowledge that is governed by conscience and a revealed knowledge that is governed by the Church, so he holds: "The end of . . . a Catholic University or of any university is 'liberal education'; though its ultimate end may be Catholicism."[4] But this requires that we acknowledge the issue in the first place. A Jesuit university president has written: "It is of little use to approach this question of the role of an academic institution by reflecting on the 'essence' of a college or a university or a research institute."[5] Such words were not spoken to the eight Jesuits and several hundred others in the Rotunda at Dublin.

Newman first was criticized by a parochialism that could not trust an alien spirit to preserve the local cultural patrimony:

> When I have given as my true opinion, that I am afraid to make
> hasty converts of educated men, lest they should not have
> counted the cost, and should have difficulties after they have
> entered the Church, I do but imply . . . that the Church must be
> prepared for converts, as well as converts prepared for the
> Church.[6]

Today he can be misinterpreted by Catholic educators if they
are insecure in their patrimony and seek the peer approval of
those sceptics Newman predicted would be the scourge of the
new age. That is my thesis, and what I have to say further is
commentary on it.

Within the space of a few days, recently, I stood in his pulpit
in the University Church of Oxford and in his pulpit of the
church he built for the university in Dublin. He was the same
man in both. More to the point, he was in both because he was
the same man. His idea of a university was the same in Oxford
and Dublin. What he says in Ireland is more than an echo of
what he said in a sermon of 1841 on the definition of wisdom,
and in his letters concerning the secular utilitarianism of Peel's
Tamworth Reading Room address.

> The Catholic Creed is one whole, and Philosophy again is one
> whole; each may be compared to an individual, to which nothing
> can be added, from which nothing can be taken away. They may
> be professed, but there is no middle ground between professing
> and not professing. A University, so called, which refuses to
> profess the Catholic Creed, is, from the nature of the case,
> hostile both to the Church and to Philosophy.[7]

A theory had not been refined by fire; it had been tested by
fire. In our own day it has been nearly destroyed by fire. And
this is because many modern Catholic teachers have lacked
Newman's confidence in the superiority of the liberal arts to
specious liberalism, or what Newman associated with Bentham's
artless concept of personal liberty as the guarantor of the
greatest happiness for the greatest number. It has been a
clerical fault, and the few signs of hope today seem to be in
lay initiatives. Newman would have expected as much, and

he urged as much. When he declined to get involved in a controversy surrounding Gladstone's Irish University Bill of 1873, he remembered how one of his chief problems with the Irish University twenty years earlier had been clerical abuse of the lay intellect: "The laity have been disgusted and become infidel, and only two parties exist, both ultras in opposite directions."[8]

One might describe the same today, though the clericalization of the laity that Newman abhorred has also come to mean a laicization of the clergy that has been publicly deplored many times by the Holy Father. But the problem of infidelity remains. And of it the most important lesson is its definition. For Newman was not content to think that fidelity could consist in less than obedience to the See of Peter. In 1851 he was one of three members of a commission that prepared a report on the organization of the proposed Catholic University of Ireland: all officers and professors of the university must make "a Profession of the Catholic Faith according to the form of Pope Pius IV". Moreover, they were required "not only not to teach anything contrary to Religion, but to take advantage of the occasion the subjects they treat of may offer, to point out that Religion is the basis of Science, and to inculcate the love of Religion and its duties".[9] To be learned in a Catholic way means to understand that such obedience is not an abandonment of ratiocination but is its freest expression. In the jargon of modern Catholic education, academic freedom has come to mean academic independence from this higher economy. The pursuit of wisdom, which is the maturity of a life intent on truth, has been replaced by the pursuit of sophistry; and sophistry marks the immaturity of a life intent on utility. He continues in words only more poignant for having been written over a century ago:

> You will be doing the greatest possible benefit to the Catholic
> cause all over the world, if you succeed in making the University
> a middle station at which laity and clergy can meet, so as to learn
> to understand and yield to each other, and from which, as from
> a common ground, they may act in union upon an age which

is running headlong into infidelity, and however evil in themselves may be the men and the measures which of late years have
had so great a success against the Holy See, they will in the
Providence of God be made the instruments of good, if they
teach us priests that the "obsequium" which the laity owe
religion is "rationabile".[10]

So his motive for the presence of laymen as university
officers is a far cry from the college president who said
recently: "In the 1960s and early 1970s most Catholic colleges
severed even tenuous ties to the Church. . . . We became
independent and named lay trustees because of accreditation,
the increased sophistication of higher education as a major
enterprise and because of the demands of growth."[11] Newman
spoke of another economy to which this gaucherie is oblivious:
"I want the educated layman to be religious and the devout
ecclesiastic to be intellectual."[12] He feared, and his fear was not
paranoia but prophecy, that the clericalization of the laity
would not only make them unfit for being Catholic in a world
that has more laymen than clergy. He saw that the ground of
modern discontent is not a *trahison des laics* but a *trahison des
clercs*. The more people are clericalized, the more people are
likely to be involved in the treason. He spoke when clericalism
was constituted by a defensive reaction against the spirit of
indifferentism; today it is almost synonymous with its embrace.
But both represent a lack of confidence in the ability of true
philosophy to civilize man.

By "philosophy" Newman has settled upon a difficult translation of the Greek *arete*: "wisdom" is not adequate as it "has a
direct relation to conduct and human life", nor do words like
"knowledge" and "science" and "judgement" convey the
sense of more than intellectual faculties. For all its ambiguity,
"philosophy" is chosen in the sixth discourse as the cipher for
an "ordering power", a reason exercised upon knowledge. It
is the enlargement, or illumination, of the mind that cracks the
egghead, dismantles the ivory tower, exposes the uselessness
of utilitarianism, and enables wisdom "to meet the great
infidel &c. questions of the day".[13] The clerical modernist no

more than the clerical reactionary can permit this philosophy and hope to perdure, for it is a habit of the mind that sees through ideology. Philosophy is the endowment conferred when mere instruction yields to education. And an institution does not educate that does not cultivate it.

Newman's account of the mentality that cannot comprehend the realities of authentic culture applies today to the modernist who rebels against attempts by the Holy See to reform the Catholic universities precisely as in his time it described the pedantry of reaction and liberalism alike. Modernism, after all, is pedantic, as it is a myopic perception of Tradition and development. Newman understood its antecedents as a refuge from reality. Modernism can continue to exist only as an anachronistic nostalgia for Victorian optimism. Consequently, academic freedom for the modernist means the guarantee of domain for ideology in opposition to philosophy. It then postures in academic dress when it cloaks an antiintellectualism as otiose as that which Newman would expose among the English Catholics:

> From their very blindness [they] cannot see that they are blind. To aim then at improving the condition, the status, of the Catholic body, by a careful survey of their argumentative basis, of their position relatively to the philosophy and the character of the day, by giving them juster views by enlarging and refining their minds, in one word, by education, is (in their view) more than a superfluity or a hobby—it is an insult. It implies that they are deficient in material points.[14]

The Irish Circumstance

At the Roman Synod on the Laity in 1987, the Father General of the Society of Jesus, Father Kolvenbach, remarked "a certain discouragement, almost a sense of desperation, regarding the possibility of assuring educational institutions of a clear Catholic identity".[15] Newman boasted that the Church in his day had an influence over her institutions that she had not in the twelfth and thirteenth centuries; and this clear refinement of Catholic identity made it easier to fight unbelief. No longer can we say what Newman was glad to say: "Secular advantages no longer present an inducement to hypocrisy and [the university's] members in consequence have the consolation of being able to be sure of each other."[16] If the Irish bishops were not desperate about Catholic identity in 1850, they were divided on the question of how to secure it. The Archbishop of Dublin, Dr. Murray, had wanted some sort of cooperation with the Queen's colleges of Sir Robert Peel's scheme. The colleges were the attempt of a worthy man to build upon the provisions of the Catholic Relief Act of 1793, giving Catholics wider access to degrees through the model of nonsectarian systems in France and Germany. They were what we should call secular schools and quite in keeping with Peel's own utilitarian theories, though not so with his aversion to state control of education. And they were the antithesis of Newman's idea of a university. Peel had honestly attempted a solution and could cite the precedent of the National Education Act of 1831 affecting primary education. But this act for "mixed education" had failed in practice; and neither the manifest goodwill of Lord Clarendon, the viceroy for Ireland, nor the arbitrations of the Irish bishops could allay doubts. The nationalist Young Irelanders favored the plan. O'Connell changed his opinion more than once. Then, perhaps not unaffected by the mental occlusion of his last days, he began to call the Queen's colleges "the Godless colleges", a phrase that in fact had been coined by the Oxford member of Parliament, Sir Robert Inglis. Godlessness first rang as a Protestant outcry against indifferentism.

We can only speculate whether the Queen's colleges of Belfast, Cork, and Galway would have eventually become Catholic by sheer demographic pressure had the Irish bishops taken advantage of Gregory XVI's hesitancy on the matter. But Dr. Murray's successor, Dr. Cullen, along with Dr. MacHale, the Archbishop of Tuam, did nothing to dissuade the new Pope, Pius IX, from outright condemnation of mixed education.

Newman was unclear about what the bishops wanted because they were unclear themselves, even after the Synod of Thurles had condemned the Queen's colleges in 1850. Cullen wanted a university in opposition to the Peel scheme, a Catholic university for the entire English-speaking world. After twenty-nine years in Rome—and the hanging of two of his patriot uncles—he was nervous about the consequences of Irish nationalism. And at the same time, though less conspicuously than Dr. MacHale, he did not imagine a universe large enough to make an Irish university convincing to anyone outside Ireland. Newman enjoyed the confidence of such as Bishop Moriarty, who belonged to the Queen's college party. And although he willingly accepted Cullen's invitation to make his Dublin discourses an argument against nonsectarian schools, he understood better than Cullen that the case must be made at a more philosophical level.

Ireland may have needed Cullen, a politician and not a philosopher; but politics needs a purpose as philosophy needs a point, and Cullen was too impetuous for a purpose. The Archbishop's neglect of Newman to the point of rudeness and his intervention to block a mitre for Newman are notorious. Cullen was not an Irish Manning, but Newman records certain tensions in his retrospective notes of 1872, though in 1867, when he was delated to Rome, he was also glad for the Archbishop's decisive support. Later Newman expressed his gratitude and affection for Cullen, some of which was the diction of a man whose lifelong inclination was to acknowledge, and sometimes to invent, the best in people.

He understood the Irish scene mostly by an intuition born of a historical sense. As Cullen was publicly denouncing Fenianism, Newman was more soberly encouraging Eugene O'Curry to recover ancient Celtic manuscripts. The Saxon diction of Newman's views on Ireland is perhaps matched for balance and expression only by Chesterton, though Newman was less of a democrat and more of an imperialist in the noble sense. For one thing, he shared Cullen's opposition to Repeal, and he once kept a low opinion of O'Connell, as the *Apologia* makes clear.[17] He later upset the neurasthenia of Gerard Manley Hopkins by saying that had he been Irish he would have (in heart) been a rebel. But he adds, "To clench the difficulty the Irish character and tastes [are] very different from the English. My fingers will not let me write more."[18] As with St. John at the end of the Fourth Gospel, one does wish that he might have gone on.

Among other things, Newman wanted his Dublin lectures to show the Irish that he could be trusted. He succeeded in part. Some of the later criticisms of the way Newman handled the university experiment sound much like attempts to justify the treatment he received in a land proud to have been a nest and refuge of saints and scholars. The faithful poor could not have been more generous. With others it was different. Part had to do with the simple difference in character and tastes. Newman was abidingly diplomatic in a land where politics and religion have long been restless subjects. And the man who measured every word was a curiosity to those for whom silence on any subject was a mortification.

He met three problem groups. First were the Protestants of the Ascendency, whom one convert described as combining "the vulgarity of the English and the brutality of the Irish".[19] Then there were the bishops: divided among themselves, parochial in their own education, and wanting imagination. Most portentous of all was his discovery of a Catholic gentry in Ireland who had so unconsciously aped the Ascendency that their Catholic instincts were disappearing and they were becoming what we would call cultural Catholics. When one of them was told that the Oxford Movement had tried to revive in England the interior life, fasting, and devotions, he answered in surprise: "Well, all that would be totally new in this country."[20] Ireland needed its own Oxford Movement. And soon Newman realized that the Irish bishops were asking him to do what they were not doing well themselves.

Thus he faced three challenges that we tend to think are

peculiar to our present situation but that in fact have rarely been absent in the pageant of Catholic education: the tension between ecclesiastical autonomy and state control, the lack of reforming courage on the part of some bishops, and the unconscious secularism of the young in quest of upward social mobility. At the same time, his attentions were distracted by the Achilli libel trial, the restoration of the English hierarchy, and the need to raise funds in a land ravaged by the Great Hunger. As he was commuting between England and Ireland for the lectures, he was engaged in many things: tracking down young Italian women who had been compromised by Achilli, preaching "The Second Spring" to the restored hierarchy of England, governing the expansion of the Oratory houses, and establishing a university. His diaries are helpful reading for latter-day academics who complain of burnout. Only incidentally does he mention collapsing one day in a regular class. And through it all he maintained his usual mortifications and use of the discipline, though these seem to have been the least of his discomforts.

The Irish years are commonly counted as a failure. It is painful to read his university reports, with their sustained hopefulness against odds, of his dream of a university that will attract upward of a hundred Yankees and become the center of English-speaking Catholicism "with Great Britain, Malta (perhaps Turkey or Egypt), and India on one side of it, and North America and Australia on the other". And which, while not yet possessing a museum of antiquities, "has received from the late Msgr. Bettachini . . . a great number of specimens of the birds, amphibia, and recent shells of Ceylon".[21]

The singular success of the medical school shows the importance of a charter, which the university itself lacked, largely because of blatant bigotry in Whitehall from all sides: Tory, Liberal, and Non-Conformist. Though fairness should ask, if, say, the Armada had won, could there have been in the nineteenth century or even until these recent years a Spanish Peel or a Spanish Gladstone providing the rudiments of mixed education in an occupied Britain? The failure to secure a charter notwithstanding, Newman's efforts were a spiritual victory and more, for they have given a philosophical guide by which we can judge ourselves when the moral and intellectual neglect of university students is one of the most serious defects of Catholic life in the United States.[22] The very name Newman has been surrendered. Nondescript religious life programs and pastoral centers are found where once there were Newman Centers. The buildings are still there, but Newman has been taken away. And with him has gone the ability to see that the renewal of education is not a program but, as he called it, a campaign. And by campaign he meant a battle. And as the end of education is learning how to think, and as the ultimate end of education is to think like the saints, then the battle must be against ignorance and falsehood. He writes at the beginning of the new adventure: "The battle there will be what it was in Oxford twenty years ago", and such men as Keble and Pusey, "who have been able to do so little against Liberalism in Oxford will be renewing the fight although not in their persons in Ireland".[23]

If we think him prophetic in measuring the residue content of the liberalism of his day, then we may also presume to acknowledge this with him: vindication of the idea of a university will not come on the campuses by bureaucratic compromise and moral innocuousness, but by genius and holiness. Divine Wisdom has been ever generous in providing these to the Church, and human wisdom consists in cultivating them as one. Newman's idea was ancient, and not ancient because it was aged but because it was true. Thus it is as new as it is old. From the isolation of modern education, the idea seems both archaic and novel. It will stay like that until the Church's universities make bold to say that an idea can be not only agreeable but also true. And Catholic leaders will recover their prophetic mantle when they publicly denounce those who rant: "Hey, hey, ho, ho! Western culture's got to go!"

Newman at Land O' Lakes

Newman's distaste for the institution of gentleman commoners at Oxford, his fund raising for needy students, and his novel provision for night classes, should purge the charge that Newman meant to foster unjust privilege by his concept of the university as a place for gentlemen.[24] The aim was against mere vocational education as instituted by the utilitarians at the University of London in 1827. Shallow populism, which has made modern American education little more than job training at the expense of cultural literacy, is based on a middle-class refinement of the naturalist assumptions of the Enlightenment. For Newman it was the most vicious threat to classical liberal knowledge, which meant to "free" the mind. This, after all, is the etymology of the liberal arts, and utilitarian liberalism was the blatant contradiction of classical liberalism.

Current best-selling criticisms of our system recognize this but do not have Newman's solution. Allan Bloom, for example, will speak of virtue but not of grace, because his sympathies are rooted in the prejudices of Rousseau, whom he would make the father of modern humanities, and of Kant, whom he even calls "a significant natural scientist".[25] He simply cannot understand the ordering of grace upon nature as Newman has it. When Bloom says the only solution is "the good old Great Books approach", he is arguing for the Burkean gentleman by whose urbanity "vice lost half its evil by losing all its grossness". When this religion of philosophy

> is strong enough to have a will of its own, and is lifted up with an idea of its own importance, and attempts to form a theory, and to lay down a principle, and to carry out a system of ethics, and undertakes the moral education of the man, then it does but abet the evils to which at first it seemed instinctively opposed.[26]

If left unchecked, it produces the mentality that thinks religion is superstition and considers an M.B.A. a scholarly degree.

Bloom's failure to mention Newman once in his entire

critique of liberal education is a thundering lacuna but no surprise. Nor is it a surprise that Newman was ignored in Wisconsin at the Land O' Lakes Conference of Catholic educators in 1967, which produced a prescription for the same sort of dilettante. In 1987, various English-speaking countries suggested that the Congregation for Catholic Education use Newman's *Idea of a University* when revising its draft schema for a pontifical document on Catholic universities.[27]

Like the Oxford Protestantism of the 1830s, neither the Bloom book nor the Wisconsin statement has been "susceptible of so high a temper" as a real campaign for university reform requires.[28] This past year in some universities, students who had been charged nearly $80,000 received Latin diplomas telling them that they now are bachelors of arts, and they also received slips of paper translating what their diplomas said. A call for higher standards will not cure this. Remedy requires a redress of the old nominalism that began the mental disorder. The closing of the American mind will not be cured by the opening of the American mind but by the strengthening of the American mind. And this means redirecting attention from the line of values to the line of the good. And only the Catholic Church is an infallible guide.

As early as his Tamworth Reading Room letters, Newman was certain that even a classical education based on other than Christianity as its element and principle would degenerate into either "a mawkish, frivolous and fastidious sentimentalism", or "a dry, unamiable longheadedness", or "an uppish, supercilious temper, much inclined to scepticism".[29] The Land O' Lakes "Statement on the Nature of the Contemporary Catholic University" succumbed to all three, expressing itself incidentally in an English as bereft of the standards Newman enjoyed as it is of his logic. It already seems dated as Newman's *Idea* cannot be, trapped in a 1960s time warp, the abject proof that thought must surrender to the slavery of contemporaneity when it is not "formed" by the liberating disciplines of the arts.

Certainly with the best intentions, a prominent churchman

upset the economy of Newman's intelligence of obedience when he said in a 1986 commencement address: "Theology will also enrich the Church if it takes into account the teaching office of the bishops and the Pope, not slavishly but with honorable fidelity."[30] Unlike Newman, he is not careful to define his terms, but he does imply that there are theologians who might enslave themselves to the Magisterium. A servile theologian would be a contradiction as Newman understands theological science. The teaching office of the Church precludes unthinking obedience precisely by the fact that it teaches essentially as the seat of authority only because it is integrally the seat of wisdom. The commencement speaker made the same dialectical faux pas that led Berengar of Tours astray in his exaggerated rejection of scholastic priorities. No one in the audience, not even all those hundreds of new bachelors of arts, seemed to have noticed this. Not even after four years in a midwestern Catholic university. Perhaps the day was too sultry. Or perhaps the microphone had failed. Or perhaps, even in a Catholic university, they had not been told about Berengar of Tours.

Servile conformity is the mark of a mind that has not enjoyed the philosophical completeness of liberal knowledge, the propaedeutic for theology and all science. Such had been the trespass of Abelard, whose biography is not without commentary on the present moral state of the Catholic university; his neglect of the liberal arts for the new philosophy cast him into a downward spiral of rebellion, impurity, and finally heresy. Here is a medieval anticipation of the Kantian antinomies to which I have alluded and which pops its head up whenever one speaks of a dialectic between slavish obedience to religion and honorable fidelity.

An intellectualism so partisan may be the romance of the natural man and even the reveries of the pagan gentleman, but it is not the logic of the Catholic scholar. Liberal education untutored by ecclesial obedience has a tendency to a "pick and choose" intellectualism.

This Intellectualism first and chiefly comes into collisions with precept, then with doctrine, then with the very principle of dogmatism;—a perception of the Beautiful becomes the substitute for faith . . . even within the pale of the Church, and with the most unqualified profession of her Creed, it acts, if left to itself, as an element of corruption and infidelity.[31]

The commencement speaker to whom I have referred remarked how, after several decades, "the Catholic community no longer lives at the edge of the society". Now, Newman spoke of the condition in Ireland, where Catholics had for centuries been deprived of their "legitimate stations, duties, employments"; and yet he explained with greater probity why his *desideratum* was not "the manners and habits of gentlemen", as such upward social mobility is the aim of utilitarianism but not of Catholic education. Newman's description of the gentleman who was not "formed" is the closest we can find to the profile of what the nominally Catholic universities seem so content to manufacture, the deontologized *arriviste* commonly called a Yuppie:

Mistaking animal spirits for vigour, and over-confident in their health, ignorant of what they can bear and how to manage themselves, they are immoderate and extravagant; and fall into sharp sicknesses. This is an emblem of their minds; at first they have no principles laid within them as a foundation for the intellect to build upon; they have no discriminating convictions, and no grasp of consequences. And therefore they talk at random, if they talk much and cannot help being flippant, or what is emphatically called *young*. They are merely dazzled by phenomena instead of perceiving things as they are.[32]

The Land O' Lakes statement begins: "The Catholic University today must be a university in the full modern sense of the word."[33] Yet it does not explain what the full modern sense of the word is or why it "must" conform to it. "Is must", asked Queen Elizabeth, "a word to be used to princes?" Jealousy for its autonomy has submitted the Catholic

university to the senile dictates of a dying liberalism. But
having accepted the hegemony of contemporaneity, the signatories of the brief Land O' Lakes text fall into the three types
Newman predicted. For mawkishness, when they rhapsodize
about "warm personal dialogue"; for longheadedness, when
they diagram "a self-developing and self-deepening society of
students and faculty in which the consequences of Christian
truth are taken seriously in person-to-person relationships";
for supercilious inclination to scepticism, when they proclaim
that "the Catholic university must have a true autonomy and
academic freedom in the face of authority of whatever kind,
lay or clerical, external to the academic community itself".[34]
But Newman has insisted that the Catholicity of a university
is secured by more than teaching theology as a branch of
knowledge:

> Hence a direct and active jurisdiction of the Church over it and
> in it is necessary, lest it should become the rival of the Church
> with the community at large in those theological matters which
> to the Church are exclusively committed,—acting as the repre-
> sentative of the intellect, as the Church is the representative of
> the religious principle.[35]

The sentimentality of the Wisconsin document is the etiquette
of an undisciplined mind and is precisely what Newman
campaigned against in both Oriel and Dublin. To wear one's
heart on one's sleeve means that it has been disconnected from
the mind. This happened to the dislocated moral interiority of
Kant, and so he quivered all his days between idealism and
empiricism. The Land O' Lakes "idea o' a university" does the
same, groping for a false independence by an unthinking
acceptance of the Kantian antinomies of will and reason. An
unconscious Kantian denial of active agency to the material
world made the signatories assume that obedience to the
historical fact of the Church compromises academic freedom.
And what is this distrust of a *cultus externus* but a banal version
of the diatribes in the fourth book of Kant's *Religion within the*

Limits of Reason Alone? They would not understand Newman's profession of faith according to the formulary of Pius IV. They do not consider the prior claim of the freedom of the Church in relation to the university, and of the freedom of the university in relation to its members, and ultimately of natural religion in relation to interior moral receptivity. Their statement materially departs from the teaching of the Second Vatican Council, which is reiterated in the revised Code of Canon Law, and the draft scheme of the Congregation for Catholic Education for a pontifical document on Catholic universities.[36] Cardinal Newman was an "absent Father" of the Second Vatican Council in no issue more than his defense of the freedom of the Church to teach. To tailor this freedom to one's personal measurement is to be like the liberal gentleman who is "merciful to the absurd".

The statutes of the Catholic University of Ireland were modeled on the revived University of Louvain, then less than twenty years old. But Newman's experience was of the Oxford collegiate system. Even in its most degenerate period, it had provided a means of personal influence necessary if the university was to be of moral consequence. Newman sided more with Edward Copleston's moderate reforming sentiments than with Pusey's bias for the tutorial arrangement. His thesis as it develops more in the *Essays* than in the *Discourses* is plain enough: the university is the province of the professorial system entrusted with the essential being of the institution, and the college is the province of the tutorial system charged with its integral well-being. The university is "a place of teaching universal knowledge", but colleges and halls of residence are the instruments that the Church uses to manifest the good of the Faith.[37] The Land O' Lakes statement assumes that the university and the college are totally distinct according to the common American model and treats them as such. Newman only wanted a true university, that is, one that "merely brought a number of young men together for three or four years and then sent them away", in contrast to an institution that "gave its degrees to any person who passed an examination in a wide range of subjects".[38] The struggle of the typical Catholic university to be like the latter is considered by many to be a mark of progress, especially if state grants are among the trophies. Such money may build libraries and gild domes, but in the end it will be used to buy a potter's field.

Newman does not disallow polytechnic study; he founded an engineering school and bought a medical school. But he reserves such to the academy according to the French and English scheme. The doctoral system as it is generally known in the United States is of the German design, which took shape after the cultural trauma of Prussian defeat at the Battle of Jena in 1806. Philosophically formed from Kantian and Fichtean subjectivism, with its deference to social evolution, it gradually came to invest scientific research with the dignity formerly enjoyed by the classical arts. Only a decade after Newman's Dublin adventure, the Johns Hopkins University introduced the German type to the United States, and Johns Hopkins is where Woodrow Wilson went for his doctorate when he had exhausted the intellectual resources of Princeton. The doctorate remained rather foreign to the English system until well into this century; and even in the United States as late as 1920, the total number of Ph.D. degrees granted by all universities and eighty-two independent professional schools was only 532.

Newman foresaw that without the obedience of faith, the aesthetic intellectualism of the German system would gradually divinize experience, dehistoricize culture, and isolate judgment by bonding it to the tyranny of immediacy. The result would be a miscellaneous erudition that cannot withstand moral fragmentation. A university is not Catholic, then, that has no unified objectivist guide for its scientific inventiveness or that countenances life-styles as alternatives to the natural law.

The Land O' Lakes statement describes a university "where the students can learn by personal experience to consecrate their talent and learning to worthy social purposes". But what are this talent and learning? Recent surveys indicate little that would have impressed Newman. In the seventh discourse Newman says, "The University, if it refuses the foremost place to professional interests, does but postpone them to the formation of the citizen."[39] But surely he means something more demanding and salutary than the consecration of a smattering of information. Of course he means the ideal of the free citizen according to the structure of *paedeia*, which, if a vague notion to twentieth-century educators meeting in Wisconsin, was as alive to Newman in nineteenth-century Ireland as it was to the Sophists in Greece twenty-five hundred years ago. The concept is of education as initiation into a culture. Protestantism could not secure it because of its tendency to sentimentalism, and liberalism could not secure it because of its tendency to gnosticism. Catholic modernism combined the two.

Plotinus astutely had located the rejection of *paedeia* at the core of Gnostic alienation. His point is germane to Newman's claim that only Catholic Christianity has been able to preserve the perduring truths of culture against dehumanizing influences. Newman's salute to the venerable Irish saints and scholars is really a salute to the Periclean ideal of the free man, the figure whose ability to reason saves him from the dictate of the cliché. And high among today's clichés is the belief that pluralism has replaced a unifying culture. "Hey, hey, ho, ho, Western culture's got to go!" This is the vulgarian's assault on *paedeia*. *Paedeia* is not conformity of thought but uniformity of conviction that there is such a thing as thought. The invocation of plural values over against the fact of culture surrenders thought to feeling. *Paedeia* was vital to the ancient Gael, as it was to St. Augustine, who did not think doctrine limited the freedom of cultured man, for it secured it; in contrast, the Gnostic distrust of Providence and its misinformed anthropology were the unspoken prompters to the utilitarian lethargy of mind. The utilitarian is ever at heart a nominalist, and the nominalist's subliminal fantasy is ever gnosticism.

The educational theory in the Land O' Lakes statement is tinged with the same sort of deracinated Gnostic impulse. One example is its call for liturgical experimentation, certainly a misplaced function in the university. The chaos that followed, no less than the moral disarray on the campuses, continues to be an unhappy ritualization of cultural amnesia. "Hey, hey, ho, ho! First the ritual language has got to go. Then the man at the altar has got to go. Then the altar has got to go." In these words of Plotinus against the Gnostics, one can imagine the voice of Newman after reading the Land O' Lakes document:

> We are not told what virtue is or under what different kinds it appears . . . we do not learn what constitutes it or how it is acquired, how the Soul is tended, how it is cleansed. For to say "Look to God" is not helpful without some instruction as to what this looking imports: it might very well be said that one can "look" and still sacrifice no pleasure, still be the slave of impulse, repeating the word "God" but held in the grip of every passion and making no effort to master any.[40]

The 1967 conference came at a time marked by concerns that occupied Newman: the temptation of mixed education, an imprecision of episcopal guidance, and a utilitarian bias in the middle class. Where Newman chose a Catholic course, the 1967 signatories succumbed to the imperative of "the infidelity of the day". The conference set the agenda for an entire generation's pedagogy; and like Friar Bacon's retreat from Aristotelian realism, it has ended up *operose nihil agendo*. The Land O' Lakes Conference was to the Catholic universities what the Yalta Conference was to Eastern Europe.

As the Church tries to recover the economy of integrity and essence in the institution, there will be new critics as Newman had his. And the Benthamites will honor the Church's champions no more than they honored Newman. But Newman understood that such neglect is its own tribute. The cynical world will decorate Catholic educators with honors only when they have become the slaves of Athens and not its free citizens. When even Newman would have expressed some things in a way Pius IX chose not, and so for instance labored over his fifth discourse, he knew that the idea of a university was not his but the sagacity of an apostle. He was no slave to that authority because he had been freed by it:

> In the midst of our difficulties I have one ground of hope, just one stay, which supports me if I begin to despond, and to which I have ever come round when the question of the possible and the expedient is brought into discussion. It is the decision of the Holy See; St. Peter has spoken, it is he who has enjoined that which seems to us so unpromising. He has spoken, and has a claim on us to trust him. He is no recluse, no solitary student, no dreamer about the past, no doter upon the dead and gone, no projector of the visionary. He for eighteen hundred years has lived in the world; he has seen all fortunes, he has encountered all adversaries, he has shaped himself for all emergencies. If ever there was a power on earth who had an eye for the times, who has confined himself to the practicable, and has been happy in his anticipations, whose words have been facts, and whose commands prophecies, such is he in the history of the ages, who sits from generation to generation in the Chair of the Apostles, as the Vicar of Christ, and the Doctor of His Church.[41]

NOTES

[1] T. Corcoran, S.J., *Newman's Theory of Education* (Dublin: University College, 1929), p. lxxi.

[2] Quoted in A. D. Culler, *The Imperial Intellect: A Study of Cardinal Newman's Educational Ideal* (New Haven, Conn.: Yale University Press, 1955), p. 304.

[3] W. Byron, S.J., in *Fellowship of Catholic Scholars Newsletter* 10 (June 1987), p. 3.

[4] "Circular and Correspondence" (manuscript, July 21 or 22, 1852). Cf. *An Essay on the Development of Christian Doctrine* (new ed.; London: Basil Montagu Pickering, 1878), p. 86.

[5] W. Sullivan, S.J., in *New Catholic World* (July–Aug. 1976), p. 164.

[6] Newman's Journal (Jan. 1863), in Culler, *The Imperial Intellect*, p. 244.

[7] *My Campaign in Ireland*, Part I. *Catholic University Reports and Other Papers* (Aberdeen: A. King, 1896), p. 270. Cf. *Fifteen Sermons Preached before the University of Oxford, 1826–1843* (London: Longman, Green and Co., 1871), Sermon XIV. See also letters on the Tamworth Reading Room address, reprinted in *Discussions and Arguments on Various Subjects* (London: Longman, Green and Co., 1885).

[8] Newman to Mr. Fottrell (Dec. 10, 1873), in W. Ward, *The Life of John Henry Cardinal Newman* (London: Longman, Green and Co., 1912), vol. II, p. 397.

[9] *My Campaign in Ireland*, p. 80.

[10] Newman to Fottrell (Dec. 10, 1873), in Ward, *Newman*, vol. II, p. 398.

[11] Sister Bridgid Driscoll, quoted in *Education: Suburban People's Spring Supplement* (Jan. 11, 1987).

[12] Ward, *Newman*, vol. II, p. 395.

[13] Newman's Journal (Jan. 1863), in Culler, *The Imperial Intellect*, p. 244. Cf. *The Idea of a University Defined and Illustrated* (London: Longman, Green and Co., 1929), pp. 133ff. The fourteenth of the *Fifteen Sermons Preached before the University of Oxford, 1836–1843* simply equates wisdom with philosophy. By enlarging upon the distinction in the sixth discourse, Newman intends no contradiction; he would consider philosophy more in terms of the intellect than of behavior.

[14] Newman's Journal (Jan. 1863), in Culler, *The Imperial Intellect*, p. 244.

[15] The Very Rev. Peter-Hans Kolvenbach, in "Seventh Ordinary General Assembly", *L'Osservatore Romano*, English ed. (Nov. 9, 1987).

[16] Newman to J. R. Mozley (Oct. 24, 1881), in Ward, *Newman*, vol. II, p. 518.

[17] *Apologia pro Vita Sua* (London: Longman, Green and Co., 1890), p. 223:

"I had an unspeakable aversion to the policy and acts of Mr. O'Connell, because, as I thought, he associated himself with men of all religions and no religion against the Anglican Church, and advanced Catholicism by violence and intrigue." A grandson of O'Connell was one of the first twenty students of the university.

¹⁸ Newman to Gerard Manley Hopkins (Mar. 3, 1887), in Ward, *Newman*, vol. II, p. 527.

¹⁹ Anonymous to Newman (Dec. 1851), in Culler, *The Imperial Intellect*, p. 142.

²⁰ See Fergal McGrath, S.J., *Newman's University, Ideal and Reality* (London: Longman, Green and Co., 1951), p. 144. In an untempered moment, Dr. MacHale remarked, "Our high Catholics are rotten to the heart's core, and our middle Catholics are fast corrupting in the same manner, by love of self and place." See W. E. Stockley, *Newman, Education and Ireland* (London: Longman, Green and Co., n.d.), pp. 101–2.

²¹ See *My Campaign in Ireland*, pp. 94 and 182. Cf. *The Idea of a University*, pp. 483ff.

²² See, for instance, E. V. Clark, "Newman and the Catholic University of Ireland", in *Newman Commemorative Essays* (New York: The Paulist Press, 1946), p. 22.

²³ Newman to Mrs. Froude (Oct. 1851), in Ward, *Newman*, vol. I, p. 312.

²⁴ See *The Idea of a University*, pp. x, xi, xvi. Also *My Campaign in Ireland*, pp. 47–48, 52–53, 128. Students in his own household at No. 6 Harcourt Street included a French vicomte, an Irish baronet, two sons of a French prince, and a Polish count; these were witnesses to confidence in him, and hardly to his confidence in them.

²⁵ Alan Bloom, *The Closing of the American Mind* (New York: Simon & Schuster, 1987), pp. 349 and 35–59. With his encomium of Kant, Bloom served evidence of a hardly ever noted facet of the closing of the American *academic* mind. It consists in systematic disregard by the "establishment" of scholarly works that discredit its hallowed clichés about cultural history. A classic illustration of this is Bloom's failure to refer to the devastating exposure of Kant's shocking incompetence in matters scientific as revealed in chap. VIII in Stanley L. Jaki's Gifford Lectures, *The Road of Science and the Ways to God*, a book published in 1978 and republished twice as a paperback by the University of Chicago Press, Bloom's own home turf. Established academic circles have also ignored Jaki's translation of Kant's cosmogony *Universal Natural History and Theory of the Heavens* (Edinburgh: Scottish Academic Press, 1981). No wonder. There a hundred-page-long introduction and about as many pages of notes place Kant in the context of a meticulously researched history of astronomy and cosmology during the eighteenth century with the result that Kant appears for what he really was with respect to science—a rank amateur.

[26] *The Idea of a University*, p. 202. Cf. ibid., Preface, p. xvi. Bloom, op. cit., p. 344.

[27] Congregation for Catholic Education, "Summary of Responses to Draft Schema of Catholic Universities", in *Origins* 17 (Mar. 24, 1988), p. 699.

[28] Newman to Mrs. Froude, in Ward, *Newman*, vol. I, p. 312.

[29] *Discussion and Arguments on Various Subjects* (London: Longman, Green and Co., 1918), p. 275. Cf. *The Idea of a University*, where he speaks in the sixth discourse (p. 145) of "a generation frivolous, narrow-minded, and resourceless".

[30] Bishop James Malone, Commencement Address at the University of Notre Dame, May 18, 1986, in *Origins*, vol. 15, p. 117. In contrast, the Second Vatican Council speaks of religious assent as the "religious submission of mind and will". *Lumen Gentium*, no. 25. Cf. *Dei Verbum*, no. 5, and the First Vatican Council, *De Fide*, in Denz. no. 1789 (no. 3008).

[31] *The Idea of a University*, p. 218.

[32] Ibid., Preface, pp. xvi–xvii.

[33] *Statement on the Nature of the Contemporary Catholic University*, Land O' Lakes, Wisconsin (July 23, 1967), sec. 1; cf. sec. 9. The definition of a university reappears in sec. 5 of "The Contemporary Catholic University", a position paper prepared by the North American section of the International Federation of Catholic Universities in *Notre Dame Report 1971–72* (South Bend, Ind.: University of Notre Dame, 1972), pp. 103ff. Its Appendix (p. 111) includes the statement: "[The Catholic university] is an independent organization serving Christian purposes but not subject to ecclesiastical-juridical control, censorship or supervision."

[34] *Statement on the Nature of the Contemporary Catholic University*, sec. 1.

[35] *The Idea of a University*, p. 215.

[36] Canons 808, 810, 812.

[37] The subject is discussed at length in *Historical Sketches*, vol. III, chaps. XV and XIX. "If I were to describe as briefly and popularly as I could, what a University was, I should draw my answer from its ancient designation of a *Studium Generale*, or 'School of Universal Learning' " (ibid., chap. II, p. 6). Cf. Newman's tribute to Copleston in *The Idea of a University*, p. 157. The Newman Movement began as an attempt to adapt Newman's vision to the American university structure. Following an experiment at the University of Wisconsin, the first "Newman Club" was organized by Timothy L. Harrington at the University of Pennsylvania in the early 1890s. Cf. John Whitney Evans, *The Newman Movement* (South Bend, Ind.: University of Notre Dame Press, 1980), pp. 19ff.

[38] *The Idea of a University*, p. 145. Here, when he says a university is "not a foundry, or a mint, or a treadmill", he echoes the scornful reference to the University of London as "Gower Street College" in *Discussions and Arguments*,

p. 274. He would certainly say the same of today's size-conscious Catholic institutions. See n. 11 above.

[39] Ibid., p. 167. Thus in *My Campaign in Ireland* (p. 249), he faults the notion of a university that is "a sort of bazaar or hotel, where everything is showy, and self-sufficient and changeable".

[40] Plotinus, *Enneads*, II, ix, 15, trans. S. MacKenna (rev. ed.; London: 1969), pp. 147–48. Cf. A. Louth, *Discerning the Mystery* (Oxford: Clarendon Press, 1983), pp. 75–77. See also W. Jaeger, *Paedeia: The Ideals of Greek Culture* (Oxford: University Press, 1939).

[41] *The Idea of a University*, p. 13. For a study of the fifth discourse and the brief of Pius IX, see McGrath, *Newman's University, Ideal and Reality*, pp. 273ff.

IAN T. KER

NEWMAN AND THE
POSTCONCILIAR CHURCH

Newman has often been called the "Father" of the Second Vatican Council. And while it might be difficult or impossible to trace his direct influence on the actual Council documents, there is no doubt that Vatican II upheld and vindicated those controversial positions that he espoused in his own time, and so often at his own personal cost.

First and most important is the dogmatic constitution on the Church *Lumen Gentium*, the cornerstone of Vatican II. It was the absence of the wider ecclesiological context in which the doctrine of the papacy needed to be placed that Newman had deplored at the time of the First Vatican Council. As he argued then, the definition of papal infallibility had not come in the right "order—it would have come to us very differently, if those preliminaries about the Church's power had first been passed, which . . . were intended." He had hoped that the Council—which broke up as a result of the invasion of Rome by Garibaldi's troops—would reassemble and "occupy itself in other points" that would "have the effect of qualifying and guarding the dogma" of papal infallibility. This was not to be, but, unlike those who supposed that the definition would render future Councils superfluous, Newman remained serenely confident that far from being the last Council, Vatican I would be completed and modified by a future Council, as had happened before in the history of the Church. Indeed, the history of the early Church showed how "the Church moved on to the perfect truth by various successive declarations, alternately in contrary directions, and thus perfecting, completing, supplying each other". The definition of papal infallibility needed not so much to be "undone, as to be completed". Faced with the exaggerations of the extreme Ultramontanes, he advised: "Let us be patient, let us have faith, and a new Pope, and a re-assembled Council may trim the boat."[1] The prophecy would take nearly a hundred years to be fulfilled, but fulfilled it was in the magnificently comprehensive teaching of *Lumen Gentium*, which reaffirmed the doctrine of papal infallibility but this time explained the primacy of the Pope as the headship of the whole college of bishops.

Newman had remarked at the time of the First Vatican Council that the definition of papal infallibility would result in "an alteration of the *elementary constitution* of the Church", because it would encourage the Pope to act alone without the bishops.[2] It was "the gravest innovation possible", for "it is a change in the hitherto recognized basis of the Church".[3] The phenomenon of so-called creeping infallibility that occurred between the two Councils would have been no surprise to Newman.

The constitution begins not with a description of the hier-archical structure of the Church but by defining the Church as a mystery before describing it in terms of the whole people of God. This new emphasis was, of course, picked up in the new insistence on the role of the laity. Newman's own constant concern as a Catholic with the failure of the hierarchy to take proper account of the laymen who constitute easily the largest part of the Church is well summed up in the famous remark to his own bishop that "the Church would look foolish without them".[4] (The separate decree on the apostolate of the laity would have been especially welcome to him.) Finally, the chapter in *Lumen Gentium* devoted to the Blessed Virgin Mary can be said to vindicate fully the balanced Mariology of Newman's *Letter to Pusey*, which, in its close adherence to Scripture and the Fathers, is also a pioneering example of ecumenical theology at its best.

Newman supported early ecumenical initiatives as an Anglican, and later as a Catholic he hoped for a reconciliation of Anglo-Catholics with Rome, which he thought should be prepared to make concessions. As in general in theological matters, he was cautious but open. He did not see his way to joining the "Association for the Promotion of the Unity of Christendom", but he deplored its harsh condemnation by the Roman authorities; unlike some enthusiastic Catholic ecumenists, he was highly sceptical about the foreseeable possibility of the reunion of Canterbury and Rome, but he deplored the bigotry of so many Catholics who, he felt, considerably underestimated the possibility of "invincible ignorance" among non-Catholics. Again, the radical statement that "all other truths and acts of religion are included" in repentance and faith in Christ[5] must be balanced against Newman's inability to accept that the Church of England was a church at all; he would have been surprised, albeit pleasantly so, by the degree of ecclesial reality that the decree on ecumenism attributes to the Christian bodies that derive from the Reformation. Nevertheless, there was no doubting his commitment to the first faint stirrings of the ecumenical movement; and he was pleased by the successful sales of a new edition of his *Parochial and Plain Sermons* among Protestants: "Whatever tends to create a unity of heart between men of different communions, lays the ground for advances towards a restoration of that visible unity, the absence of which among Christians is so great a triumph, and so great an advantage to the enemies of the Cross."[6]

There are three other major conciliar documents that Newman anticipated. The dogmatic constitution on revelation insists on the intimate connection of Scripture and Tradition, refusing to endorse the post-Tridentine "two sources" theory. As an Anglican, Newman had assumed the inseparability of Scripture and Tradition, and later as a Catholic he held that the disagreement on this point between Anglicans and Catholics is a purely verbal one, since Scripture requires Tradition for its interpretation and Tradition needs the authority of Scripture. The constitution's teaching that the inspiration of Scripture extends only to "that truth which God wanted put into the sacred writings for the sake of our salvation" (art. 11) vindicates Newman's own tentative approach in the article he wrote in the last years of his life "On the Inspiration of Scripture".

The possibility of religious truth outside the Christian revelation is explicitly allowed for not in this constitution but in the decrees on non-Christian religions and on the Church's missionary activity. Newman himself in his first book had boldly affirmed, "There never was a time when God had not spoken to man", for although it was true that "the Church of God ever has had, and the rest of mankind never have had, authoritative documents of truth, and appointed channels of communication with Him", still "all men have had more or less the guidance of Tradition, in addition to those internal notions of right and wrong which the Spirit has put into the heart of each individual". Calling this "vague and uncertain family of religious truths, originally from God . . . the *Dispensation of Paganism*", Newman came to what was then the radical conclusion that the Christian apologist or missionary should, "after St. Paul's manner, seek some points in the existing superstitions as the basis of his own instructions, instead of indiscriminately condemning and discarding the whole assemblage of heathen opinions and practices", thus "recovering and purifying, rather than reversing the essential principles of their belief".[7]

The pastoral constitution on the Church in the modern world *Gaudium et Spes* encouraged exactly that creative and positive engagement with the secular world that Newman so vainly desiderated in his own time, and particularly with those intellectual problems raised by scientific progress and secularization. Newman has often been criticized for his lack of involvement in pressing contemporary social questions; he himself noted at the end of his life, "It has never been my line to take up political or social questions, unless they come close to me as matters of personal duty."[8] But there was one political idea, quite radical then, that he embraced from the beginning of the Oxford Movement and to which he continued to adhere as a Catholic—with, it should be said, much greater hope of its practical realization: I refer to his conviction that the Church, as in the first centuries, must once again become a *popular* Church, a Church of the people. I think that there can be no question that the emergence of the Church as a popular institution in countries such as the Philippines and in Latin America would have delighted Newman. Deeply shocked as he was by what he called the "great scandal" of Pius IX being "protected against his own people by foreign bayonets",[9] Newman surely would have rejoiced at the sight of John Paul II personally upholding the rights of the poor and oppressed in so many Third World countries. Long before it happened, Newman had seen that "establishment Catholicism" was not only anachronistic but also in practice ultimately harmful to the interests of the Church. The disengagement or distancing of the Church from the state in so many Catholic countries since the end of the Second Vatican Council Newman would have seen as inevitable and in the long term thoroughly beneficial. In 1864 he wrote:

> I am not at all sure that it would not be better for the Catholic religion every where, if it had no very different status from that which it has in England. There is so much corruption, so much deadness, so much hypocrisy, so much infidelity, when a dogmatic faith is imposed on a nation by law, that I like freedom better. I think Italy will be more religious, that is, there will be more true religion in it, when the Church has to fight for its supremacy, than when that supremacy depends on the provisions of courts and police.

He also saw very clearly that the refusal to grant religious freedom to non-Catholics in Catholic countries, however justifiable (as it then seemed) on the abstract ground of the truth of the Catholic religion, was utterly impractical and self-defeating in a modern, pluralist world. Catholicism had to be defended "by reason, not by force".[10] The declaration, in fact, on religious freedom would have been seen by him not only as a useful practical measure but also as an example of the development of doctrine called for by the times.

If we turn now to the postconciliar period, we may first note that however dismayed Newman would have been by the chaos and conflict that came in the wake of the Council in many parts of the Church, he would certainly not have been in the least bit surprised by it. Indeed, his reflections on the aftermaths of Councils make interesting and consoling reading today. From his lifelong study of the early Church, he knew only too well how much confusion and dissension those first crucial, formative Councils had caused. Because Councils "generally acted as a lever, displacing and disordering portions of the existing theological system", they were naturally often followed by bitter controversies within the Church.[11] It was, he said, one of the "disadvantages of a General Council . . . that it throws individual units through the Church into confusion and sets them at variance".[12] The secession of the Old Catholics under Döllinger after Vatican I was as predictable as the extremism of the Ultramontane party. The more overdue the reforms of Vatican II, the more bitter was the polarization likely to be between the conservative and liberal wings of the Church. Newman could have predicted the rise of both Archbishop Lefebvre and Professor Küng, and he would have enthusiastically endorsed the condemnations by Pope Paul VI and Pope John Paul II of both "integralism" and "progressivism". But while deploring the excesses of extreme so-called progressive Catholics, he would surely have placed a large part of the blame on those Ultramontanes who by encouraging the tendency to "creeping infallibility" had helped to provoke a bitter reaction, as well as on the authorities of the Church for failing to adapt sooner to the modern world.

Apart from the relation of Vatican II to Vatican I, can one from Newman's writings draw any theological insights into the ways in which the specific teachings of Vatican II were likely to disturb the peace of the Church by "displacing and disordering portions of the existing theological system"?

To take *Lumen Gentium* first, it would have been obvious to Newman that the new emphasis placed on the rights of both the episcopate and the laity was bound to cast a shadow over both the papacy and the clergy. Because bishops and laymen came out of Vatican II with greatly enhanced roles, it was inevitable that both the Pope and the priests would seem to be correspondingly downgraded. It was yet another instance of his general maxim that the Church develops "by various successive declarations, alternately in contrary directions, and thus perfecting, completing, supplying each other". And so at the present a reaction seems to be setting in as the realization grows that just as in spite of sharing in a common priesthood through Baptism, the laity loses its true character by being "clericalized", so the ordained ministry is different precisely because of the sacrament of Holy Orders from other legitimate forms of ministry in the Church. Newman would have been struck by the paradox that, in spite of the tendency of Vatican II to cut the Pope down, as it were, to ecclesial size as head of the college of bishops, ironically the advances in technology have ensured that the modern Pope has access to a universal audience on a scale undreamed of in the past. The televised pastoral visits of Pope John Paul II have given a whole new meaning to the claim of the Pope to exercise a pastorate over all Christians. There is, incidentally, a strange prophecy of the Pope's highly successful visit to England in 1981 in Newman's *Lectures on the Present Position of Catholics in England*, when he writes:

> I will say a bold thing,—but I am not at all sure, that . . . the Pope himself, however he may be abused behind his back, would not be received with cheers, and run after by admiring crowds, if he visited this country, independent of the shadow of Peter which attends him, winning favour and attracting hearts,

when he showed himself in real flesh and blood, by the majesty
of his presence and the prestige of his name.[13]

The point is not without theological interest. As an Anglican,
Newman had maintained that because human nature needs
individuals as guides and leaders, "Christianity has met our
want in the Episcopal system."

> Increase the number of our Bishops. Give the people objects on
> which their holier and more generous feelings may rest. After
> all, in spite of the utilitarianism of the age, we have hearts. We
> like to meet with those whom we may admire and make much
> of. We like to be thrown out of ourselves. . . . Human nature is
> not republican.

Newman thought hopefully that "the sight" of the bishop
was sure to bring out "the purer and nobler feelings of our
nature" and a "flame of devoted and triumphant affection".[14]
Although Newman would have approved not only of *Lumen
Gentium*'s idea of the apostolic college but also of the opportunity for collective and concerted action provided by
episcopal conferences, he would also, with his lifelong personal antipathy to boards and committees, have deplored any
diminution of the personal influence of the bishop in his
diocese. Nor can there be any question that Newman's
imagination would have been fired by the heroic nature of
Pope John Paul II's often highly dangerous journeys abroad.
This development in the role of the papacy may not have been
intended by the Fathers of Vatican II, but Newman would
have seen it as a providential if unexpected corrective of a
certain depersonalizing democratization that followed Vatican II.

It is highly characteristic of Newman's extraordinary genius
for seeing all sides of a question and for keeping very different
considerations in balanced perspective that, in spite of having
originally opposed the definition of papal infallibility as "in-
opportune", once the doctrine had been defined he was ready
to admit that, although he had "always inclined to the notion
that a General Council was the magisterial exponent of the

Creed", unfortunately, it had to be admitted that "a General Council may be hampered and hindered by the action of infidel Governments upon a weak or time-serving episcopate". He even went so far as to concede:

> It is . . . better that the individual command of Christ to Peter to teach the nations, and to guard the Christian structure of society, should be committed to his undoubted successor. By this means there will be no more of those misunderstandings out of which Jansenism and Gallicanism have arisen. [15]

Moreover, his study of Church history and his knowledge of the intriguing and lobbying at the recent Council had led him to the depressing conclusion that if the proceedings of Councils "are to be the measure of their authority, they are, with few exceptions, a dreary, unlovely phenomenon in the Church". [16] A few years later he felt even more negative about Councils, but correspondingly even more positive about the papacy: "The more one examines the Councils, the less satisfactory they are . . . [but] the less satisfactory *they*, the more majestic and trust-winning, and the more imperatively necessary, is the action of the Holy See." [17]

Naturally, this was only one side of the question. Nobody was more opposed to an autocratic papal curia than Newman: the threat of Garibaldi's invasion of Rome and the prospect of a secular government of the Eternal City seemed to Newman to be not without potential benefit to the Church, for "it would cut off a great deal of unprofitable gossip sent to Rome . . . and of crude answers sent back from Rome by men who seem to have authority, but have none—and it would throw power into the hands of the local Bishops every where." [18] But concerned as he was for the legitimate self-government of the local Church and opposed as he was to the heavy hand of Roman bureaucracy, he was never tempted to imagine the evolution of the Petrine office into a kind of general presidency over a federation of local Churches—as some in recent times have envisaged. At the very time of his worst collision with

Cardinal Barnabò, the Prefect of Propaganda, over the question
of Catholics going to Oxford, he did not hesitate to insist to
Pusey on the "unlimited" and even "despotic" jurisdiction of
the Pope, albeit as a "principle" rather than "doctrine" of the
Catholic system. Although he modifies this by observing that
papal authority is more an "abstract power" than a "practical
fact", he is very forthright that

> there is no use in a Pope at all, except to bind the whole of
> Christendom into one polity; and . . . to ask us to give up his
> universal jurisdiction is to invite us to commit suicide. . . . An
> honorary head . . . does not affect the real force, or enter into the
> essence, of a political body, and is not worth contending about.
> We do not want a man of straw, but a bond of unity. . . . Now
> the Church is a Church Militant, and, as the commander of an
> army is despotic, so must the visible head of the Church be.[19]

Before leaving *Lumen Gentium*, a word should be said about
Marian devotions. Although, as has been said, Newman would
have welcomed the constitution's balanced Mariology and
although, in view of past distortions and exaggerations that he
himself had deplored, he would have appreciated the difficult
decision the Council Fathers took not to treat our Lady in a
separate document but to view her in the context of the whole
mystery of the Church—there is no doubt that the recent
tendency to deprecate and depreciate devotion to Mary would
not have struck any responsive chord in Newman. An unease
at certain manifestations of emotional devotionalism by no
means meant that Newman himself did not have a deep
Marian piety. Although he had deliberately refrained from
invocatory prayer while he was an Anglican on the ground
that it was not allowed by the Church of England, this did not
mean that even then he did not have "a high exaltation of the
Blessed Virgin", "a true devotion to the Blessed Virgin".[20]
Indeed, even then he had felt that the doctrine of the Immaculate
Conception was "the most natural and necessary of doctrines
—and I cannot enter into the minds of those who feel it

difficult". In a sermon preached ten years before he became a Catholic, called "The Reverence Due to the Virgin Mary", he had made this quite clear when he had said that the sinless human nature of Christ could not have come from sinful flesh.[21] As a Catholic, in the *Letter to Pusey*, he warned that "on the whole . . . just those nations and countries have lost their faith in the divinity of Christ, who have given up devotion to His Mother, and that those on the other hand, who had been foremost in her honour, have retained their orthodoxy": "In the Catholic Church Mary has shown herself, not the rival, but the minister of her Son; she has protected Him, as in His infancy, so in the whole history of the Religion."[22] It can be stated with categorical certainty that the opinion of certain modern theologians, including Catholic theologians, that the virginal conception is not central to Christianity would have profoundly shocked Newman.

The new emphasis on Scripture in both theology and liturgy stems, of course, from the dogmatic constitution on divine revelation. Again, welcome as this would have been to Newman, his writings contain many warnings of the dangers of Bibliolatry. Already, before the Oxford Movement began, he had pointed out in his first book on the Arians that the early Church did not use the Bible to teach the Faith; rather, it was the Church that taught what had to be believed, only appealing to "Scripture in vindication of its own teaching".[23] As a Tractarian, Newman never ceased to inveigh against the "ultra-Protestant principle", according to which "every one may gain the true doctrines of the gospel for himself from the Bible".[24] The idea that one gains today from reading certain Catholic authors that Church and Tradition can somehow be dispensed with was dismissed in a memorable passage in the *Essay on the Development of Christian Doctrine*:

> We are told that God has spoken. Where? In a book? We have tried it and it disappoints us, that most holy and blessed gift, not from fault of its own, but because it is used for a purpose for

which it was not given. . . . The Church undertakes that office;
she does what none else can do, and this is the secret of her
power.[25]

But even if Scripture was not intended like the Church to
teach doctrine ("a book does not speak; it is shut till it is
opened"),[26] Newman never meant to slight its importance for
faith. As an Anglican, he took the reading of the Bible for
granted and was only intent on preventing its misuse for
purposes for which it was not intended. But as a Catholic, his
attitude changed because he found himself in a Church where
the reading of the Scriptures was the exception rather than the
rule. On becoming a Catholic, he had been struck very favor-
ably by the simple, objective faith of Catholics, but he came to
see that that was only one side of the picture, and that the lack
of the Bible in the lives of ordinary Catholics was gravely
damaging:

> It is the best book of meditations which can be, because it is
> divine. This is why we see such multitudes in France and Italy
> giving up religion altogether. They have not impressed upon
> their hearts the life of our Lord and Saviour as given in the
> Evangelists. They believe merely with the intellect, not with the
> heart. Argument may overset a mere assent of the reason, but
> not a faith founded in a personal love for the Object of Faith.
> They quarrel with their priests, and then they give up the
> Church. We can quarrel with men, we cannot quarrel with a
> book.[27]

Newman's concern that Catholics should know their Bible is,
of course, commonplace now in the Church; but his warnings
as an Anglican against the limitations of Scripture are applicable
in the postconciliar period when signs of a creeping Biblicism
can be detected in some quarters.

There is no indication that Newman ever contemplated or
wanted any radical changes in the liturgy. The scene in the
Passionist church at the end of *Loss and Gain* has sometimes

been cited by those opposed to the liturgical reforms of Vatican II. But against that should be placed the plainer liturgical setting at the end of *Callista*, where a simple Mass of the early Church is celebrated facing the people. Not only, of course, was Newman well aware of the many and varied changes in the Church's liturgy over the centuries, but change was to be expected, for, to use his own famous words, "to live is to change",[28] while on the other hand "an obsolete discipline may be a present heresy".[29] It is quite clear that Newman would have seen the importance and inevitability of adapting the liturgy to a cultural and religious milieu very different from that of the Council of Trent. That is not to say that all the contemporary expressions of eucharistic worship would have appealed to his reserved and shy temperament. But it has to be said that what chiefly impressed Newman when he became a Catholic was not the numinous quality of the Latin Mass or the ritual or the chant but rather the *objectivity* of the worship, symbolized in particular by the Real Presence of Christ in every Catholic church or chapel. There are numerous references in his postconversion letters to his reaction to the reservation of the Blessed Sacrament in the tabernacle. In the following passage, for example, written from Maryvale, it is noteworthy how the emphasis falls not so much on the Mass as on the Blessed Sacrament:

> We went over not realizing those privileges which we have found *by* going. . . . I could not have fancied the extreme, ineffable comfort of being in the same house with Him who cured the sick and taught His disciples. . . . When I have been in Churches abroad, I have religiously abstained from acts of worship, though it was a most soothing comfort to go into them—nor did I know what was going on; I neither understood nor tried to understand the Mass service—and I did not know, or did not observe, the tabernacle Lamp—but now after tasting of the awful delight of worshipping God in His Temple, how unspeakably cold is the idea of a Temple without that Divine

Presence! One is tempted to say what is the meaning, what is the use of it?[30]

When he was in Milan on his way to study for the priesthood, Newman wrote, "I never knew what worship was, as an objective fact, till I entered the Catholic Church." He was overwhelmed by what he saw in the Duomo:

A Catholic Cathedral is a sort of world, every one going about his own business, but that business a religious one; groups of worshippers, and solitary ones—kneeling, standing—some at shrines, some at altars—hearing Mass and communicating— currents of worshippers intercepting and passing by each other —altar after altar lit up for worship, like stars in the firmament —or the bell giving notice of what is going on in parts you do not see—and all the while the canons in the choir going through matins and lauds, and at the end of it the incense rolling up from the high altar, and all this in one of the most wonderful buildings in the world and every day—lastly, all of this without any show or effort, but what everyone is used to—every one at his own work, and leaving every one else to his.[31]

This powerful passage may well evoke nostalgia in some people, but it is not intended to suggest that Newman would have been opposed to the liturgical movement, which he would have seen as a necessary development in the life of the Church and as an essential adaptation in a changed world. Obviously, to some extent Newman was responding to the actual situation in the Church as he knew it, and one would not expect a modern liturgist, any more than a modern ecumenist, necessarily to endorse all his views. But what still bears repeating, and what still needs to be stressed, is the objective aspect of the Church's liturgical life, which is objective precisely because of its supernatural character. Is there not a tendency in the contemporary liturgy to reduce the transcendent element, to substitute the immediate presence of the people gathered in eucharistic worship for that objective Real Presence of Christ on the altar, which alone makes possible such a community?

As an Anglican, Newman had criticized those "who come to the Lord's Table without awe, admiration, hope; without that assemblage of feelings which the expectation of so transcendent a marvel should raise in us".[32] The Tractarian Newman called for more frequent Communion, but the thought of the casual practice of receiving Communion as a matter of course at every Mass would have shocked the preacher who spoke of the "calm worship, the foretaste of heaven" of those "who for a season shut themselves out from the world, and seek Him in invisible Presence, whom they shall hereafter see face to face".[33]

The constitution on the liturgy called for a revision of the sacrament of Penance, but the actual reform has not prevented a widespread neglect of the use of the sacrament. Of course, this may prove to be a passing phenomenon, due in part perhaps to an overfrequent use in the past of a sacrament that was often administered no doubt in too juridical and mechanical a way. As a Catholic priest, Newman was diffident about hearing confessions in rather the same way that he was diffident about writing theology—in both cases he felt he lacked the technical expertise. The more liturgical and pastoral approach to the sacrament of today, with a fresh emphasis on spiritual direction, would have made him feel much less uneasy. But let there be no mistake about Newman's opinion of the value of the sacrament. Once again, in order to correct a contemporary imbalance in the Roman Catholic Church, we have to turn to the Anglican Newman. Just before Christmas 1842, he wrote with some vehemence to John Keble:

> As to reminding my People about Confession, it is the most dreary and dismal thought which I have about my Parish that I dare do so little, or rather nothing. I have long thought it would hinder me ever taking another cure. Confession is the life of the Parochial charge—without it all is hollow.[34]

It is generally agreed that, no doubt inevitably, there has been a negative side to that long-overdue engagement and sympathy with the secular order that *Gaudium et Spes* encouraged.

Now in spite of all his disappointment at and disapproval of the Catholic Church's refusal to come to terms with the modern world, Newman never lost that pessimism about the natural world that is so prominent a feature of his Anglican sermons. In "Faith and the World", for example, after citing several warnings from the New Testament about "the world", Newman declares severely and uncompromisingly:

> Let us be quite sure, then, that the confederacy of evil which Scripture calls the world, that conspiracy against Almighty God of which Satan is the secret instigator, is something wider, and more subtle, and more ordinary, than mere cruelty, or craft, or profligacy; it is that very world in which we are; it is not a certain body or party of men, but it is human society itself.[35]

There is in Newman no facile, superficial optimism about the world such as we find sometimes in Catholic writers today. But, in spite of his admitted lack of expertise in political and social matters, there was never any question in his mind about the right and duty of the Church to intervene in the temporal sphere. Where Newman strikes a cautionary note is in his frequent warnings against obscuring the true role of the Church, the "direct and primary aim" of which is the worship of God, whereas "the sole object . . . of the social and political world everywhere, is to make the most of this life".[36] Or, as he put it in a famous, even notorious, passage, the Catholic Church

> holds that it were better for sun and moon to drop from heaven, for the earth to fail, and for all the many millions who are upon it to die of starvation in extremest agony, so far as temporal affliction goes, than that one soul, I will not say, should be lost, but should commit one single venial sin, should tell one wilful untruth, though it harmed no one, or steal one poor farthing without excuse . . . she would rather save the soul of one single wild bandit of Calabria, or whining beggar of Palermo, than draw a hundred lines of railroad through the length and breadth of Italy.[37]

In the context of the hopeful optimism of *Gaudium et Spes*, it may be legitimate to note a certain preoccupation since the

Council with the "success" of the Church's mission and to set it against the pessimistic realism of Newman. He admitted in his Anglican sermons that he was "suspicious of any religion that is a people's religion, or an age's religion", for the "token" of "true religion" was rather "the light shining in darkness". As for the Church, "she attempts much, she expects and promises little". The idea of a faithful remnant runs through the Bible, and "when Christ came, the bulk of His own people rejected Him". Redemption *"has* come to all the world, but the world is not changed thereby as a whole". There should be "no vain imaginings about the world's real conversion". Indeed, Jesus spoke of the "Gospel being preached, not chiefly as a means of converting, but as a witness against the world". A realist would have to ask whether the world is not "as unbelieving now as when Christ came", and whether Christians, "except a small remnant", would not, like the Jews, reject Christ if he came again.[38]

A few remarks may be useful about Newman's spirituality and that of contemporary Catholicism. Although the deeply scriptural and Patristic sermons he preached as an Anglican anticipate more recent theology in their profound awareness that the Resurrection was more than the affirmation of Christ's divinity and of his victory over sins, the Crucifixion and the Cross nevertheless cast their dark shadow over every page of Newman's preaching. Again, through his study of the New Testament and the Fathers, Newman had recovered for himself the great doctrine of the "indwelling" of the Holy Spirit,[39] but because of his mistrust of the evangelical emphasis on salvation by faith alone, he deliberately stressed not so much the Spirit as the Christian's responsibility to obey the Commandments and the Law of Christ. The theological rediscovery of the Resurrection in recent times as well as the Charismatic Renewal movement's emphasis on Pentecost have both sometimes seemed to lead to a neglect of the Crucifixion. One of the most impressive aspects of Newman's integrated theology is his balanced view of the whole mystery of redemption beginning with the Incarnation and concluding with Pentecost. As a

result, his spirituality avoids the two extremes into which
Christians can easily fall. If it may be alleged that the pre-
Vatican II Church, with its emphasis on sin and Penance,
appeared to be more interested in Good Friday than in Easter,
then it may also be suggested that there is perhaps a reverse
imbalance in contemporary Catholicism. In his sermons, as in
his other writings, Newman was always insistent on both
sides of Christianity, on both the Crucifixion and the Resurrection. Christianity must be cheerful and joyful, but it must
also be sorrowful and fearful. As he puts it succinctly in one
sermon, "None rejoice in Easter-tide less than those who have
not grieved in Lent." Or again, "The duty of fearing does but
perfect our joy; that joy alone is true Christian joy, which is
informed and quickened by fear, and made thereby sober and
reverent." But he also writes:

> Gloom is no Christian temper; that repentance is not real, which
> has not love in it; that self-chastisement is not acceptable, which
> is not sweetened by faith and cheerfulness. We must live in
> sunshine, even when we sorrow. . . . All through Lent we must
> rejoice, while we afflict ourselves.

Anxious to avoid a merely negative spirituality of repentance,
contemporary Catholic spirituality seems sometimes to lay
itself open to Newman's severe rebuke: "I wish I saw any
prospect of [an] element of zeal and holy sternness springing
up among us, to temper and give character to the languid,
unmeaning benevolence which we misname Christian love."[40]

Such are some of the ways in which Newman's thought
may complement or correct some of the imbalances or in-
adequacies that have accompanied the implementation of the
Council that Newman himself anticipated and to which he
looked forward. As we have seen, Newman had a theology of
Councils that is relevant to our own times. He also had what
may be called almost a theology of the vicissitudes of the
Church, which, following the pattern of the Crucifixion and
Resurrection, dies in one place and one time only to rise to new

life in another place and at another time. As an Anglican, he wrote:

> The whole course of Christianity from the first . . . is but one series of troubles and disorders. Every century is like every other, and to those who live in it seems worse than all times before it. The Church is ever ailing. . . . Religion seems ever expiring, schisms dominant, the light of Truth dim, its adherents scattered. The cause of Christ is ever in its last agony.[41]

Again, in the *Essay on the Development of Christian Doctrine* he spoke of the "wonderful revivals" of the Church "while the world was triumphing over her".[42] As a Catholic he returned to the theme more than once. The Church always "seemed dying" but then "triumphed, against all human calculation". It was "impossible to forecast the future" when there were "no precedents—and the history of Christianity is a succession of fresh trials—never the same twice". There was "a continuous history of fearful falls and as strange and successful recoveries". The sheer variety of the catastrophes, "each unlike the others", was a "pledge that the present ordeal, though different from any of the preceding, will be overcome". It seemed to Newman in his old age that they were not "entering on quite a new course—for which the civil ignoring of Christianity may be the necessary first step, and we may have centuries of confusion —but the Church has steadily worked her way out of over-whelming misfortunes in time past, and will . . . again."[43]

Scholars may criticize Newman's credentials as a historian. What is not in doubt is his historical imagination or his profoundly historical cast of mind. For Newman the study of theology necessarily involved the study of history. His views on the Church of his day were also highly colored by his historical vision. It is surely the lack of a proper historical sense that is the salient characteristic of both the extreme conservatives and liberals in the Church today. Newman's calm perspective, derived from his reflections on the history of the Church, is one of the great gifts he has to offer postconciliar Catholicism.

NOTES

[1] *Letters and Diaries*, vol. XXV, pp. 278, 310.

[2] *Letters and Diaries*, vol. XXIV, pp. 377–78.

[3] *Letters and Diaries*, vol. XXV, p. 100.

[4] *Letters and Diaries*, vol. XIX, p. 140.

[5] *Letters and Diaries*, vol. XX, p. 172.

[6] *Letters and Diaries*, vol. XXIV, p. 22.

[7] *The Arians of the Fourth Century* (London: Longman, Green and Co., 1908), pp. 80–81, 84.

[8] *Letters and Diaries*, vol. XXX, p. 209.

[9] *Letters and Diaries*, vol. XXV, p. 217.

[10] *Letters and Diaries*, vol. XX, p. 477.

[11] *Letters and Diaries*, vol. XXVI, p. 76.

[12] *Letters and Diaries*, vol. XXVII, p. 240.

[13] *Lectures on the Present Position of Catholics in England* (London: Longman, Green and Co., 1913), p. 61.

[14] *Via Media* (London: Longman, Green and Co., 1911), vol. II, pp. 66–68.

[15] *Letters and Diaries*, vol. XXV, p. 259.

[16] *Letters and Diaries*, vol. XXVI, p. 120.

[17] *Letters and Diaries*, vol. XXVIII, p. 172.

[18] *Letters and Diaries*, vol. XXII, p. 317.

[19] *Letters and Diaries*, vol. XXIII, p. 106.

[20] *Letters and Diaries*, vol. XXX, p. 233; *Apologia pro Vita Sua* (Oxford: Clarendon Press, 1967), p. 152.

[21] *Letters and Diaries*, vol. XIX, p. 346.

[22] *Certain Difficulties Felt by Anglicans in Catholic Teaching* (London: Longman, Green and Co., 1908), vol. II, pp. 92–93.

[23] *The Arians of the Fourth Century*, p. 50.

[24] *Letters and Diaries*, vol. V, p. 166.

[25] *An Essay on the Development of Christian Doctrine* (London: Longman, Green and Co., 1908), p. 88.

[26] *Sermon Notes of John Henry Cardinal Newman, 1849–1879*, ed. Fathers of the Birmingham Oratory (London: Longman, Green and Co., 1913), p. 53.

[27] *Letters and Diaries*, vol. XXVI, p. 87.

[28] *Essay on the Development of Christian Doctrine*, p. 40.

[29] *The Idea of a University*, ed. I. T. Ker (Oxford: Clarendon Press, 1976), p. 81.

[30] *Letters and Diaries*, vol. XI, p. 131.

[31] Ibid., p. 253.

[32] *Parochial and Plain Sermons* (San Francisco: Ignatius Press, 1987), vol. VI, no. 11, p. 1267.

[33] Ibid., vol. VII, no. 11, p. 1498.

[34] *Letters and Correspondence of John Henry Newman*, ed. Anne Mozley (London: Longman, Green and Co., 1920), vol. II, p. 362.

[35] *Sermons Bearing on Subjects of the Day* (London: Longman, Green and Co., 1902), p. 80.

[36] *Letters and Diaries*, vol. XXVII, p. 388.

[37] *Certain Difficulties Felt by Anglicans in Catholic Teaching*, vol. I, p. 240.

[38] *Parochial and Plain Sermons*, vol. I, no. 5, pp. 43–44; vol. IV, no. 10, p. 821; vol. V, no. 18, p. 1111; vol. II, no. 31, p. 470; vol. II, no. 17, p. 351; vol. VI, no. 6, p. 1227.

[39] See C. S. Dessain, *John Henry Newman* (London: A. and C. Black Ltd., 1966), pp. 19–21.

[40] *Parochial and Plain Sermons*, vol. II, no. 23, p. 406; vol. V, no. 5, pp. 992–93; vol. V, no. 19, p. 1120.

[41] *Via Media*, vol. I, pp. 354–55.

[42] *Essay on the Development of Christian Doctrine*, p. 444.

[43] *Letters and Diaries*, vol. XXVIII, pp. 191 and 196.

JOSÉ MORALES

NEWMAN AND THE
PROBLEMS OF JUSTIFICATION

The doctrine on the Justification of sinners by God is one of the central aspects of the Christian Faith. It occupies a place of singular importance within the history of the religious opinions held by Newman, it has been one of the salient points at the center of disputes and discussions among Reformed and Catholic theologians, and it constitutes an obligatory topic within the current ecumenical dialogue.

While expounding on the fundamental lines of thought of John Henry Newman on the matter of Justification, we shall have to consider as well whether his ideas can contribute fully and clearly to appreciating the terms according to which the theological debate between the Catholic Church and the denominations arising from the Reform of the sixteenth century is being approached and developed at present.

The questions bearing on the topic of Justification are, along with the doctrine on the Church, the most decisive matters within Newman's long spiritual evolution. When he suggested in 1826 to Samuel Rickards the task of systematizing the theological opinions of traditional Anglican theologians, he expressed himself in this manner: "The leading doctrine to be discussed would be (I think) that of regeneration—for it is at the very root of the whole system. . . . It is connected with the doctrine of free will, original sin, justification, holiness, good works, election, education, the visible Church, etc."[1]

The doctrine on Justification is not to be set, according to Newman, within a merely theoretical framework. It represents in his life a matter of great existential repercussions, closely linked to the religious trajectory that, by means of High Church Anglicanism, led him away from the Calvinism of his youth toward the Roman Church. As is well known, the starting point of this process is to be found in the Evangelical positions that affirmed Justification *only by faith* to the exclusion of any other means, questioned regeneration through Baptism, separated Justification and sanctification, and denied, finally, all justifying value to good works.

Newman's gradual abandoning of these principles began as of 1822 and culminated around 1837, when he felt capable of elaborating a synthesis of his thought that would be part of the Anglican *Via Media* between Protestantism and Romanism. This Anglican synthesis had the intent of satisfactorily responding to all the debated points and of keeping in mind the valid aspects of the doctrine sustained by Protestants and Catholics.

Before examining in some depth the contents of the *Lectures on the Doctrine of Justification*, written in 1838, it would seem convenient briefly to comment on some of the stages of the intellectual and religious process that gave rise to this work.

In 1820 we find a young Newman convinced that he had not received in Baptism any type of spiritual regeneration and that the needed interior change in order to enter the Kingdom of God had been produced in him through his 1817 conversion: "I believed that the inward conversion of which I was conscious . . . would last into the next life, and that I was elected to eternal glory."[2] He also thought at the same time that whereas Justification is instantaneous, regeneration is progressive and gradual, and that the sacrament of Baptism is an accidental accessory of this regeneration that does not concede any type of clear title vis-à-vis eternal life.

In January of 1825 Newman's convictions had sufficiently become modified so as to enable him to write: "I must give up the doctrine of imputed righteousness and that of regeneration as apart from baptism."[3] There thus began a period in which

Newman increasingly spoke of Baptism as a means of grace and Justification. Although he still doubted whether the sacrament was wholly sufficient, Baptism became overtly associated in his writings with the donation of the Holy Spirit, which regenerates. That is, Newman rejected the subjective criterion of the Evangelical conversion and embraced the objective criterion of the baptismal rite. Around this same time he declared that "good works are required . . . because they are the means, under God's grace, of strengthening and showing forth that holy principle which God implants in the heart".[4]

As of 1830 Newman delved more deeply into the Anglo-Catholic vision, and, with the aid of the Greek Fathers, he discovered the great topic of the deification of Christians by means of uncreated grace. In his sermon entitled "Human Responsibility", preached in January or February of 1835, Newman formulated for the first time one of the central ideas of the *Lectures on Justification*: "The grace of Regeneration . . . is a definite and complete gift conveyed, not gradually, but at once; and it is a state distinct from every other, consisting in the Sacred presence of the Spirit of Christ in soul and body".[5]

The *Lectures* of 1838 are, according to Newman, one of the five *constructive* books written throughout his life.[6] It was elaborated by Newman with great effort and with some doubts as to the validity of the viewpoints he was defending. "My book is now in press", he wrote to his sister Jemima in January. "I am very anxious about the unity of the composition. . . . I should say for certain that nothing I have done has given me such anxious thoughts and so much time and labour. I have written it over, and recast parts, so often that I cannot count them."[7] At first the book was greeted with little reaction. The most interesting and keen-sighted response was a long and slightly unfavorable review written by the Anglican C. Lebas and published in the *British Critic*.[8] The most favorable Catholic comment around that time is probably the one that appeared six years later in the *Tübinger Theologische Quartalschrift*.[9]

In 1840 a second edition was published. The third appeared

much later, in 1874. It contained the same text without additions or modifications, but Newman included an advertisement of six pages and a total of sixteen notes[10] in which he clarified nuances or in some cases completed affirmations in the first edition. New observations of greater importance refer to the so-called *only formal cause* of Justification and tend to include in the *Lectures* the teachings of the Council of Trent on this decisive point of Catholic doctrine.

The main finality of the *Lectures* of 1838 is to show that the doctrine of Justification by faith alone is not unreconcilable, except in its extreme versions, with Tractarian ideas that spoke of baptismal regeneration, emphasized the sacramental aspects of Justification, and attributed an essential role to charity and obedience in the latter.

But Newman goes beyond his primary intention and offers a relatively systematic treatise in which he takes a stand on all the salient points brought out by the topic of Justification, both in itself as well as within its general religious and theological framework. Needless to say, there are some excessively subtle lines of reasoning, theses that can be sustained only with difficulty, and paradoxical affirmations that border on contradiction. In spite of everything, the whole work provides a substantially valid synthesis, which we will now describe in its basic lines.

The most outstanding merit of this book lies, in my view, in the Trinitarian perspective that Newman adopts in consonance with Holy Scripture in order to develop the Christian doctrine of Justification and to solve some of its thorniest and most debated aspects. It can be seen that, over and beyond terminological discussions and simply controversial considerations, Newman comes face to face with a mystery of faith of which he has a true grasp, not a purely nominal one, which he tries to transmit.

Our author tries to discern and expose the role corresponding to each of the Divine Persons in the Justification and sanctification of man. Justification unequivocally appears as an exclusive action of God that, upon the basis of the merits and the saving grace of Christ, declares and truly makes sinful man to be just by means of the inhabitation of the Holy Spirit.

The theological analysis of the creating action of God the Father in the soul of the just man will allow Newman to examine and defend the *declaratory* aspects of Justification. The saving and atoning operation of the resurrected Christ, grasped and made part of themselves by believing men and women, provides the possibility of situating the role of faith and of reasoning out the correct meaning of the *sola fides* as an instrument of Justification. The gift of the Holy Spirit, which deifies man, finally explains why in Justification we can speak of the *inherent* sanctity of the justified person.

The *Lectures* are characterized by a strong polemical tone with regard to Luther's opinions as interpreted by Newman. His critique of the ideas of the German reformer is usually the starting point of the positive construction he offers. I do not believe it is necessary now to examine whether Newman's theological image of Luther faithfully responds to the view currently provided by sources and studies at our disposal. Although Newman's information may have contained some unprecise points and some debatable affirmations, it seems to respond to the Lutheran doctrine in its essential nature and reflects well, in any event, the central aspects of the Protestant and Evangelical Tradition on the topic of Justification.

Newman first of all refutes the distinction between deliverance from guilt and deliverance from sin, which are called Justification and renewal, respectively, by non-Catholics, and considered to be independent benefits. Newman states: "Now, in opposition to this, it may surely be maintained that Scripture blends them together as intimately as any system of theology can do. This distinction, so carefully made by many men at present, between being righteous and being holy, is not scriptural."[11]

Newman calls received doctrine to the teaching according to which Justification is something inherent and truly wrought in us. The doctrine of Luther, on the contrary, speaks of Justification that is external, reputed, nominal.[12] The Lutheran notion of Justification is therefore tantamount to a declaration, not a making, of righteousness on the part of God.

But Newman does not despise those aspects according to which Justification is, apart from divine justice wrought in us, a genuine declaration of justice on the part of God. This is not a concession to Luther or to the Evangelicals, as might seem to be the case, but rather an attempt to expose this doctrine in its entire biblical and religious scope.

"As Christ's justification did not supersede but implied His inherent righteousness," writes Newman, "so is our Justification God's announcement, concurrent with His own deed so announced; yet in our case, preceding, not following."[13] The divine Justification of sinners therefore presents a *judicial* aspect, which is scriptural and which Newman wishes to incorporate within his synthesis. It "is a word of state and solemnity"[14] whereby God repeals the sentence of wrath that lies against us.

It is not, however, an ordinary declaration because it is not man's word but rather the Word of God. We read in Newman:

> This declaration is the cause of that being which before was not and henceforth is. . . . He declares a fact, and makes it a fact by declaring it. . . . God's word effects what it announces. . . . Then it appears that Justification is an announcement or *fiat* of Almighty God. Justification *declares* the soul righteous, and in that declaration, on the one hand conveys *pardon* for its past sins, and on the other *makes* it actually righteous.[15]

Principles of lucid biblical theology on the divine *dabar*, which includes word and deed, sustain these affirmations, which come in Newman to be tantamount to a de facto equivalence between Justification and renewal: "They are practically convertible terms."[16]

Having come to this point, it has to be stressed that Newman does not completely renounce speaking of Justification as the beginning of sanctification and not as something absolutely coincidental with it. There is thus manifested an evident tension in the course of his reasonings, which seem to oscillate between two poles: the equivalence between Justification and regeneration, and gradualness in the fulfillment of the latter.

States Newman: "Justification tends to sanctity."[17] Later on he affirms: "Not that there is not abundant evil still remaining in us, but that Justification, coming to us in the power and 'inspiration' of the Spirit, so far dries up the fountain of bitterness and impurity, that we are forthwith released from God's wrath and damnation, and are enabled in our better deeds to please Him."[18] He continues, "By Grace we are gifted not with perfection, but with a principle hallowing and sweetening all that we are, all that we do religiously, sustaining, hiding, and (in a sense) pleading for what remains of sin in us."[19]

We get the impression that Newman has begun a slight retreat with regard to the direct sanctifying capacity of Justification. This impression is strengthened when we read in another place: "In justifying, God takes away what is past, *by* bringing in what is new. But is it not plain that in its beginnings it [justification] will consist of scarcely anything but pardon? Because all that we have hitherto done is sinful in its nature, and has to be pardoned; but to be renewed is a work of time."[20]

It is obvious that our author is trying to compromise between the letter of Article XI (On the Justification of Man), which states, "We are accounted righteous before God, only for the merit of Our Lord and Saviour Jesus Christ by faith, and not for our own works or deservings", and the affirmation of the justifying power of obedience shown in good works. In order to achieve this compromise, Newman has to attribute supernatural efficiency to the obedient and justified man, but at the same time he must establish a certain distance between Justification and regeneration, because experience tells him that the recently justified person still shows remnants of sinful habits that are capable of attenuating the efficiency of good works. For this he writes: "The justified are just, really just, in degree more or less, but really so far as this, that their obedience has in it a gracious quality, which the obedience of the unregenerated has not."[21]

Close consideration of these texts makes it appear that Newman in fact opts for what the theology of the sixteenth century called the doctrine of *double Justification*, according to which in order to be true and complete our justice must be completed by that of Jesus Christ, which would come to make up for the deficiencies that the previous sinful condition always leaves in the justified individual.[22] "Our righteousness is a resemblance", he writes, "and therefore a partial communication or infusion into our hearts, of the superhuman righteousness of Christ, which is our true Justification. . . . He implants in part within us the very thing which in its fulness He imputes to us."[23]

In spite of the hesitations that are observed in this approach and that can be considered as one of the insufficient aspects of the *Lectures*, the Christological approach is full of excellent results in Newman's construction. In this sense we must mention the particular justifying efficiency that, drawing from a typically Pauline topic, he attributes to the Resurrection of our Lord, who "died for our sins and resurrected for our Justification". Our author here shows himself clearly to be a pioneer of theses and developments that for the better would be adopted by future theology.

Righteousness is for Newman the fruit of our Lord's Resurrection: "He Himself was raised again and 'justified' by the Spirit; and what was wrought in Him is repeated in us who are His brethren. . . . What took place in Him as an Origin, is continued on the succession of those who inherit His fulness, and is the cause of its continuance."[24]

The most original and fertile aspect of the *Lectures on Justification* is, nonetheless, the decisive and unique role that Newman attributes to the Holy Spirit in the realization of the Justification of sinners. C. S. Dessain observes that "the East has always emphasized that the grace of Justification is a personal union with God, the result of our deification. In the West grace has tended to be thought of more as a remedy for sin and as a quality of the soul. Newman's emphasis, in his sermons and in his treatises, is on our deification and on the indwelling of the Holy Trinity that follows from it."[25]

It can be said, in effect, that Newman brings up to date an essentially Patristic topic and that he situates himself in the modern theological line, which goes from Petavius to Mathias Scheeben and focuses its attention not only upon created grace but rather also and above all upon the indwelling of the Holy Trinity in the justified soul.

The topic is raised by Newman in Lecture VI—"The Gift of Righteousness"—where he asks: What is the state of a justified man? Or in what does his Justification consist? Or, stated in other words, what is that object or thing, what is it in a man, that God seeing it there, therefore calls him righteous?[26]

Newman responds that it is neither Christ's obedience imputed nor a new and spiritual principle imparted to us by the Holy Spirit. With this answer our author believes to have avoided the erroneous Protestant affirmation of extrinsic justice and what he calls the insufficient Roman stand on quality created in the soul and to have unified in practice the notions of Justification and regeneration.

After declaring that "justifying righteousness consists in the coming and presence of the Holy Spirit within us",[27] Newman formulates his thesis in what comes to be one of the most important passages of the *Lectures*:

> It is the Divine Presence that justifies us. . . . The word of Justification is the substantive living Word of God, entering the soul, illuminating it and cleansing it, as fire brightens and purifies material substances. He who justifies also sanctifies, because it is He. The first blessing runs into the second as its necessary limit; and the second, being rejected, carries with it the first. And the one cannot be separated from the other except in idea.[28]

Uncreated grace seems to replace, in the conception reflected in the *Lectures*, created grace, and the Divine Presence thus directly plays the role of inherent justice.

Although these obscure points do not invalidate the fundamental basis of the theses on Inhabitation defended by Newman,
later on he had to clarify nuances and in part rectify his
opinions on the existing relationship between created and
uncreated grace. We shall see to this later on.

We must finally examine the function that the *Lectures*
attribute to faith within the process of Justification. It is
evident that Newman denies the justifying capacity of faith
alone in the Lutheran sense. The cause, properly said, of the
Justification and regeneration of man is not faith but rather
grace.

Our author, however, makes an effort to determine with the
greatest precision possible the role played by faith in the
Justification of sinners. He does not do so in order to remain
faithful to a religious Tradition whose fundamental principles
he had abandoned, nor is he urged to do so in a search for
a compromise, but rather because he considers that faith in
any event is a factor of great importance in the process of
Justification.

Newman writes: "While when we reserve to Baptism our
new birth, and to the Eucharist the hidden springs of the new
life, and to love what may be called its plastic power, and to
obedience its being the atmosphere in which faith breathes,
still the divinely appointed or the mysterious virtue of Faith
remains."[29]

Newman admits that "faith has an office for which we have
not a word, as not having a definite idea".[30] But he is willing
tentatively to concretize his conception, and he describes faith
first of all as the *emblem* of the *image* of grace, which saves us
and redeems us. For Newman, faith typifies the free nature of
our Justification and the decisive fact of our being saved
exclusively by the mercy of God and on the overabundant
merits of our Lord Jesus Christ. In this sense the word "faith"
represents a true abstract principle much more than it does a
concrete reality. Newman even comes to summarize his thought
with the following words: "Salvation by faith only is but
another way of saying salvation by grace only."[31]

Our author knows in spite of all that the interdenominational discussions concerning faith as the supposed cause of Justification are not a mere *lis de verbis*, and that the Catholic doctrine on human merit and the positive role of good works does not whatsoever diminish the exceptional and unique importance of the merits of Christ and the fact that we are justified in the ultimate end by the pure grace of God.

Newman must then distinguish between faith and charity and assign to the former a role that is distinct from the properly justifying and sanctifying role of grace. The solution, for Newman, is found in conceiving faith as an *internal* condition and instrument of Justification. He states: "Before Baptism faith is not the instrument of Justification, but only one out of a number of qualifications necessary for being justified."[32] Faith is first a *condition*, and only after Baptism does it convert itself into an instrument of Justification. It is well understood that we are not dealing with an external instrument—such as Baptism —but rather with an internal instrument. Baptism and faith are at the same time instruments of Justification, but they are so, according to Newman, in a different sense: "Baptism might be the hand of the giver, and Faith the hand of the receiver."[33]

C. Lebas, a contemporary of Newman, was the first to manifest in writing in the *British Critic* some of the difficulties brought about by this explanation. Commenting upon some words that summarize it, namely, "the highest praise of faith before baptism, is, that it leads to it, and its highest efficacy, after, that it comes from baptism", Lebas observes:

> Why—if faith comes from baptism, surely it cannot have existed, even in the most imperfect condition, before baptism; and therefore, could have led to nothing! And yet, that it had some sort of existence before baptism, seems to be admitted by Mr. Newman, for he afterwards allows that faith must be, *substantially*, the same habit of mind, under all circumstances; otherwise it would not be called faith. So that we must presume his meaning to be, that faith, after all, *does* precede justification; but that it does not acquire any justifying dignity or power, till the process of justification has commenced; in short that although

it is a necessary pre-requisite to justification, it has, in fact no justifying efficacy but what it derives from justification.

We cannot but reverentially hope, that there is something more of directness and simplicity in the divine counsels, than we are able to discover in the views here adopted and expounded by their interpreter![34]

Alongside the excessive subtlety and the petition of principle that Lebas politely denounces, it could also be objected from the Catholic viewpoint that the notion of instrument applied to faith has no precedent within Christian theological Tradition. If faith is an instrument of Justification, it must be so with respect to the principal divine cause. In what intelligible sense could faith be the instrument of God in man's Justification?

Newman himself felt the shakiness of his position and realized that the idea of faith as an internal instrument only with difficulty could be squared with the remaining aspects of his system. Only the desire to retain and keep for faith the important place it occupies in the New Testament stopped him from rapidly and expressedly abandoning his position. Yet while summarizing his theses at the end of the *Lectures*, Newman characterizes the role of faith in Justification in a slightly different and much less concrete manner. He states: "We are then justified by grace, which is given through Sacraments, impetrated by faith, manifested in works."[35]

It cannot, therefore, be maintained that the *Lectures on Justification* are Newman's last word on the topic.[36] Even if we keep in mind the notes introduced in the 1874 edition, which mainly refer to the formal cause, the book has to be completed by diverse texts and commentaries by Newman that are found in his writings and letters after 1838. Only then does Newman's true thinking on the matter appear. Without substantially modifying the approaches of the *Lectures*, Newman occasionally added abundant observations that get rid of the ambiguities and insufficiencies found in the doctrinal construction contained in the original work.

Some of these defects derive from the dialectic approach,

which prompted the establishment of a forced symmetry between Protestantism and Romanism and which did not always allow the author clearly to express his points of view. This artificial methodology disappeared from all of Newman's statements on the subject from 1840 on, when he began to oppose Protestantism and Pelagianism instead of Protestantism and Romanism as incorrect extremes.[37] The new focus permitted him to formulate his thought with greater coherence.

The additions and clarifications carried out concerning the *Lectures* in a more or less implicit manner refer mainly to three points: (1) the relationship between Justification and sanctification, (2) the presence of *iustitia inherens* in justified man, and (3) the role of faith in the justifying process.

In my view, Newman succeeds in harmonizing a unitarian vision of Justification and sanctification with the idea that between the two there exists a healthy and necessary tension. He upholds the doctrine of the Council of Trent, according to which "Justification is a passing from the state in which man is born a son of the first parents to the state of grace and adoption as son of God", and he understands at the same time that sanctification is a reality *already* present in the justified man, although of a markedly eschatological nature. A few lines from his *Discourses Addressed to Mixed Congregations*—written apropos of St. Philip Neri—express well Newman's thought in this regard. "Saint Philip", he writes, "never lost his state of grace, from the day he was put into it, and proceeded from strength to strength, and from merit to merit, and from glory to glory, through the whole course of his long life."[38]

The Word made Flesh is the means chosen by God to regenerate our nature, so that the sanctification accompanying Justification is from the very beginning a stable reality—a state—in the justified person.[39] Says Newman: "The Divine Baptism, wherewith God visits us, penetrates through our whole soul and body. It leaves no part of us uncleansed, unsanctified. It claims the whole man for God."[40]

Although the Christian is *holy* from the moment baptismal

grace penetrates within him, sanctification is also a process that unfolds throughout his life and never finds its end in this world. The many divine callings that span the Christian's existence are added onto the first great calling and are the origin of nonstop progress in the path toward salvation. Newman writes: "We are all in course of calling, on and on, from one thing to another, having no resting-place, but mounting towards our eternal rest, and obeying one command only to have another put upon us. He calls us again and again, in order to justify us again and again—and again and again, and more and more, to sanctify and glorify us."[41]

The sanctification of Christian men and women is thus a fact already wrought in them from the moment of Justification, and it is at the same time a dynamic process that unfolds through time, because the spiritual perfection of the human creature requires continuous change in this life. To be perfect means in man many changes for the better during the course of his temporal existence.

Man's capacity for sin and offense is only comparable to his capacity for sanctity with the help of grace. "No degree of sin, however extreme, precludes the acquisition of any degree of holiness, however high. No sinner so great, but he may, through God's grace, become a saint ever so great."[42] Newman's ideas inevitably remind us of those of Gregory of Nyssa, for whom the coming closer to God knows no end in this life and consists of a permanent effort of approximation toward an infinite limit. In this effort there is constant passage —from glory to glory—from a certain stage of perfection to another, more elevated, stage.

Without diminishing the importance of man's direct sanctification through the inhabitation of the Holy Spirit, Newman increasingly dwells upon *created grace* as the cause of Justification. He begins to do so in a decisive sermon written in January of 1840,[43] insisting on the topic in his *Discourses Addressed to Mixed Congregations* of 1849, and definitely formulating it in different texts published during the 1860s.

Newman is concerned with maintaining, above any other affirmation, the idea that God is the unique, principal, and absolute cause of our Justification. But divine justice becomes really and truly ours not in a figurative, metaphorical, or external sense but in a real and proper sense. He writes:

> This then is one of the first elements of Christian knowledge and a Christian spirit to refer all that is good in us, all that we have of spiritual life and righteousness, to Christ our Saviour; to believe that He works in us, or, to put the same thing more pointedly, to believe that saving truth, life, light, and holiness are not *of* us, though they must be *in* us.[44]

Later on he writes: "While truth and righteousness are not of us, it is quite as certain that they are also in us if we be Christ's; not merely nominally given to us and imputed to us, but really implanted in us by the operation of the Blessed Spirit."[45]

The vocabulary used by Newman henceforth clearly suggests the idea of *inherent* justice, which he avoided in the *Lectures*. This inherent justice theologically implies the category of created grace, which certainly derives from the Divine Presence of the Holy Spirit in the soul but which is a quality or habit distinct from uncreated grace and proper to regenerated man. It is in him a permanent possession.[46] Our author writes: "When God, for Christ's sake, is about to restore any one to His favour, His first act of mercy is to impart to him *a portion of His grace*."[47] Newman refers here to *created grace*.

Such an approach carries with it the literal acceptance of the Tridentine doctrine on the formal cause of Justification as a state of the soul[48] and the resulting rejection of any version of the doctrine of double Justification.[49]

At the beginning of the 1840s Newman abandoned the notion of instrumentality in favor of a more sober opinion closer to the Patristic Tradition with regard to the role faith plays in Justification.[50] He says: "A man may have true faith and still not yet be justified; he may have a faith for Justification, yet the time of Justification not yet have arrived."[51] Faith, of course, keeps all its religious importance in the ideas of our author, but within the process of Justification it is, for him, more a symbol of the free nature of salvation than a decisive specific factor. It is evident, in any event, that it cannot be compared in importance to love. "Whereas faith is the essence of *all* religion, and of the Jewish inclusive, love is the great grace of Christianity."[52]

Newman now frequently speaks not only of faith in itself but also of true faith, to signify a fertile faith that is united to love and accompanied by good works. "No faith justifies *but* true faith," says Charles Reding in *Loss and Gain*, "and true faith produces good works. In other words, I suppose faith, which is certain to be fruitful, or fruitful faith, justifies. This is very much like saying that faith and works are the joint means of Justification."[53]

Having reached this point, we must ask ourselves where Newman's pulse really is to be found when he writes and speaks on Justification throughout his life and must also see to what degree his ideas can contribute to the ecumenical dialogue of today.

We must bear in mind that non-Catholic Christian theology lacks a common stand on the topic of Justification. There does not exist, for example, complete agreement among Lutherans over whether Justification is a fundamental doctrine of faith. Whereas some attribute to it a historical and symbolic importance, others consider it the *articulus stantis et cadentis Ecclesiae*.

Many Protestants, along the lines of Albrecht Ritschl, vaguely consider that Justification is simply the forgiveness of sins and understand it as the acceptance of sinners into that fellowship with God within which their salvation will be effected and developed into eternal life.[54]

Well known is the position held by R. Bultmann, for whom Justification is part of a process of self-understanding that occurs in man's conscience and in which he discovers himself to be forgiven by God through Jesus Christ after having admitted to being a sinner.

Karl Barth, finally, represents a position that places the divine revelation to sinful man at the point where Luther placed the divine Justification of sinful man, and he affirms that the *articulus iustificationis* is not central to the Christian proclamation.

Nonetheless, there would seem to exist today a certain consensus within the most representative Protestant theology on how man's Justification by God is to be understood. It is said that the human condition has been changed through the action of God in Jesus Christ. This divine action is considered as based upon grace alone. Although man is generally understood to be involved in his Justification in some manner, this theology emphasizes the priority of the divine action.[55]

Catholics and Protestants are currently stressing different aspects of the doctrine. The former do not deny, as is logical, the primacy of grace, but they underline that grace is also manifested in the human cooperation and the interior transformation of the person. That is, the *justice* of God also becomes the justice of regenerated man, although he never possesses it as something properly his own independently from its source. Protestants usually insist, rather, on divine initiative and on the absolute and almost exclusive primacy of the action of God.

Within this framework it might be adequate to consider the declaration of the Mixed Roman Catholic—Lutheran Evangelical Commission on the Augsburg Confession (1530). It was drawn up in 1980 and reads as follows: "On the doctrine of Justification . . . an ample consensus is to be observed: only through the grace and through the faith that we have in the saving action of Christ, and not through our own merits, are we accepted by God and do we receive the Holy Spirit, who renews our hearts and qualifies and impulses us toward good works."[56]

This is a text of great interest that—like others of a similar nature—must provoke legitimate hope in all Christians. I believe at the same time that if this declaration constitutes a point of arrival, it is also a point of departure, given the fact that the expressions used herein can be interpreted according to more than one meaning.

Newman's thought is very apt in order to contribute toward endowing the quoted words with the most correct meaning among the various possible interpretations. There are three basic ideas in the writings of our author that in my view represent the nucleus of his final doctrine on Justification and that are most relevant in this moment of interconfessional dialogue.

To state that God accepts us through grace must include the affirmation that justified man attains through divine mercy a justice that really belongs to him. It is not sufficient to speak of *sola gratia* if by so doing we are only indicating a free gift and not the existence of a quality created in the soul.[57] Newman clearly saw that Justification must not be held as an abstract idea but rather as something that really is wrought in justified man. This man needs to have his own justice. Otherwise, there would exist a dualistic anthropological stance, and we would be speaking of two men: an ideal justified man and, juxtaposed to him, another real, concrete, and sinful man. Man's unity requires inherent justice and not merely the free gift of justice.

God's generosity, second, allows us to offer him his own free gifts as if they were our own. Newman says:

> Our salvation from first to last is the gift of God. It is true indeed that we merit eternal life by our works of obedience; but that those works are meritorious of such a reward, this takes place, not from their intrinsic worth, but from the free appointment and bountiful promise of God; and that we are able to do them at all, is the simple result of His grace.[58]

The unique and overabundant merit of Christ makes our own merit possible, without eliminating it or separating it from his own. The liturgy of the Church expresses this idea very well when in the Preface of Holy Men and Women it addresses itself to God with the following words: "You are glorified in your saints, for their glory is the crowning of your gifts."

It is necessary, finally, to affirm with no hesitation and with no ambiguity both man's freedom and his active part in the operation of his Justification. "It is the very triumph of God's grace", Newman writes, "that He enters the heart of man, and persuades it, and prevails with it, while He changes it. He violates in nothing that original constitution of mind which He gave to man: He treats him as man; He leaves him the liberty of acting this way or that."[59]

Justification is an action of God, but it is at the same time an event that is wrought in man and through man himself. Newman resists the antihumanist conceptions that do not come seriously to consider either the human freedom or the human reality of Christ as the effective Mediator of salvation.

NOTES

[1] *Letters and Diaries*, vol. I, p. 310.

[2] *Apologia pro Vita Sua*, ed. M. J. Svaglic (Oxford: Clarendon Press, 1967), p. 17. See *Autobiographical Writings* (New York: Sheed & Ward, 1957), p. 165.

[3] *Autobiographical Writings*, p. 203.

[4] *Parochial and Plain Sermons* (San Francisco: Ignatius Press, 1987), vol. I, no. 1, p. 9.

[5] Ibid., vol. II, no. 26, p. 434.

[6] "I have written in all (good or bad) 5 constructive books. My Prophetical Office (which has come to pieces)—Essay on Justification—Development of Doctrine—University Lectures (Dublin) and this Grammar of Assent. Each took me a great deal of time and tried me very much." *Letters and Diaries*, vol. XXIV, p. 390.

[7] *Letters and Diaries*, vol. VI, p. 186. On the seventeenth he communicated to John Bowden: "Then about my own work. . . . It is a terra incognita in our Church, and I am so afraid, not of saying things wrong so much, as queer and crotchety—and of misunderstanding other writers for really the Lutherans etc. as divines are so shallow and inconsequent." *Letters and Diaries*, vol. IV, pp. 188–89.

[8] July 1838, *Letters and Diaries*, vol. XXIV, pp. 82–119.

[9] *Tübinger Theologische Quartalschrift* 26 (1844), pp. 417–57. After Newman's conversion, Döllinger did not hesitate in declaring on the *Lectures*: "It is in my estimation one of the best theological books published in this century."

[10] The notes appear in pp. 31, 73, 96, 101, 154, 186, 187, 190, 198, 201, 226, 236, 260, 343, 348–49, and 353.

[11] *Lectures on the Doctrine of Justification* (London: Longman, Green and Co., 1908), pp. 39–40.

[12] Ibid., p. 62.

[13] Ibid., p. 77.

[14] Ibid., p. 73.

[15] Ibid., pp. 78–79.

[16] Ibid., p. 88.

[17] Ibid.

[18] Ibid., pp. 90–91.

[19] Ibid., p. 91.

[20] Ibid., p. 102.

[21] Ibid., p. 91.

[22] Ibid., pp. 156, 158, 160.

[23] Ibid., pp. 92, 95.

[24] Ibid., pp. 206–7.

[25] Charles S. Dessain, "Cardinal Newman and the Eastern Tradition", *Downside Review* 94 (1976), p. 95.

[26] *Lectures*, pp. 130–31.

[27] Ibid., p. 137.

[28] Ibid., p. 154.

[29] Ibid., pp. 236–37.

[30] Ibid., p. 238.

[31] Ibid., p. 283.

[32] Ibid., p. 241.

[33] Ibid., p. 226.

[34] *Letters and Diaries*, vol. XXIV, p. 105.

[35] *Lectures*, p. 303.

[36] Thomas L. Sheridan holds the opposite opinion in his *Newman et la justification* (Paris: Desclée, 1968), p. 388.

[37] See *Parochial and Plain Sermons*, vol. V, no. 10, pp. 1037–38.

[38] *Discourses Addressed to Mixed Congregations* (London: Burns & Oates, 1876), p. 51.

[39] "Our Lord, by becoming man, has found a way whereby to sanctify that nature, of which His manhood is the pattern specimen. He inhabits us personally, and this inhabitation is effected by the channel of the Sacraments." *Select Treatises of Saint Athanasius* (London: Rivingtons, 1881), vol. II, p. 193.

[40] *Sermons Bearing on Subjects of the Day* (London: Rivingtons, 1879), p. 131.

[41] *Parochial and Plain Sermons*, vol. VIII, no. 2, pp. 1569–70.

[42] *Sermons Bearing on Subjects of the Day*, p. 17.

[43] "Righteousness, not of us, but in us", in *Parochial and Plain Sermons*, vol. V, pp. 1032–40.

[44] Ibid., p. 132.

[45] Ibid., p. 136.

[46] See *The Via Media* (London: Rivingtons, 1877), vol. II, p. 167.

[47] *Discourses*, p. 170.

[48] See *Decree on Justification*, chap. 7.

[49] It is surprising that in 1874, in his Advertisement to the third edition of the *Lectures*, Newman should affirm that "their drift is to show that there is little difference but what is verbal in the various views of Justification, found whether among Catholics or Protestant divines" (*Lectures*, p. ix).

[50] See *Loss and Gain* (London: Rivingtons, 1891), p. 137.

[51] *Parochial and Plain Sermons*, vol. VI, no. 13, p. 1286.

[52] Ibid., p. 1291.

[53] *Loss and Gain*, p. 138.

[54] See *The Christian Doctrine of Justification and Reconciliation* (Clifton, N.J.: Reference Books Publishers, 1966), pp. 35ff.

[55] See A. McGrath, *Iustitia Dei* (Cambridge: Cambridge University Press, 1986), vol. II, pp. 189–90.

[56] See *Lutherische Welt-Information* 12 (1980), pp. 3–7.

[57] See W. Joest, *Dogmatik* (Goettingen: Vandenhoeck, 1980), vol. II, p. 454.

[58] *Discourses*, p. 124.

[59] Ibid., pp. 71–72.

LOUIS BOUYER

THE PERMANENT RELEVANCE
OF NEWMAN

What struck me at a first reading of Newman's works and what has remained my personal interest (throughout many years) to this day is how Newman manages to develop in both his personality and teaching an immediate and spontaneous union between fidelity to God and intellectual integrity without these being in conflict.

For Newman, God is never seen as an idea, a notion, but as a concrete reality confronting man in the consciousness of his own human situation in being—the supreme reality, who as such commands of man not only an attitude of absolute respect but the total commitment and surrender of his existence. From the time of what Newman calls his first conversion, when he was still in his teens, this recognition of God appears as neither exclusive of nor opposed to intellectual honesty; rather it is grounded in the basic intuition that the voice of genuine reason and the voice of conscience are not two disparate voices but only two aspects of the single voice of the one true God worthy of the name.

This was the immediate, intimate conviction of his youth, following a period of doubt which he clearly perceived as intellectual pride. This same conviction permeates his *Oxford University Sermons* of his Anglican period, as well as the *Grammar of Assent*, the masterwork of his whole life, written in the full maturity of his later years. It is the common thread of these two books, evolving to final form in the second. Reason is not to be used in a kind of vacuum, skirting those details of reality bearing a special relation to our fully human development. Otherwise, what takes place is not a genuinely rational process, but an artificial, unhealthy, even cancerous development. It will not lead to a conclusion drawn from reality, but just a variety of pretentious, unreal words, devoid of justification. In producing such elucidations, we have simply forgotten that our mind has been revealed to itself as a moral conscience, as Augustine says: "the witness of someone more intimate to myself than I myself am". As God is unconditionally the master of our thinking as of our acting, rationality and obedience cannot be opposed, being one in their root: that mysterious presence, at the ultimate ground of our personality, which is its divine origin, or, as Saint Thomas says, "Him in whom we live more truly even than he lives in us".

It is only when we realize this as the background or foundation of the whole life of Newman, as of everything that Newman would develop in the most diverse fields of theological speculation, that both the deep organic unity and the equilibrium of his work may be justly appreciated. First of all, this is at the root of his treatment in the 15th and last of his *Oxford University Sermons* as in the famous *Essay on the Development of Christian Doctrine*. He has been misinterpreted by the modernists first, and later by interpreters like Jean Guitton, as a champion of the idea that development for its own sake is the chief characteristic of the life of the Catholic Church, while all the distortions of Christianity in the most varied heresies were imagined to be sterile. No greater mistake could be made not only about the real intention of Newman, but about what he himself stated most explicitly. For him, development as a characteristic of every living thing, healthy or unhealthy, leads either to the fulfillment of life or to the decomposition of irreversible death. Calvinism itself, he said, and all the possible Christian "isms", are either stillborn or develop; their development either leads to lasting life or is a deadly decomposition. He disappointed the modernists precisely because he is not interested in development for development's sake, but in how to distinguish a development that leads to death and decomposition from the development that retains the integrity of its germ. Therefore, his attempt will not be to demonstrate how abundantly, how gloriously the Catholic tradition has developed, as compared to spurious or partial traditions of Christianity, but to elaborate a series of "notes" which may enable us to distinguish genuine, faithful developments from the more or less unhealthy ones.

Here again we catch Newman in the same search for integrity which animated his unswerving fidelity to rational consistency as well as to authentic obedience to God, the two complementary aspects of the right use of reason, above all concerning ultimate truth. The integrity of Newman's reflection on aspects of Christian belief and practice (and also in opposition to all forms of integrism and all forms of pretention to exclusive modernity or actuality or futurity), far from opposing genuine ecumenism, brought him to see how and in what manner authentic Catholicism and ecumenism are mutually inclusive, rather than contradictory.

From this perspective his often neglected *Lectures on Justification* has been acknowledged by such an ecumenist as Archbishop Michael Ramsey as a model for realistic ecumenism.

Protestants have tended in effect to oppose justification by faith alone to a justification including works of salvation, or a justification wrought for us by Christ alone to a justification wrought by our own human merits. However, according to Newman, we ought rather to see justifying faith as involving, not only what Christ has done for us on the Cross, but also his presence in us now as the author of our actual sanctification. Without this sanctification our justification would have no substance. Is this not the ultimate meaning of the affirmation of Saint Paul: "It is no longer I who live, but Christ who lives in me"?

This corresponds exactly to the conclusion reached a century earlier by one of the greatest and most popular spiritual authors of Protestantism, Johann Ardnt, in his book *Wahres Christentum*.

It is revealing that this same book, published anonymously, would later be translated by Cardinal de Noailles for Catholics as well as by Saint Tikhon of Zadonsk for the Orthodox!

It may be when we consider Newman's work on ecclesiology, however, that we discover at its best how this permanent relevance proceeds from what we have described as his integrity. I am thinking of his lectures on the *Prophetical Office of the Church*, written while an Anglican, yet reprinted when he was a Cardinal under the title *Via Media* with no modifications but only some supplementary material and a preface. It is often quoted, but not so often well understood.

In the main body of this work Newman gives us a view of the Catholic tradition which is not only a most inclusive but a most synthetic one. It may be considered at the same time a most illuminating vision of, not only the place of the laity in the Church, but its actual relation to episcopal authority.

For Newman there is a single tradition of the truth of life in the Church, but it presents two aspects which are clearly distinct yet ultimately inseparable. These are what he calls the prophetic and the episcopal traditions, or again, more precisely, two aspects of a single and indivisible tradition.

The truth of the gospel with its vision of faith develops in the whole body of the Church, in the whole Christian people —among the simple faithful as well as the clergy, including the bishops themselves. Now its most intimate development is the development of the truth of life, the development of personal holiness. As to the expression in words of this basic development, it implies, together with personal holiness, intellectual capacities. This latter is a gift no less personal than that of holiness, and could be equally granted to anybody in the Church, clerical or lay, man or woman. This is what Newman calls the prophetic tradition. We must consider the episcopal tradition as inseparable from this, and to some extent indistinct. This latter corresponds to a gift which is not properly that of every Christian, but only of those who have received a share in the supreme pastoral responsibility concerning the whole body of the Church, that is, the bishops acting all in communion under the leadership of the Bishop of Rome. What distinguishes the specifically episcopal form of the tradition is an ultimate capacity, when controversy arises, for judging expressions of the faith to be authentic or inauthentic, determining which are to be received as faithful or rejected as lacking in authenticity or clarity. Only those who have received as a collective, indivisible responsibility the charge of shepherding the flock of Christ are endowed with this capacity as an essential part of this charge committed to them by Christ himself: "He who hears you hears me, he who rejects you rejects me."

In itself, as is emphasized by Newman, this does not necessarily mean that only a bishop will be able to find the needed doctrinal formula. In the very first Ecumenical Council of the Christian Church, which had to define the reality of the divinity of Christ, it was Athanasius of Alexandria who suggested the word finally canonized: Homoousios (of the same nature) as the Father; at that time Athanasius was only a deacon.

We may add that even a simple priest such as Thomas Aquinas may be acknowledged and proclaimed by the supreme authority in the Church as a Doctor, that is, a teacher having authority. And not only laymen, but lay women as well have been given this same title—Saint Catherine of Siena and Saint Teresa of Avila.

These views provide us with a firm basis for a proper recognition of the relation between the laity and what we have come to call the hierarchy, meaning the different ordained ministries or just the episcopal ministry. It is significant to note, however, that Pseudo-Dionysius, who introduced the term, meant not the ministers but the influx of grace, through them but from Christ alone, which establishes all the Church in a communion of grace. In the same way, the epistle of Clement of Rome (probably the most ancient Christian text after the New Testament) comparing Christian worship with that of the Jews, did not hesitate to say that in the Church of the

New Testament there is no longer a merely passive laity, but that lay people themselves correspond now to what were the ordinary priests of the old covenant. This is typical of that patristic Christianity which Newman did so much to restore to our knowledge and imitation. Also the bishop in the New Testament (or the "presbyters" who are now associated with his presidential function) fulfills, as representative of the Head (Christ), in the midst of his whole body, the function formerly reserved to the high priest alone.

It is in the same spirit that Newman today sees the whole body of the Church, laity included, cooperating in its active development of the truth of life. This development once again is realized through the holiness of individuals with the gift of a capacity for expressing their own experience, notwithstanding the fact that only those responsible for the common life of the whole body will possess the gift to judge, that is, to distinguish with authority between the expression of truth which is genuine and that which is not. Nonetheless, this special episcopal gift itself would have no object if it were not for the constant contribution of all the members to the life, and to the intelligence of that life, of Christ in us.

Closely connected with this comprehensive view of the situation of life and light in the Church, Newman as a cardinal insists on the triple aspect of that life of the light of truth in the Church in his *Via Media* (a point later emphasized and much developed by Friedrich von Hügel). Newman distinguishes between the three offices of the Church: the doctrinal, the cultic and devotional, and the regal. From his exposition it becomes clear that mankind being what it is, still fallen even in the process of recovering holiness, will not expect a simultaneous development of these three aspects, however inseparable they are, without more or less serious conflicts or at least tensions between them. The doctrinal development at times may obscure that of holiness. In addition, the latter may degenerate if needed doctrinal developments are lacking. And both, at times, may appear to hinder a peaceful exercise of authority, which itself, in turn, may be tempted to be in-attentive or too easily afraid of the other factors.

Here again, Newman has too often been misunderstood by apologists only too anxious to make use of his calm and patient analyses. Newman does not mean in the least that a lack of coherence between these three items, at times unavoidable owing to human weakness, is not to be deplored. On the contrary, for any attentive reader, it is clear that for Newman this means no reform of the Church will ever be made once and for all. The Church always has to be both "semper reformata" and "semper reformanda", even as she remains the one true Church, indubitably willed by Christ, but willed as ever prone to see her weaknesses and ready to correct them.

Another aspect of the problem of the laity and its role in the Church is treated in the *Idea of a University* and the related essays. Here again Newman undertakes to clarify the relation between culture—especially intellectual culture, but more generally "humanism" as widely understood today—and properly religious culture tending directly to the development of the spiritual life itself. It is amusing to see how many superficial readers have completely misunderstood his descrip-tion of the gentleman as the aim of the formation expected of universities. For Newman, however, it is clear that the gentle-man, as the free and liberal citizen, is meant to be a first sketch of what a full Christian should become. (It is only as an unconscious caricature that it degenerates from within, while taking care to keep the appearances.) Humanist culture, per-fected by Christianity, although having its first roots in Greco-Roman civilization, is a necessity for the Christian in the world. It is there he develops his human activities, always illuminated from above and rectified by the light of the gospel. Conversely, there will never be an effective influence of the gospel on man at large and human society if a properly Christian formation for clerics and laity persists in ignoring the common culture of the day, in both its good points and its possible defects.

More importantly, we are in danger of trivializing our Christianity, both when we disdain and ignore culture at large and when we submit to it passively, uncritically. The Christian not only must know what it means to be "a man of the world" and eventually be capable of acting as such; but he must also take care not to reduce his Christianity to the level of the more refined authentic humanism of his day or a fortiori, to allow the development of his properly Christian culture to fall below the level of his humanistic culture.

Together with these basic problems, and as a component part of them, Newman has treated in a way no less lasting in its relevance the more special question of the relation between the formation of man as such and his specialized professional formation. And regarding a more specific aspect of this problem, Newman has some extraordinarily interesting views on the relation of science both with technology on the one hand and with human formation at large, whether directly religious or not.

Here I would emphasize the importance of a much neglected passage of the *Idea of a University*, in which he comes unexpectedly near to observations made quite recently by philosophers such as Wittgenstein (in the *Brown* and the *Blue* books of his last period), and also Karl Jaspers. I mean first that, like Wittgenstein, he underlines the fact that there are different views of the world which simply correspond to different practical approaches to its reality. According to the different angles of vision implied, they may appear to be contradictory at first sight, while in truth they are simply complementary. Still it is not possible to combine them into a pseudo-synthesis, which would afford only an incongruous hodge-podge. But, as Jaspers has shown in his turn, some may be more "englobing" than others, without being substituted for them. And this appears to be the case, eminently, for an authentic religious view of the world, compared to either a scientific or merely philosophical approach. No less does this intuition (so typically Newmanian, albeit none of his readers until now seems to have grasped it) correspond to what is suggested by the best specialists of the comparative history of religions, having rejected as pure fantasy all attempted reductions of the religious phenomenon to anything else. (One could compare, for example, what Mircea Eliade says in his book *The Quest*.)

My impression is that we Christians at the end of the twentieth century are still very far from having grasped the importance of such considerations or, even more, from having drawn all the implications of such views for our present cultural situation.

The modern apologists of Christianity are apparently not much more aware of the exact significance of Newman's considerations in his *Grammar of Assent* which treat not just probability in understanding the assent of faith (in the line of Joseph Butler's argumentation in his famous *Analogy*), but also treat what he himself calls the convergence of independent probabilities. With his discussion, we have a fully modern and most illuminating explanation (as well as an exposition in terms of modern psychology) of the very Thomistic view of faith as being both supernatural and, owing to that supernatural character itself, without any implicit contradiction, at the same time free and rational.

But, however important all that we have tried to summarize may be, the most lasting element in Newman's approach to the Christian faith, in a world which he was one of the very first to describe as post-Christian, lies elsewhere. Bremond, in his strange book entitled (in the English translation) *The Mystery of Newman*, has a whole chapter, pleasant to read, on Newman as a poet. His own conclusion is clearly that all this is only the final evidence of a lack of sound rationality in Newman. This is the typical view of an incurable sceptic, combining an unbelieving reason with a lack of spiritual experience, but taking refuge in an attempted confusion between mysticism and poetry. Here as elsewhere, Bremond simply lends his own unsolved contradictions to the object of his brilliant but finally highly subjective studies.

Newman, undoubtedly, is almost unique in the way he uses

poetry, not so much in his own verses, which are usually rather indifferent in poetic quality, as in his ordinary approach to religion. But by poetry we must understand here, as has been so well shown, especially by Coulson, something not very far from what Coleridge, following Schelling, calls "imagination" (meaning truly creative or rather re-creative imagination rather than the mere "fantasy" of any waking dream). Here there would be too much to say. Let us once more observe only that Newman simply makes more concrete for us another formula of Saint Thomas. This formula, completely forgotten (if not implicitly rejected) by too many of our modern "Thomists", is that the best evidence for the truth of Christianity is just what he calls its "sublimity".

MICHAEL SHARKEY

NEWMAN'S QUEST FOR HOLINESS IN HIS SEARCH FOR THE TRUTH

An Anglican Bishop was once heard to remark, "There is too much name-dropping in the Church of England, and the Queen and I are very worried about it!" Well, there is too much name dropping in the Church of Rome, too, and the Pope and I are very worried about that! One of the most droppable names at the moment is that of Newman. It is a name that is usually dropped with a label or two: freedom of conscience, development of doctrine, advance of the laity, defense of the episcopacy, and so on. Unfortunately, Newman is often reduced to this—a name and a few labels. There is even danger of his name and his labels being hijacked and used for purposes for which he himself was not sympathetic and to which in fact he was diametrically opposed. Because he was a critic of the way authority was exercised in the Roman Catholic Church, he is suspected of insubordination. His melancholy looks are attributed to the way he was thwarted by Roman Catholic authorities. Wrong again: he himself accounts for the change in his appearance, dating it to 1839, six years before he became a Catholic.

> O how forlorn & dreary has been my course since I have been a Catholic! here has been the contrast—as a Protestant, I felt my religion dreary, but not my life—but, as a Catholic, my life dreary, not my religion. Of course one's earlier years are (humanly speaking) best—and again, events are softened by distance—and I look back on my years at Oxford & Littlemore with tenderness—and it was the time in which I had a remarkable mission—but how am I changed even in look! till the affair of No 90 and my going to Littlemore, I had my mouth half open,

and commonly a smile on my face—& from that time onwards
my mouth has been closed and contracted, and the muscles are
so set now, that I cannot but look grave and forbidding.[1]

This reduction of Newman to a name and a few labels leads
the honest enquirer to ask, would the real J. H. Newman,
theologian, please stand up! Would the real J. H. Newman,
candidate for canonization, please stand up!

There are a number of ways to sanctity and canonization in
the Roman Catholic Church. I would like to identify the way
that would fit Newman's course. It was not the way of the
martyr, the person who gives his or her life for the Faith.
Newman did have his crosses to carry but not to the point of
martyrdom. It was not the way of the healer and miracle
worker. He did not cure the sick and raise the dead. He did
work miracles of the mind in helping people to come to faith,
to find God as the source of their consciences, to recognize the
historic revelation of God as embodied in the Church, but this
is a spiritual application of the meaning of the word *miracle*.
Newman's way was not that of the miracle worker, nor was it
the way of asceticism, though he tried it. In his "personal and
most private" journal, for instance, he records the details of the
fast and abstinence he had undertaken in 1839, and which he
was to repeat throughout the 1840s.

March 28. 1839. Good Friday.
   During this Lent I have observed the following rules, Sundays
being altogether excepted.
   I have used no sugar—I have eaten no pastry fish fowl or
toast—and my rule has been not to be helped a second time to
meat at dinner. I have eaten no meat at any other time. I have not
dined out.
   Exceptions have been, dining out three times—with Iffley
Trustees, at the Provost's, & once in hall with Williams when I
came away early—And the first two of these I ate pastry, I was
frequently helped twice to meat as time went on. I have not
abstained from wine.
   On Wednesdays and Fridays I abstained from any food whatever till 5 P.M. when I ate a biscuit—I ate no breakfast or dinner,

but generally an egg at tea—sometimes barley water at 5 o'clock. Twice or three times I ate a biscuit in midday.

The Tempus Passionis, the week before this and this week, I left off butter and milk, besides. Several times, however, I took milk.

The Hebdomada Magna (Passion week) I have abstained hitherto from breakfast and dinner every day, breaking fast on a biscuit at midday; yesterday (Thursday) & today I have abstained, & mean to abstain, from tea also & egg; tasting nothing either day but bread & biscuit & water. This I purpose to continue till evening tomorrow, when the fast being over, I may perhaps eat some meat.—This I *did* observe to the end—but I shd say that on Wednesday I took a glass of port wine. The only great inconvenience I have found has been face ache—for which I have used sulphate of quinine pills successfully.[2]

Eventually he abandoned these rigors, realizing that God did not require them of him, though he always maintained a certain self-denial.

Newman did not regard himself in any way as a saint, but he did have his own *way*, an *ordinary way* to holiness. He frequently explained it to the priests of the Oratory. The clearest summary statement of it is found in his *Meditations and Devotions* under the title of "A Short Road to Perfection".

He, then, is perfect who does the work of the day perfectly, and we need not go beyond this to seek for perfection. You need not go out of the *round* of the day.

I insist on this because I think it will simplify our views, and fix our exertions on a definite aim. If you ask me what you are to do in order to be perfect, I say, first—Do not lie in bed beyond the due time of rising; give your first thoughts to God; make a good visit to the Blessed Sacrament; say the Angelus devoutly; eat and drink to God's glory; say the Rosary well; be recollected; keep out bad thoughts; make your evening meditation well; examine yourself daily; go to bed in good time, and you are already perfect.[3]

Newman profoundly believed in this ordinary path to holiness, but we have not assembled here in his memory simply because he got up in good time, said his prayers, and went to bed early! There was something special about Newman: he is the epitome of *credal-shaped holiness*. We are hallowed not only by prayer, by obedience to commandments, growth in virtue, and reception of sacraments. We are hallowed in believing and by believing. We are nourished by the teaching, tales, and word pictures in the Scriptures. We are made holy by receiving, dwelling on, and entering into doctrine, especially the propositions of the Creed. Newman is both the explainer and the exemplar of this way to holiness.

There is an intimate relationship between right belief and right behavior, including right feeling. Although some heretics have been particularly good and kind people, and some defenders of orthodox faith have been very difficult people, nevertheless, these are exceptions to the general rule that right belief breeds right behavior and feeling, and right behavior and feeling lead eventually to the fullness of right belief.

An illustration of this may be seen in the way our Church authorities have now linked together the declarations of someone as saint and Doctor of the Church. It used to be possible for someone to be declared Doctor without being canonized as a saint. That is no longer possible. There is something essentially wise about linking the two, though. A number of Newman scholars have suggested in the past that Newman be declared a Doctor of the Church without canonizing him. The majesty of his theology is more obvious than the heroic sanctity of his personal life. These scholars have wanted him declared Doctor as the endorsement and promotion of his theology. Sometimes this way has been proposed because a number of people find the process of canonization to be an embarrassment. At times this betrays a sort of spiritual snobbery, at other times it betrays doubts about Newman's sanctity, and at other times again it betrays scepticism about miracles. For instance, it has been said that Newman should be canonized on the strength of the sort of miracle associated with his ministry: the miracles of conversion and the discernment of God's providence for individuals. It is as though some people do not believe in the possibility of classical miracles of the physical kind, or perhaps they simply find them distasteful, embarrassing. But Newman believed in miracles and wrote in their defense. As part of the cause for Newman's canonization we need a miracle or two, since miracles are the sign of *God's* approbation and use of Newman's intercession.

When I have explained in some high academic circles this need for a Scripture-type miracle at Newman's intercession, I have usually found agreement, though one wit did say that if we had to have a Scripture miracle he would prefer a repeat of the miracle of Cana: dry, white, if you please, to go with the loaves and fishes, the bread whole meal and the fish grilled! More seriously, I should also point out that the priests of my diocese, for instance, have prayed for Newman's intercession for the recovery of three priests, each suffering from cancer. The miracles did not happen. Our priests tend to be of that alternative spirituality of seeking God's grace to carry one's cross, not to be relieved of it. In short, we are still waiting on a miracle as proof on earth of Newman's intercession in heaven and as a sign that he is a Servant of God. For Newman to be declared a Doctor of the Church, he must first be canonized as a saint. For him to be canonized, his heroic sanctity must be made evident. There is a *cultus*, which is quiet and unostentatious, but the proof of his heroic sanctity has yet to cross a hurdle or two.

To read his theology in his published works is to experience his profound understanding of the Revelation of God, expressed with such grace, elegance, and clarity that, applying the old maxim that the style is the man, the reader already senses Newman's personal greatness, as though if he were only half as holy in personal life as his theology is holy, then the Church has here a champion indeed. Then, to follow his biography, is to have this impression confirmed. Newman the Anglican was bright, full of sparkle and vigor, in spite of his shyness. He was warm and sensitive. He could also be cuttingly sarcastic and a bit of a bigot. The great line in his book on *The Development of Christian Doctrine* that "to live is to change, to be perfect is to have changed often" is not only a statement of historical hermeneutics; it is also a personal confession. Newman was mellowing. When he became a Roman Catholic in 1845, he joined a Church whose authorities did not understand him. He was abused, suspected, and neglected. He had to bear many trials. These are the marks of a saint. Almost in spite of himself, he still produced great works of theology. These are the marks of a Doctor.

However, he was also hypersensitive. His wit was brilliant, but it could also be cutting. Although the revelation of himself in the *Apologia*, written in only six weeks, is entirely without vanity, some of his letters seem to reveal a sense of great self-importance and an indignation with opponents. My own view is that most of Newman's tough remarks are to be attributed to his candor. Furthermore, his very candid remarks were made within the parameters of the confidentiality of close friendships, or the objectivity that belongs to professional cooperation, such as in founding the Oratories and the Catholic University in Dublin, and in his dealings with Wiseman and Manning. The most seemingly damning example is his reply on the eve of Vatican I to Bishop Brown's invitation to come to the Council as his expert. Bishop Brown had become a supporter of Newman, but ten years earlier Brown had delated him to Rome on a charge of heresy for his essay "On Consulting the Laity". He did not inform Newman of his charge. Wiseman failed to pass on to Newman the Curia's questions, and the Curia misjudged that Newman had simply chosen to ignore them. Newman's letter to Brown in answer to his invitation seems cold and unforgiving:

TO THOMAS JOSEPH BROWN, BISHOP OF NEWPORT
        The Oratory, Birmm November 3, 1869
My dear Lord
 I thank your Lordship for your kind letter; but I am not able to say more than I have said already.

There was an English Bishop, just ten years ago, who, without
a word to me, (which would have settled every thing,) and in
spite of the sacred direction, Matth. xviii, 15, denounced a
writing of mine to the Authorities at Rome.

He it is, who has created a prejudice against me there, such, as
to be my sufficient justification in acting upon those positive
inducements, which lead me at this time to remain quietly in my
own place at home.

I am, My dear Lord, Your Lordship's faithful Servt in Xt
John H. Newman of the Oratory
The Rt Revd The Bp of Newport[4]

In fact, Bishop Brown had been badgering Newman. Newman
had already declined politely. Within the terms of their now
warm relationship, one can see that the letter was a wry
kindness, not a cold cruelty. There are a number of incidents
like this in Newman's life. They cannot be swept under a
carpet, but they can be explained. However, this reinforces the
need for a miracle or two through Newman's intercession as
proof of God's vindication of him.

Newman's understanding of what happens to a person in
believing and in progressing through life may be illustrated
from his works, beginning with the first of his *Parochial and
Plain Sermons*, the one that is entitled "Holiness Necessary for
Future Blessedness". If I punch you on the nose, say, which I
really should not do, I not only offend you, your nose, God,
and our relationship, but I also offend my own being. When I
sin, I warp myself. I become bent, kinked, corrupt, twisted.
The more I sin, rob, lie, punch noses, and so on, the more
corrupt my very being becomes. I need forgiveness. A mere
juridical forgiveness is not enough. It is not enough simply to
be told that my offenses are no longer held against me, that I
have been excused punishment, released from the dock, and
given my freedom. I am still bent and kinked and warped and
twisted. I cannot come to God in that condition. I could not
bear God in that condition. In that condition the very sight of
God would be an unendurable agony. I need the sort of

forgiveness from him that will penetrate my very being. I need a medicinal forgiveness that will unbend, unkink, unwarp my being. I need straightening out, cleaning up; the moral quality of my very self needs to be restored to the image and likeness of God. God in his mercy will not bring me to himself until that process is complete. The word of forgiveness that is spoken over me penetrates me because the word of forgiveness is the Word of God himself, and he comes to indwell me.

This is a caricature of Newman's theology, but it is not unfair, and it does bring out the existential dimension of it. The heroine of his novel *Callista* is a young woman of family, wealth, and beauty. She is obedient to her conscience and begins to search for a manifestation or revelation of the Person whom she senses is echoed in her conscience. She finds her way to faith, and in making her spiritual journey she loses all her worldly gifts, including her elegance and good looks, but Newman identifies in her and in her bedraggled dying the beauty of her godliness, the glow of grace, and the pure image of what we are called to be.

We are to be transformed and glorified in order to fit us for heaven. Our Lord himself was transformed and glorified, and it is that same transformation and glorification that he communicates to us. In the *Lectures on Justification* Newman paints a picture of the Risen Lord encountering Mary Magdalen in the garden:

> 5. And these considerations will serve to throw some light on a difficult passage in the end of St. John's Gospel, where our Lord says to St. Mary Magdalen—"Touch Me not, for I am not yet ascended to My Father." The question arises here, *Why* might not our Lord be touched *before* His ascension, and how *could* He be touched *after* it? But Christ speaks, it would seem, thus (if, as before, we might venture to paraphrase His sacred words)— "Hitherto you have only known Me after the flesh. I have lived among you as a man. You have been permitted to approach Me sensibly, to kiss and embrace My feet, to pour ointment upon My head. But all this is at an end, now that I have died and risen again in the power of the Spirit. A glorified state of existence is

begun in Me, and will soon be perfected. At present, though I bid you at one moment handle Me as possessed of flesh and bones, I vanish like a spirit at another; though I let one follower embrace My feet, and say, 'Fear not,' I repel another with the words, 'Touch Me not.' Touch Me not, for I am fast passing for your great benefit from earth to heaven, from flesh and blood into glory, from a natural body to a spiritual body. When I am ascended, then the change will be completed. To pass hence to the Father in My bodily presence, is to descend from the Father to you in spirit. When I am thus changed, when I am thus present to you, more really present than now though invisibly, then you may touch Me,—may touch Me, more really though invisibly, by faith, in reverence, through such outward approaches as I shall assign. Now you but see Me from time to time; when you see most of Me I am at best but 'going in and out among you.' Thou hast seen Me, Mary, but couldst not hold Me; thou hast approached Me, but only to embrace My feet, or to be touched by My hand; and thou sayest, 'O that I knew where I might find Him, that I might come even to His seat! O that I might hold Him and not let Him go!' Henceforth this shall be; when I am ascended, thou shalt see nothing, thou shalt have everything. Thou shalt 'sit down under My shadow with great delight, and My fruit shall be sweet to thy taste.' Thou shalt have Me whole and entire. I will be near thee, I will be in thee; I will come into thy heart a whole Saviour, a whole Christ,—in all My fulness as God and man,—in the awful virtue of that Body and Blood, which has been taken into the Divine Person of the Word, and is indivisible from it, and has atoned for the sins of the world,—not by external contact, not by partial possession, not by momentary approaches, not by a barren manifestation, but inward in presence, and intimate in fruition, a principle of life and a seed of immortality, that thou mayest 'bring forth fruit unto God'."[5]

This passage would have a great deal to offer to the contemporary debate on the Empty Tomb and the nature of the Resurrection event, but I quote it at length here in order to illustrate Newman's understanding of our transformation and glorification, our being made holy.

To complete Newman's imagery, we need to go to *Gerontius*,

the long poem about the moment of an old man's death, his last sigh on earth, and his being taken by his guardian angel to the Judgment Seat of God. This is a poem of excellent theology and modest poetry that in Elgar's setting to music becomes a great work of art. Gerontius has been hallowed in believing. His holiness has been shaped and nourished by the Creed. Newman puts the Creed into Gerontius' mouth in the form of a hymn, which has become much loved and widely known:

> Firmly I believe and truly
>   God is three, and God is One;
> And I next acknowledge duly
>   Manhood taken by the Son.
> And I trust and hope most fully
>   In that Manhood crucified;
> And each thought and deed unruly
>   Do to death, as He has died.
> Simply to His grace and wholly
>   Light and life and strength belong,
> And I love, supremely, solely,
>   Him the holy, Him the strong. . . .
>
> And I hold in veneration,
>   For the love of Him alone,
> Holy Church, as His creation,
>   And her teachings, as His own.[6]

Gerontius has believed. He has been a man of faith. Now he rises to meet his God, but he has not yet been perfected, for God in his mercy will not bring us to himself until we are fit for him. When Gerontius gets his first glance of God, when the veil is drawn back, he is struck in agony. "Take me away, take me away", he calls out, knowing that he is not yet ready. He needs his final purging, and the last words of the poem are given to the Angel:

ANGEL

> Softly and gently, dearly-ransom'd soul,
>   In my most loving arms I now enfold thee,

And, o'er the penal waters, as they roll,
  I poise thee, and I lower thee, and hold thee.

And carefully I dip thee in the lake,
  And thou, without a sob or resistance,
Dost through the flood thy rapid passage take,
  Sinking deep, deeper, into the dim distance.

Angels, to whom the willing task is given,
  Shall tend, and nurse, and lull thee, as thou liest;
And masses on the earth, and prayers in heaven,
  Shall aid thee at the Throne of the Most Highest.

Farewell, but not for ever! brother dear,
  Be brave and patient on thy bed of sorrow;
Swiftly shall pass thy night of trial here,
  And I will come and wake thee on the morrow.

The Oratory   January 1865[7]

Words are human. They are limited and conditioned, but they are used by God to communicate to us truths that transcend this world and to give us a participation in those truths. The language of Revelation has a sacramental character and office. Dogmas and doctrines are expressions in language of *aspects* of God in his saving work in Christ through his Body, which is the Church. These word pictures and propositions are given to us for our assent. By meditating on them, we gain an insight into them. Our apprehension and assent to them become *real*, and we are challenged, changed, and hallowed in believing.

I was born about a mile from Newman's Oratory. I was educated in the classrooms that he built and where he taught. While I was at school, I learned very little about Newman but a lot about St. Philip. I began to read his works because his name kept being quoted during the preparations for Vatican II. For more than twenty-five years I have been a student of his works, and for the last six years I have taught courses about his theology in Rome to students from all over the world. These are graduate students. They have all done at least two years of philosophy and three years of theology. They have all heard Newman's name, and they know a few labels. A few have a good knowledge of Newman, but for most of them the discovery of what Newman actually taught comes as a surprise, usually a comfortable one. They find his theology nourishes their own faith. In this busy, modern world, Newman offers them an intellectual method of integrity, that by receiving the Revelation of God as it comes to us in history, maintaining its true identity and wholeness as it comes down the centuries, they too become hallowed by it. Newman promoted a *liberal education*, but he was opposed to *liberalism in religion*, a phrase that has a very distinct meaning for him. Many a student has admitted to having been brought back from liberalism by Newman. He also, however, has a profound effect on some of those who are tempted to be "Rambos of orthodoxy", those who would police the Church and who are inclined to a sort of loveless "orthodoxy". Right belief breeds right behavior. Newman explains this and promotes it. I think he also exemplifies it.

NOTES

[1] John Henry Newman, *Autobiographical writings*, ed. Henry Tristram (London and New York, 1956), pp. 254–55.

[2] Ibid., pp. 215–16.

[3] John Henry Newman, *Meditations and Devotions*, in *Prayers, Verses and Devotions* (San Francisco: Ignatius Press, 1989), pp. 328–29.

[4] *The Letters and Diaries of John Henry Newman*, vol. 24, pp. 361–62.

[5] John Henry Newman, *Lectures on Justification* (London: Longman, Green and Co., 1874), pp. 216–17.

[6] John Henry Newman, *Verses on Various Occasions*, in *Prayers, Verses and Devotions* (San Francisco: Ignatius Press, 1989), pp. 693–94.

[7] Ibid., p. 725.

STANLEY L. JAKI

NEWMAN'S ASSENT TO REALITY,
NATURAL AND SUPERNATURAL

On Tuesday, March 15, 1870, Newman's *Essay in Aid of a Grammar of Assent* was published and sold out on that same day.[1] A week later, to Newman's great surprise, there followed a second edition.[2] Still another ten days later a long review of it was carried in the *Spectator* throughout the intellectual and literary world. The reviewer, Richard Holt Hutton, began with a reference to the title as "superfluously modest" and a "deprecation by Dr. Newman of extravagant expectations on behalf of his readers".[3] Pressed by a correspondent about the title, Newman pointed in its defense to the difference between an essay and a grammar. The word "essay" mainly meant an "analytical" probing, which his book was, instead of being a "systematic" work, which any grammar was supposed to be.[4] Another justification he offered was that as it stood, the title "would prepare people for a balk"[5] and diminish thereby the measure of their disappointment.

Whatever the defense of the title, Newman's remark that the book was a "semi-logical fancy" was subtly to the point. In the *Grammar* Newman aimed at unfolding the distinction between mere assertions and assertions that were so many assents, not so much from the logical as from the phenomenological or psychological viewpoint. Not that he put this clearly when, six weeks before its publication, Newman warned Bishop Ullathorne that the *Grammar* was about a "dry logical subject, or semi-logical. Assent".[6] However, insight into the logical peculiarity of assent was, in Newman's own admission, the factor that enabled him to write the book. In his letter of February 21, 1870, to his sister Jemima, he recalled his having been seized, while on vacation in Switzerland, with the meaning of assent: "We went up to Glion, and then suddenly the idea came into my head, which have [*sic*] been a clue to the treatment of my subject; and my first pages stand pretty much as I wrote them in August 1866."[7]

In those first pages of the *Grammar* Newman offers some distinctions, almost pedantic at first sight. He tells his reader that a verbal proposition is either a question, or a conclusion, or an assertion. But then he warns that when we conclude we still argue, but when "we assert we do not argue".[8] In other words, he warns that we must be most logical with words, that we must take them in their pristine meaning, a point that should seem prophetic in this age when respect for meaning is being victimized by advertising, the media, and analytical philosophy. Newman then lists the three mental acts—doubt, inference, and assent—corresponding to those three verbal propositions. The *Grammar*, he states, will deal almost entirely with assent, with inference hardly, and with doubt not at all. Finally he points out the difference between assenting to a notional or abstract proposition and assenting to a concrete fact, especially to one vividly visual. Throughout the *Grammar* Newman lays much emphasis on the primacy of the sense of vision over the other senses. Indeed, from the very start he stresses the superiority of single facts as objects of sight over universal notions, a strategy that has not failed to perplex philosophically sensitive minds.

Another and rather different account given by Newman about the genesis of the *Grammar* is worth recalling for two details in it. One shows Newman's own recurring perplexity: "I felt I had something to say upon it [assent], yet, whenever I attempted, the sight I saw vanished, plunged into a thicket, curled itself up like a hedgehog, or changed colours like a chameleon." The other is the importance that Newman attributes to his having found the right start after so many tries.

Once more he refers to the visit to Glion, where "a thought came into my head as the clue, the 'Open Sesame', of the whole subject, and I at once wrote it down, and I pursued it about the Lake of Lucerne. Then when I came home, I began in earnest, and have slowly got through it."[9]

Newman's references to the *Grammar* as "disappointing",[10] as a "Lenten reading for one's mortification",[11] as a "dry and humdrum" discourse,[12] that would make people ask "what is it all about?"[13] could be disappointing to not a few. Even more so his warning that the book would not be a refutation of rationalism on a grand scale. To be sure, instead of combating Huxley, Tyndall, Lyell, or other chief representatives of the day "or anything necessarily of this day", the book was on a "far more abstract level". But then, almost as if to contradict himself, he added that the book "combats views of friends of my own rather than any popular orthodoxies".[14] As will be seen, those views were quite rationalistic and very much the product of the day.

That in writing the *Grammar* Newman had some friends of his in view was an almost open secret in the circle of his confidants. Few of them knew, however, the long story of the making of the *Grammar*. In that letter to Jemima, already quoted, Newman speaks of a most laborious tunneling process;[15] elsewhere he describes it as a work that, unlike many of his other writings, was a toil for him.[16] He expected its reading as well to be a toil.[17] To a correspondent who read it twice, he wrote: "To have read it once is a real kindness; I take it as a personal one—but it is more than kind to have read it twice." Then he indulged in another superfluously modest self-deprecation: "Of course I can't tell the worth of it myself."[18] Yet, Newman never for a moment doubted the importance of the *Grammar*. He kept telling his correspondents that time will prove the full worth of so laborious a work.[19]

A labor it was, and a labor of love that excels by patient endurance. Newman spoke to Jemima about the half a dozen versions dating back to 1846, 1850, 1853, 1854, and 1865.[20]

Even from 1866 on he rewrote parts of the *Grammar* several times. He spoke of those years as a particularly taxing period in his life. But his resolve to resume the ever heavier task of writing had more to it than the urge to accomplish: "All I know is that I was unhappy till I had done it. I felt it a sort of duty on my conscience."[21] Rarely was conscience invoked in a fuller sense. For, as will be seen, Newman rested the objective truth about assent more on the objectivity he ascribed to the voice of conscience than to the objective truth of the external world. Such an esteem of the voice of conscience called for a heroic measure, both in sensing the magnitude of responsibility and in the resolve to live up to it. Once more the burden assumed proved the truth of his often-quoted words: "I have not sinned against light."[22]

Indeed, he never refrained from taxing himself if he could save a soul. The one who kept saying in later years that he was neither a philosopher nor a theologian was wont to identify himself as a mere "controversialist".[23] Such was a touch of saintly modesty on the part of the shepherd of souls he was. In the entire "General Staff" of the Oxford Movement, he alone engaged in down-to-earth pastoral work. Newman senior, a banker, was shocked on learning that his son, an Oriel don, regularly visited the often-illiterate working-class families of Littlemore. In doing so, Newman pursued the same goal that he did in writing, publishing, and disseminating the Tracts. They were to alert souls to their being called to holiness as the sole reason for the existence of the Church. It was most logical that the *Grammar* should come to a close with an encomium on holiness. Newman presented it as the chief characteristic of the assent given by the first Christian martyrs to the truth, natural as well as supernatural, of the existence of God the Creator but especially the Moral Lawgiver.

Working with simple souls, Newman, great logician as he was, could not help noticing the difference between their vast ignorance of the proofs of the Christian Faith and their firm, unshaken attachment or assent to it. They were never absent from his mind as he struggled in writing the *Grammar*, which in fact is aimed at defending the mass of the faithful against the accusation of fideism. In making this appraisal of the *Grammar*, Fr. Charles Stephen Dessain could have quoted not a few passages from it. Fortunately for those far away from the manuscript treasures of the Birmingham Oratory, he quoted from a draft of the *Grammar* dated January 5, 1860: "Mrs L comes and says, 'I want to be a Catholic.' Her catechist is frightened, for he can find no motivum. . . . A factory girl comes and can only say, 'So and so brought me,' etc. . . . a boy comes and says he wishes to get his sins forgiven."[24]

For all his concern for these simple folk, Newman did not expect them to read the *Grammar*. Its readers were to be above all some of his friends who, the more they had learned about the proofs of Christian Faith, the more they refused to give their assent to them. One of those friends was William Froude (1803–79), a prominent civil engineer, who saw his wife and later his four children, one after the other, become Catholic. For Froude this was a protracted trial, which he bore with great tactfulness. Although everybody expected him to become a Catholic, and countless prayers were said for his conversion, he stuck by his argument that the complete assent implied in Catholic faith presupposed absolutely certain proofs that no theologian could provide.[25] Such was as rationalistic a posture as there could be.

Newman was very much privy to the spiritual drama enveloping the Froudes. For over twenty years he hoped to work out an argument to his own satisfaction to help the conversion of Froude and others trapped in the fallacy of that rationalist argument. The counterargument was to show that absolute assent is given on countless occasions in daily life as well as in general intellectual and moral domains, though absolute proofs are not on hand. Dispensing with "absolute" proofs would but invite a shift toward tactful persuasion. Thus Newman did not send a copy to William Froude, but rather to his son, Edward. "Thank Eddy", he wrote to Froude, "for his letter, for me—and tell him I mean to send him my book—I don't send it to you, lest I should seem controversial."[26]

Still another point, very important for understanding the *Grammar*, is that it may appear a systematic abdication of scholarship. Today, the very first thing expected from a scholar is to serve evidence that he has indeed read everything available on the subject. Newman was resolved not to read anything that others had written on a number of subjects pertaining to the *Grammar*, although, to quote his words, "there has been much written in this day". Newman gave two reasons for this rather unusual policy. One was that he would have been drawn too much into controversies with others to the detriment of clarity. The other was outspokenly personal and personalistic: "My own work would vanish."[27] In the words of the *Grammar*, it was his most personal book, in which he wanted to offer arguments that moved him personally. A consequence of this, again pointed out by him, was that far from being systematic, the *Grammar* contained seemingly unnecessary digressions.[28] He could not, therefore, mean systematic philosophical strength as he listed the *Grammar* as one of his five "constructive" books that do not have a controversy for their chief aim.[29]

A book with many digressions, unnecessary or not, is bound to appear obscure. This is one of the reasons why the *Grammar* has remained Newman's least-read, and hardly ever digested, major work. Half a century after its publication, Father Francis Joseph Bacchus of the Birmingham Oratory, an authority on Newman's thought, felt the need to write an article to facilitate the reading of the *Grammar*. He recalled that there had been some who spoke of it as "one of the most obscure books ever written" and that some "distinguished philosophers" had openly avowed that "they could make nothing of it". Fr. Bacchus admitted that the book was obscure "by its outward appearance" and because "of the eagerness with which its critics fasten upon irrelevant side issues when discussing it".[30]

In trying to dissipate the apparent or real obscurity of

the *Grammar*, Fr. Bacchus urged one to concentrate on the enormous degree of its originality, for which, as he rightly put it, most of its readers were unprepared. This unpreparedness should seem even greater in these times, when more than ever science is viewed as the exclusive source of rational certainty. A much broader and deeper view of certainty was, according to Fr. Bacchus, the *Grammar*'s chief contention as well as originality. Warnings, such as the one by the editor of the *Month*, one of the earliest reviewers of the *Grammar*, that Chapter Seven on certitude holds the book together,[31] may, because of that unpreparedness, remain ineffective in allaying the perplexity caused by the *Grammar*.

Another and very different source of that perplexity is a series of barbs in the *Grammar* at metaphysics that must have given some pleasure to Newman himself. Otherwise Charles Meynell, professor of theology at Oscott College, near Birmingham, who helped in reading the proofs of the *Grammar*, would not have thought of congratulating Newman for having defied the scholastic system of argumentation:

> Since you look at man in the concrete, it is not so much for you to reconcile yourself with metaphysics as for the latter to reconcile itself with you. If metaphysics doesn't account for the concrete man, I say so much the worse for metaphysics! as for the writer who says that *the book* does not follow the scholastic system, I say What is the scholastic *system*? I never heard of it. The ultra-realism of the writer who considers the *ideas* as separate *entities* was not held by *all* the scholastics, nor is it held by the modern Catholic metaphysicians. And Liberatore and the Sacred congregation suspect it.[32]

All this can only whet one's curiosity about Newman's handling in the *Grammar* basic philosophical or epistemological questions, especially that of the universals, the chief target of Meynell's remarks. Newman did not handle the universals with gloves in hand or with much consistency, except for the consistency that whenever he felt himself being carried to the edge of the precipice of unorthodoxy, he resolutely pulled back. If he had the strength to do so, the strength has much less to do with philosophy, or with logic for that matter, than with his quest for holiness, a quest anchored in his enormous sensitivity and faithfulness to the voice of conscience, a principal point in the *Grammar*. But this is to anticipate. Thus the very same Newman who repeatedly and emphatically stated that assent was an intellectual act, that the illative sense (a term that he did not invent but certainly made popular) was an intellectual operation, and that certitude was supremely intellectual,[33] also claimed personal dislike, in fact plain incompetence, for his not giving philosophical answers to essentially philosophical and fundamentally epistemological questions. Thus at the very start of Chapter Nine on illative sense, in a sense the philosophical finale of the *Grammar*, Newman invokes a sort of philosophical agnosticism as he tries to defend the very objective of the *Grammar*:

> My object in the foregoing pages has been, not to form a theory which may account for those phenomena of the intellect of which they treat, viz. those which characterize inference and assent, but to ascertain what is the matter of fact as regards them, that is, when it is that assent is given to propositions which are inferred, and under what circumstances.[34]

In the hands of most present-day phenomenologists, this passage might serve as their endorsement by that very high authority that Newman has become. The phenomenologists in question are, of course, those who forget that the methodical avoidance of ontological and metaphysical questions does not prove the nonexistence of those questions. But those forgetful of the inevitability of metaphysics may derive ample support from Newman's apparent agnosticism as he hints at the impossibility or unfeasibility of epistemology (the genesis of reasoning that gives a hold on the real insofar as it is intelligible) on the ground that even the "acutest minds"[35] could not convince their opponents. Did Newman remember, as he wrote this, that he repeatedly argued in the *Grammar* against those who took widespread disagreement for an impossibility of reaching the truth and with certainty?

In the same context Newman, who certainly opposed those philosophers who admitted only probabilities but no certainties, refused to accept the aid of philosophers who held high the trustworthiness of intellectual certainty about realities, physical and spiritual. He was not impressed by their efforts whereby "in order to vindicate the certainty of our knowledge they make recourse to the hypothesis of intuitions, intellectual forms, and the like, which belong to us by nature, and may be considered to elevate our experience into something more than it is itself". As he distanced himself, firmly and almost contemptuously, from even the good philosophers, Newman made an appeal, most unphilosophical on a first look, to public opinion: "In proof of certainty, it is enough to appeal to the common voice of mankind."[36] An ironical appeal it was and easily to be turned into a boomerang, a point of which Newman could hardly be unaware.

The *Grammar* is a storehouse of evidences not only of Newman's keeping some very good philosophers out of sight but also of his strange choice of philosophical heroes. Not once does he quote Aquinas. His sympathy is not for Aristotle, the master of syllogisms, but for the Aristotle who in the *Nichomachean Ethics* makes much of the personal characteristics of each intellect, according to its aim and profession.[37] In none of the three different occasions when he speaks of Francis Bacon, "our own English philosopher", does Newman note the chinks, very fateful ones, in the intellectual armor of Lord Verulam. He praises Bacon for having inculcated the maxim that "in our inquiries into the laws of the universe, we must sternly destroy all idols of the intellect"[38] but fails to note that Bacon's empiricism could not lead to a single law and much less to the assurance that there is a universe ruled by laws.[39] As he recalls Bacon's separation of mechanical from teleological causes,[40] Newman does not as much as hint about the disastrous consequences of that separation for natural theology, which for Newman very much includes a purposeful Providence, which, philosophically at least, is nonexistent for Bacon.

One wonders whether Locke was ever put on a higher and more undeserved pedestal than the one provided by Newman. Clearly, if Newman had "so high respect both for the character and the ability of Locke, for his manly simplicity of mind and his outspoken candor" and if there was "so much in Locke's remarks upon reasoning and proof with which he [Newman] wholly concurred", then disagreement with Locke on any point could be but painful for Newman. Newman, the great logician, did not seem to perceive anything of the chain that made one particular point (very fateful in Newman's eyes) a logical consequence of Locke's basic presuppositions. Newman merely deplored Locke's "slovenly thinking" for not seeing a contradiction between two claims of his. One was that it was not only illogical but also "immoral to carry our *assent* above the *evidence* that a proposition is true" or to have a "surplusage of *assurance beyond* the degree of evidence". The other was that some first principles, though only most probable, were to be allowed "to govern our thoughts as absolutely as the most evident demonstration".[41]

Yet Newman did not probe into either of two most pertinent aspects of the inconsistency that Locke espoused. One aspect related to the very root of that inconsistency, the other to its moral. There was more to that inconsistency than, as Newman put it, Locke's *animus*, or resolve to form men or human thinking "as he thinks they ought to be formed, instead of interrogating human nature as it is".[42] To give a glimpse, however brief, of the root of that inconsistency, would have been rather easy, as Locke himself plainly stated and prominent admirers, such as Voltaire, loudly repeated that he wanted to chart the human mind in the light of Newton's physics.[43]

Newman's failure to probe this point was all the more surprising because, both in the *Grammar* and many years beforehand in a still not sufficiently appreciated writing of his, Newman spoke prophetically of the limitations of the quantitative method.[44] There he decried the fashionable infatuation with that method as a cultural curse and as the chief mental obstacle to the recognition of spiritual and ethical realities. But he would not on that score inculpate Locke in the *Grammar*, although Locke was most instrumental in spreading Newtonianism as the only sound form of philosophy.[45] There the quantitative method ruled supreme, with the consequence that complete certainty in any formal assent was legitimate only if a mathematical proof was on hand—the very opposite to Newman's chief contention in the *Grammar* that on that basis human life would be both impracticable and unthinkable. Would it not have been most logical to exploit Locke's inconsistency as a striking evidence of the traps opened up by mechanistic philosophy taken for reasoning? In fact, it would have been most philosophical, but this was the very posture Newman was not too eager to take in the *Grammar*.

Newman's disagreement on a particular point with Bishop Butler, his third favorite British philosopher, is equally revealing, though in a positive sense. In speaking about the range of illative sense, a particular aspect of prudent judgment, Newman considers among various objections to its validity in matters religious the rationalist Thomas Paine's claim that if there is a divine revelation, it should be as clear "as if it were written in the sun". The claim, Newman noted, appeals to common sense through an assumption that Butler would not admit because it is unphilosophical. The assumption is part of that probabilism with respect to the real that follows from Locke's seeking in philosophy full certainty in terms of quantitative or Newtonian exactness. While Newman here parts ways with Butler, he does not see that above all he is parting with Locke as he turns the tables on Paine and does so by endorsing "philosophical cogency". The Visible Church, Newman says, "was at least to her children the light of the world, as conspicuous as the sun in the heavens". Newman was willing to admit at most that "owing to the miserable deeds of the fifteenth and sixteenth centuries", some clouds may have come over the sun, yet he would not allow that "the Church fails in this manifestation of the truth any more than in former times". While the countenance of the Church, Newman continues, "may have lost something in her appeal to the imagination, she has gained in philosophical cogency".[46]

Rarely in the history of philosophy did a great mind speak so emphatically of "philosophical cogency" and speak with so little conceptual cogency about its very foundation. The foundation, here as in many other cases, is the question of universals. The answer to that question controls whatever generalization is offered about the real as universal truth. This point is forcefully brought home in our times by the reluctant awakening of Darwinists to the fact that all talk about species, genera, classes, phyla, and kingdoms is talk about universals before it becomes scientific talk. Another modern aspect of the fateful presence of universals relates to the impossibility of talking rationally about such ethical problems as abortion and euthanasia, without coming to terms with the reality of human nature as a universal. Much less can certitude be claimed about universal truth (Newman's chief task in the *Grammar*), without setting forth the truth about the universals.

To be sure, Newman holds high universal truth throughout the *Grammar*, and especially in that pivotal chapter on certitude: "Truth cannot change; what is once truth is always truth."[47] In the section on complex assent leading to the chapter on certitude, Newman defines certitude as "the perception of a truth with the perception that it is a truth".[48] Newman is defending the universality of truth when he distinguishes it from the "conclusiveness of a proposition".[49] Even when he extols probability as the practical guide in life and reasoning, he takes pains to point out that "probability does presuppose the existence of truths which are certain".[50] He has no patience with the claim that "truth need not be universal".[51]

Yet, the "universals", without which there can be no consistent discourse about universal truths, fare badly in the *Grammar*. Newman does not refer to the word itself, as he states that comparing and classifying things are among the "most prominent of our intellectual faculties". There he also states that those functions act "instinctively" and "spontaneously", even before we set about apprehending "that man is like man, yet unlike; and unlike a horse, a tree, a mountain, or a monument, yet in some, though not the same respects, like each of them". Without having studied Thomas' doctrine on universals and the analogy of being, Newman almost articulates them. Yet almost in the same breath he almost undercuts his insights. By being reduced to the class *man*, he states, the individual man is "made the logarithm of his true self, and in that shape is worked with the ease and satisfaction of logarithms".[52]

The remark is a descriptive marvel and a philosophical near-disaster. Well in advance of their times logical positivists received in that remark a devastating portrayal, but at the same time neo-Thomists too were dealt a great injustice. In the latter respect the only saving grace was Newman's admission about his remark as being a "harsh metaphor". For when Newman explicitly speaks of universals, he comes very close to denying any real content in them. "There is no such a thing as a stereotyped humanity", he declares.[53] He has little use for general man, which he calls the *auto-anthropos*. For him universals are wholly subservient to individual things: "Let units come first, and (so-called) universals second; let universals minister to units, not units be sacrificed to universals." A middle road could not seem important to the one who declared, "What we aim at is truth in the concrete."[54]

Newman was taken up so much with the concrete, tangible facts as to create time and again the momentary impression of being a latter-day follower of Ockham, if not a replica of Mister Gradgrind teaching but facts and nothing but facts. "Experience", Newman declares, "tells us only of individual things."[55] He ties belief "to things concrete".[56] His stated preference is "to go by facts", not by abstract reasoning.[57] The weak point of logic is, according to him, that "it does not give us to know even one individual being".[58] Newman's world is a "world of facts, and we use them; for there is nothing else to use".[59] On a cursory look it is a world of empiricism that beckons, not surprisingly, also in the *Apologia*, which Newman wrote by putting aside momentarily the writing of the *Grammar*. The latter comes to a close with an apotheosis of Roman Catholic religion as not so much a religion of notions as a religion of facts, and for this reason the only true religion. Even less than in the *Grammar* is that insistence on facts as pregnant with universal truths put by Newman in the *Apologia* into a coherent philosophical proposition.

Resolute insistence on facts may have immediate advantages. Thus in dealing with Gibbon's famous "five causes" of whole-sale conversions to Christianity in late imperial Rome, Newman certainly scores with his question: "Would it not have been worth while for him [Gibbon] to have let conjecture alone, and to have looked for facts instead?"[60] Yet, how would Newman have countered the objection that the lopsided imbalance be-tween his praises of facts (individual things) and plain suspicion about universals makes him a mere conceptualist? Did he realize that conceptualism failed to prevent Protestant thought from being fragmented and caught in subjectivism? Was it not the very fragmentation and subjectivism that he tried to over-come first by reading Catholicism into the Thirty-nine Articles? Did he not recognize that the *Via Media* was a mere system on paper, precisely because it was ultimately an exercise in con-ceptualism? Would he not have protested from all his heart the claim that in espousing Roman Catholicism, he did not espouse a universally valid reality?

As the author of the *Grammar*, Newman would have been entitled to offer two answers. Although philosophically neither could be satisfactory, both could be forceful to the point of dissipating any doubt about his orthodoxy, philosophical and theological, and could cut short any future attempt (by modernists, neomodernists, and phenomenologists) to misconstrue his true position. One of his answers would have been his pointing out some forceful statements in the *Grammar*, though, if I may say so, they amount to a series of rescue operations. Time and again, when he seems to commit himself to mere empirical facts, he reasserts, and in a matter-of-fact way, the validity of objective truths transcending those facts. The most telling of such cases occurs when he insists on the personal conditions that decide whether a proposition is assented to or not. But he immediately balances his act by asking, as if to prevent any misreading of his train of thought: "Shall we say that there is no such thing as truth and error?"[61]

All those personal features, color as they might one's assent to a proposition, are subordinated to the truth of the proposition: "Assent is the acceptance of truth and truth is the proper object of the intellect."[62] Newman had no use for the principle of universal doubt, perceiving as he did its contradictory character. He held, and did so most reflectively, that the starting point in reasoning was a plain surrender to the obvious, an assent "to the truth of things, and to the mind's certitude of that truth". Ultimately there was no other criterion for recognizing truth in the real as that sense that was primarily a good or common sense rather than scientific. Behind that position of his there lay a most considered stance: "I owe I do not see any way to go further than this."[63]

A particular aspect of that sense was that illative sense that Newman defined as a judgment of prudence in which he saw a preeminently personal characteristic. Whenever he noted that the illative sense opened the door to subjectivism, he right away shut that door: "Duties change, but truths never."[64] The recognition that "the rule of conduct for one man is not always the rule for another" did not prevent him from stating in the same breath: "The rule is always one and the same in the abstract and in its principle and scope."[65] Again, the fact that "men differ so widely from each other in religion and moral perceptions" does not prove, he warns, "that there is no objective truth".[66]

Newman could, in addition, refer to more than one place in the *Grammar* where the human mind is celebrated as made for truth, objective truth, that is. Of course, he knew that the human mind was not infallible. But if its errors were not to land one in a wholesale doubt about reasoning, one had to have the highest esteem for the mind's structure pivoted on truth: "It is absurd to break up the whole structure of our knowledge, which is the glory of the human intellect, because the intellect is not infallible in its conclusions."[67] This passage is from the section "Indefectibility of Certitude", where he anchors that indefectibility not in some intangible subjective disposition but in objective truth insofar as the human mind has an intrinsic affinity for it:

> Now truth cannot change; what is once truth is always truth; and the human mind is made for truth, and so rests in truth, as it cannot rest in falsehood. . . . It is of great importance then to show . . . that the intellect, which is made for truth, can attain truth, and, having attained it, can keep it, can recognize it, and preserve the recognition.[68]

Newman must have been thinking of that passage when, after Leo XIII redirected, with the *Aeterni Patris*, Catholic philosophers to the doctrine of Aquinas, he has asked about an eventual Thomistic scrutiny of his ideas: "I have no suspicion, and do not anticipate [any suspicion] that I shall be found in substance to disagree with St. Thomas."[69]

Newman certainly opposed doctrines irreconcilable with basic Thomistic positions. Newman's thinking is poles apart from Kantianism, and even from that Aquikantianism that is transcendental Thomism, as shown by his flat declaration: "By means of sense we gain knowledge directly."[70] The Kantian principle whereby the mind's categories create reality is contradicted by Newman's statement: "We reason in order to enlarge our knowledge of matters, which do not depend on us for being what they are."[71] His most devastating anti-Kantian declaration is in a note that he attached from one of his early Catholic sermons to the *Grammar* ten years after its first publication. In that sermon Newman urges that assent to natural and supernatural truths or realities (which may appear sheer mysteries to rigid logicians) is based on the same, we would say today, epistemological considerations. Without ever having read Kant's *Critique*, Newman hit its very core by his emphatic declaration: "When once the mind is broken in, as it must be, to the belief of Power above it, when once it understands that it is not itself the measure of all things in heaven and earth, it will have little difficulty in going forward."[72] Newman rejects mind as the measure of all things not only because he has the moral sensitivity about a fallen human nature but also because of his readiness to assent to natural reality and truth as given independently of man.

Since Newman did not have Kant in mind, why did he make statements so forcefully anti-Kantian? The answer is simple. In philosophy in general, and epistemology in particular, the basic options are few. Actually, there are only two fundamental alternatives. In one the starting point is the objective thing, in the other the subjective ego. By casting his lot with the former, Newman inevitably had to censure the latter. This is why one finds in the *Grammar* gemlike phrases that cast a devastating light on such latter-day intellectual preoccupations as artificial intelligence, the subconscious, logicism, and the information explosion.

When Newman denounces the claim that "whatever can be thought can be adequately expressed in words",[73] a basic assumption of artificial intelligence is denounced in advance. The same is true when Newman asserts that the acts of man's intellectual growth are "mental acts, not the formulas and contrivances of language",[74] or when he notes that we arrive at our most important conclusions not by "a scientific necessity independent of ourselves, but by the action of our own minds, by our own individual perception of the truth in question, under a sense of duty to those conclusions and with an intellectual consciousness".[75] In fact, Newman sees intellectual activity in such a nonmechanical perspective (of which the "sense of duty to conclusions" operative in any assent is a graphic reminder) as to endorse what in our times has become spoken of as "tacit knowledge". He does so as he notes that in performing acts of the illative sense, the mind often perceives the connection of data with first principles "without the use of words, by a process which cannot be analyzed".[76] But this absence of explicit analysis did not mean a general falling back on the subconscious. On assent that comes unconsciously, Newman states, "I have not insisted, as it has not come in my way; nor is it more than an accident of acts of assent, though an ordinary accident."[77]

Great logician as Newman was, he did not miss an opportunity to put logic in its place. If logical positivists had an advance antagonist, it was Newman. Close as was the connection between assent and logical conclusions, it was not more than the one "between the variation of the mercury and our sensation; but the mercury is not the cause of life and health, nor is verbal argumentation the principle of inward belief. If we feel hot or chilly, no one will convince us to the contrary by insisting that the glass is at 60. It is the mind that reasons and assents, not a diagram on paper." Then he points out the rank inconsistency of a "class of writers" who keep acting on many a truth as do their unsophisticated neighbors while pretending "to weigh out and measure" truths and warning them that "since the full etiquette of logical requirements has not been satisfied, we must believe those truths at our own peril".[78] It is not certain whether he meant by that "class" the followers of J. S. Mill or of Whateley, but his strictures certainly apply to the claims and behavior of logical positivists.

Present-day academics, fond of dissecting and wary of assenting, are aptly described in Newman's reference to the claim of some in the academies of Greece of old who claimed that "happiness lay not in finding the truth, but in seeking it". Their abdication of finding the truth was as much an evasion of the duty to assent to truth as the claim, fashionable among modern academics, that all intellectual pursuit is a mere game. Newman grants that in matters that do not "concern us very much, clever arguments and rival ones have the attraction of a game of chance or skill, whether or not they lead to any definite conclusion".[79] But in matters of grave human concerns the claim, Newman argued, was as hollow as the alleged happiness of Sisyphus.

Taking all intellectual pursuit for a mere game, as an excuse for dispensing with assent, had in part to do, according to Newman, with what is called today the information explosion: "The whole world is brought to our doors every morning, and our judgement is required upon social concerns, books, persons, parties, creeds, national acts, political principles and measures. We have to form our opinion, make our profession, take side on a hundred matters on which we have but little right to speak at all."[80] Such is a prophetic anticipation of our educational and public situation. There any and all are continually invited to offer their opinionated judgments as if they were so many assents. The result is the general feeling that assents can be readily reversed, the very point that Newman held to be impossible.

The very fact that Newman was writing the *Grammar* when he took out ten feverish weeks to write the *Apologia* may in itself suggest that the *Grammar* too was autobiographical, in a sense of being very personal. The *Grammar* contains Newman's most personalist philosophical statements. He spoke of a sentiment that came over him habitually "about egotism as true modesty" as he turned to discussing inference and assent in the matter of religion, natural and supernatural: "In religious inquiry each of us can speak only for himself, and for himself he has a right to speak." Of course, here, too, he immediately went to the rescue of objective truth. The individual "knows what has satisfied and satisfies himself; if it satisfies him, it is likely to satisfy others; if, as he believes and is sure, it is true, it will approve itself to others also, for there is but one truth."[81]

Precious and all important as are Newman's almost instinctive moves to safeguard objectivity and the universal
validity of truth, those moves were never systematic. The
Grammar is as much more than a treatise as concrete life is far
more than a book. Books come and go, and their arguments
will forever be controverted. Such a perennial pattern would
least surprise the one who once spoke about the "wild living
intellect of man".[82] The phrase is from the concluding part of
the *Apologia*, which has so much in common with the theme of
the *Grammar*, namely, that religion is not about notions but
about facts. No fact commanded Newman's assent more than
the fact of what he called "the giant evil", or original sin.[83] A
chief evidence of it was, in Newman's eyes, the cacophony of
the human scene. To reconcile it with the evidence of God ("*if*
there be a God, *since* there is a God"), one had no choice but to
assent that "the human race is implicated in some terrible
aboriginal calamity. It is out of joint with the purposes of its
Creator. This is a fact, a fact as true as the fact of its existence;
and thus the doctrine of what is theologically called original sin
becomes to me almost as certain as that the world exists, and as
the existence of God."[84]

In the *Grammar* the last argument on behalf of the supernatural origin of Christian religion is that "it has with it that
gift of stanching and healing the one deep wound of human
nature, which avails more for its success than a full encyclopedia
of scientific knowledge and a whole library of controversy,
and therefore it must last while human nature lasts. It is a living
truth that never grows old."[85] Newman would find exceedingly
illogical the present-day emphasis on the Church's healing
power, which underemphasizes to a shocking degree the
existence of that deep wound. This is certainly true about the
intellectual part of that wound, the result of man's desire to
become, through knowing, like God. In trying to rise above
everything, man becomes bewildered by the variety of things,
all of which clamor for assent but to none of which is the fallen
man able to give it with certitude.

Certitude, in this fallen state, was therefore for Newman more than a question of epistemology. It was a question of healing grace, which could not operate except in an ambience that constantly reverberated with the call: "Your whole nature must be re-born, your passions, and your affections, and your aims, and your conscience, and your will, must all be bathed in a new element, and reconsecrated to your Maker, and, the last not the least, your intellect."[86] The call was the call of that Church that alone, among all churches, showed similarity with the Church of the Apostles and of the Fathers. This is why Newman became a Catholic. Once a Catholic and a priest, he saw closely other priests and found two things about them. One was their unaffected outspoken manners. The other was that they had certitude about all mysteries of the Creed, and that certitude was never a burden for them. Sharp-sighted an intellect as he was, Newman would even today spot the large number of priests, perhaps not in this or that particular country but on a global scale, who still exude certitude and feel none unhealthier for it. He would also easily note the obvious, or the certitude carried all over the world by the occupant of that chair that he once apotheosized as "cathedra sempiterna".[87]

He would spot that obvious partly because his perception was eminently visual. Although an excellent violinist, he celebrated the sense of sight throughout the *Grammar*. Its thirty or so analyses of particular cases of assent are so many graphic portrayals of psychological processes true to life. Above all he paints his own mental portrait, and therein lies the lasting instructiveness of the *Grammar*. The picture shows him as a great mind even in the ordinary sense. One of the first reviews of the *Grammar*, the one in the *Spectator*, a prominent and widely read British weekly, came to a close with a homage to that greatness: "The work of a really great man may fairly be allowed, for some time at least, to speak for itself, before smaller men begin to praise or censure."[88]

Most of those who praised the *Grammar*, let alone those who censured it, failed to see his real greatness and the reason why the *Grammar* was to remain a great book. For the culture, national and ecclesiastic, into which Newman was born and which educated him and which he hoped to restore to its ideal vigor, was vigorous only in producing opinions that could not encourage assent. Most of those who labored with Newman in the Oxford Movement were unable to assent to the truth of that fatal symptom. Thus by the time Newman set forth in twelve public lectures, delivered in London in 1850, his penetrating diagnosis of the national church,[89] it was clear that his hopes for a mass conversion among the intelligentsia were unrealistic. Men of unquestionably vigorous intellect and of more than average good will refused to follow him and his few dedicated associates on the path to Rome. They bemoaned Newman's conversion as the error of an overzealous conscience, without pondering the nature of their own "zeal".

Others not so close to him, such as the undergraduates who listened in awe to his university sermons in which several themes of the *Grammar* had been anticipated, conveniently forgot his message in the measure in which they became part of the establishment. That the lay as well as clerical factors of that establishment kept undermining, however unwittingly at times, genuine Christianity had become crystal clear to Newman by the time he finished the *Development*. But he, the *Apologia* is the witness, had to go through many shadows and free himself of many illusory images, such as the *Via Media*, before he could see the light. His chief accomplishment was that he could state with no touch of boasting that on that arduous quest for light he never sinned against the Light, or the voice of God speaking through man's conscience. The epitaph—*ex umbris et imaginibus ad veritatem*—he wrote for himself could just as well be a reminder of his spiritual odyssey. Little of this was seen by the established order, which, steeped as it was in Locke's "common sense", had eyes only for opinions, however opinionated, but not for real assent even in worldly matters. Much less had it eyes for that assent that is to be given to the most challenging aspect of human existence, the voice of conscience speaking continually of matters otherworldly and eternal.

Newman's sensitivity to that voice was so great as to put him on the path to sainthood from his late teens on. On that path all signposts—actual and historical, personal and social—were reminders of a God who, if he is truly God, has to reveal above all his holiness to sinful man. Hence Newman's search for that Church in which the standards of revealed holiness have always been held high, whatever the failures of those whose duty is to proclaim those standards. If he said that the Fathers made him a Catholic, it was only because he had eyes for the holiness of the Fathers.[90]

Newman's relentless quest for personal holiness is the explanation of the fact that in articulating his epistemology or grammar of assent he keeps going back to the reality of the voice of conscience. He would have been trapped in subjectivism had he centered on the voice itself and not on the objective moral content of that voice. No wonder that he always finds his way to the external objective world and even to that witness of that world which sustains the cosmological argument.[91] Though not particularly fond of it, he would have been the last to deny its validity. Yet for all his readiness to go to the objective external reality and to endorse, at least in principle, all that is implied in its knowledge, he failed to the end to see clearly the epistemological nature of that road.

Yet how close he could be to seeing the obvious. A passage in his *Philosophical Notebooks* has it in a nutshell. There he argues that the sense of consciousness is not immediate but "external" to his sensing it. From his hypothetical opponent, who sees in his insistence on consciousness a straight road into utter scepticism or solipsism, Newman asks but one concession: "You must allow *something*—and all I ask you to allow is *this*—that it is true that *I am*—or that my consciousness that I am represents the fact external to my consciousness (viz) of my existence. Now see what is involved in this one assumption. Viz My consciousness."[92] Taken up so much with his consciousness, Newman could not see that he was mistaken in using the word "external" in the context. He was entitled to no more than to use the word "different". Most importantly, he did not see the obvious. The very fact of arguing with an opponent provided him with the external world as an indispensable condition for arguing at all, an act securing him the external objective world and with it the only safe basis for working out one's philosophy.

This is not to suggest that Newman necessarily would have found that philosophy had he been born a Catholic. But philosophical clarity, which has never been a permanently widespread commodity even within the Church, may seem simply nonexistent in non-Catholic Christian ambiences. No less extraordinary should therefore seem the fact that he kept adhering to that clarity even though little enlightenment could come to him from inside that Church, which was still to be reawakened to the teaching of Thomas Aquinas. A chief instructiveness of the *Grammar* may therefore lie in the disproportionality between Newman's philosophical resources and his philosophical achievement. The point was already made in far more graphic terms, which Newman, so keen on graphic portrayals, would have no doubt greatly cherished. There he is described as "the genius who, following the gleam, cut his way through the undergrowth of a jungle where the weaker Pusey, with perhaps equal piety and goodwill, remained lost *in umbris*". His intellectual odyssey, which is inseparable from his spiritual quest to find the proper place and object for a final and supreme assent, remains indeed "one of the most palpitating dramas in the history of the human soul. It tugs at the heart-strings like that of Augustine, and is surely not less beautiful because there is nowhere in the early background any trace of those aberrations which are so frankly revealed in the *Confession*."[93]

What remains to be done is to sketch briefly the bearing of all this for the intellectual aspects of our own ecclesiastical times. Seeing it with Newman's eyes, the first thing to be noted is the status of the Church of England. Today he would be immensely saddened, though not surprised, on seeing that church go not so much the way of all flesh but all the way of the flesh. He would see in the performance of the latest Lambeth conference on homosexuality and polygamy an illustration of a principal contention of the *Grammar*: Breaking with an assent is a proof that the assent has never been truly present. He would point out that it was for the same reason that the same church could not see that its own male ordinations lost the last shred of credibility when the ordination of its females was not seen above all as a question of validity.[94] Newman could certainly see the intimate connection between dissent from truth relating to sacramental ontology and dissent from truth relating to morals or holiness.

After that Newman would direct his gaze to the Catholic Church. He would again be saddened, though not surprised, that assent to truth has been all too often replaced by disputes about inferences in order to justify dissent. As the author of the *Grammar* he would engage in passionate controversy with many priests, theologians, nuns, and laymen. He would show them that they have destroyed the faith of much of an entire generation of Catholics. He would show them that by withholding their assent to the teaching of the Church, they incapacitated themselves for the task of eliciting in their youthful charges that assent that is the backbone of faith. He would show them that their game with assent was a result of their unwillingness to give assent to the fact that there is sin in the strict spiritual sense, the very fact that, as he insisted in the *Grammar*, is the basis of natural as well as of revealed religion.

On one point he would cross swords with the world at large, just as he did when the moral integrity of the Catholic clergy was called in doubt. He would not mind that just as in the secularist court he lost his case, he would lose again today in the kangaroo courts of the media. He would be satisfied for making it clear that Catholics cannot obtain justice in the supreme courts of publicity. The darlings of those courts are those Catholic clergymen and religious (if they still have religion) who use his personalistic philosophy of assent as their noblest excuse for refusing their assent to legitimate Church authority. He would challenge them to appear with him in the Court of Conscience, which he rightly held high as the ultimate and supreme forum, provided it was not a mere fancy, whim, and social fashion. There he would ask them whether it was not he who wrote in connection with the See of Peter that even when it speaks outside its special province and errs, "it still has in all cases a claim to our obedience".[95]

That Newman has become a battleground and possibly the great intellectual battleground within the Church shows more than anything else his greatness. Just as in Arian times, when both orthodox and unorthodox parties tried to secure the vote of Anthony, *the* saint of the day, so today both parties try to claim Newman to themselves. It seems that the unorthodox Catholic and the non-Catholic parties have better perceived the monumentality of his vote. Newman was still to become a cardinal when Gladstone, a chief Anglican opponent of his in the disputes about infallibility, admitted the monumentality of Newman's assent to it. "In my opinion," Gladstone wrote in 1876, "his secession from the Church of England has never yet been estimated among us at anything like the full measure of its calamitous importance. It has been said that the world does not know its greatest men; neither, I will add, is it aware of the power and weight carried by the words and by the acts of those among its greatest men it does know."[96]

Today, on the eve of the centenary of Newman's death, his fellow Roman Catholics still have to go a long way toward realizing the magnitude of the gain they may derive from his assent to reality, natural and supernatural. The longer they go along that way, the better prepared they will be to play a constructive role in the great contestation between the prince of lies and the angel of Truth. Newman's account about that contestation, or about the coming of the Antichrist, was prophetic because he, as did any true prophet, gave his full assent to his God-given role to explain and help implement assent to Truth.

NOTES

¹ As stated in the entry for that day in Newman's diary. See *Letters and Diaries*, vol. XXV, p. 54.

² To Mrs. Mozley (Jemima Newman), Mar. 21, 1870, ibid., p. 59.

³ "Dr. Newman's *Grammar of Assent*", *The Spectator*, Apr. 2, 1870, p. 436.

⁴ To Canon J. Walker, Apr. 8, 1870: "You see I called it an Essay, as it really is, because it is an analytical inquiry—a Grammar ought to be synthetical." *Letters and Diaries*, vol. XXV, p. 84.

⁵ To Jemima, Feb. 21, 1870, ibid., p. 35.

⁶ To Bishop Ullathorne, Jan. 28, 1870, ibid., p. 19.

⁷ To Jemima, Feb. 21, 1870, ibid., p. 35.

⁸ See pp. 25–31 in the Image Book (Garden City, N.Y.: Doubleday, 1955) edition of *An Essay in Aid of a Grammar of Assent*, which, in addition to being its most widely available edition, also has the extra feature of a penetrating introduction by Etienne Gilson.

⁹ To Aubrey de Vere, Aug. 31, 1870, *Letters and Diaries*, vol. XXV, p. 199.

¹⁰ Ibid., pp. 24, 35, 43, 46.

¹¹ Ibid., pp. 38 and 39.

¹² Ibid.

¹³ To Jemima, Feb. 21, 1870, ibid., p. 36.

¹⁴ To Canon Walker, Jan. 25, 1870, ibid., p. 14, and also to Bishop Ullathorne, Jan. 28, 1870, ibid., p. 19.

¹⁵ Ibid., p. 35.

¹⁶ Ibid., pp. 10 and 12.

¹⁷ Ibid., p. 65.

¹⁸ To Sir Frederic Rogers, June 30, 1870, ibid., p. 155.

¹⁹ Ibid., pp. 160 and 279.

²⁰ Ibid., p. 35. Newman gives elsewhere (p. 155) the years "1846, 1847, 1850, 1853, etc."

²¹ Ibid., p. 155.

²² In the context of his first reminiscences on his almost fatal sickness in Sicily. See *Letters and Correspondence of John Henry Newman during His Life in the English Church*, ed. A. Mozley (London: Longman, Green and Co., 1890), vol. I, pp. 365–66.

²³ *Letters and Diaries*, vol. XXV, p. 100.

²⁴ Quoted from a draft (Jan. 5, 1860) of the *Grammar* by C. S. Dessain, *John Henry Newman* (new ed.; Oxford University Press, 1980), pp. 152–53.

²⁵ See P. Flanagan, *Newman, Faith and the Believer* (London: Sands, 1946), pp. 92–95. Froude's argument was called "equationism" by F. R. Ward in his

review of the *Grammar* in *The Dublin Review* (17 [April 1871], p. 255), of which he was the editor.

²⁶ To W. Froude, Jan. 31, 1870, *Letters and Diaries*, vol. XXV, p. 22.

²⁷ Ibid., p. 36.

²⁸ *Grammar*, p. 172.

²⁹ *Letters and Diaries*, vol. XXV, p. 11. He refers to them as 2 Protestant and 3 Catholic. In another letter (ibid., p. 35) he begins describing them with the *Grammar* as "the hardest, though all have been hard—my Prophetical Office [*Via Media*], which has come to pieces—my Essay on Justification, which stands up pretty well—and three Catholic—Development of doctrine—University Education, and the last which I have called an Essay in aid of a Grammar of Assent".

³⁰ F. J. Bacchus, "How to Read the Grammar of Assent", *The Month* 1 (1924), p. 106.

³¹ *The Month*, 1 (1870), p. 360.

³² May 24, 1870, *Letters and Diaries*, vol. XXV, p. 39.

³³ *Grammar*, p. 86.

³⁴ Ibid., p. 270.

³⁵ Ibid.

³⁶ Ibid.

³⁷ Of the eight references in the *Grammar* to Aristotle, four deal with the shortcomings of syllogisms and four with the *Nichomachean Ethics*. It is among the latter that one finds Newman endorsing Aristotle as "my master" (p. 335).

³⁸ Ibid., p. 275.

³⁹ On fatal defects in Bacon's philosophy with respect to natural science, see chap. IV, "Empirical Scouting", in my Gifford Lectures, *The Road of Science and the Ways to God* (Chicago: University of Chicago Press, 1978).

⁴⁰ Actually, Newman speaks of Bacon's separation "of the physical system of the world from the theological" (*Grammar*, p. 282), which is a signal misunderstanding on Newman's part of Bacon's rejection of the "teleological".

⁴¹ See *Grammar*, pp. 137–39. The quote is from Locke's *Essay on Development of Doctrine*, chap. VII. Later (p. 251) Newman remarks that Locke "does not tell us what these propositions are".

⁴² *Grammar*, p. 139.

⁴³ For details on both Locke and Voltaire, see chap. 6, "The Role of Physics in Psychology", in my *The Absolute beneath the Relative and Other Essays* (Lanham, Md.: University Press of America and Intercollegiate Studies Institute, 1988).

⁴⁴ The importance that Newman attached to that writing, "The Tamworth Reading Room", a long critique addressed to the editor of the *Times* apropos a speech by Sir Robert Peel at the dedication of a public library in Tamworth in early 1841, can be seen from Newman's quoting from it at length in the *Grammar* (pp. 88–92).

[45] A fact all the more ironical as Locke had to gain assurance from Huygens that the *Principia* contained not only good mathematics but also reliable physics.

[46] *Grammar*, p. 295.

[47] Ibid., p. 181.

[48] Ibid., p. 162.

[49] Ibid., p. 158.

[50] Ibid., p. 192.

[51] Ibid., p. 196.

[52] Ibid., pp. 44–45. Whereas some of the first Catholic reviewers, Fr. Harper, S.J., in particular, expressed deep concern about Newman's cavalier treatment of the universals, little trace of such concern is found in the studies of the *Grammar* written recently by Catholics who cannot be suspected of anti-Thomist preferences. That Newman was inconsistent on the problem is set forth in some detail by Dr. Zeno, the Dutch Capuchin Newmanist, in his *John Henry Newman: Our Way to Certitude: An Introduction to Newman's Psychological Discovery: The Illative Sense and His Grammar of Assent* (Leiden: E. J. Brill, 1957), pp. 63–75. The problem, which Dr. Zeno calls "Newman's inconsistency", is passed over by E. J. Sillem in his long study preceding his edition of *John H. Newman: The Philosophical Notebook* (New York: Humanities Press, 1969) and is not discussed by I. T. Ker in his long introduction to his meticulous critical edition of the *Grammar* (Oxford: Clarendon Press, 1985).

[53] *Grammar*, p. 224.

[54] Ibid., p. 223.

[55] Ibid., p. 44.

[56] Ibid., p. 87.

[57] Ibid., p. 136.

[58] Ibid., p. 226.

[59] Ibid., p. 272. Such and similar emphases put by Newman on objective truth found no echo in N. Lash's introduction, which disgraces the edition of the *Grammar* by the University of Notre Dame Press (1979). Lash sees in Newman's thinking an anticipation of T. S. Kuhn's evaluation of all intellectual process as a series of paradigm shifts without noting its irrationalist character. The latter point was made in my Gifford Lectures, *The Road of Science and the Ways to God* (Chicago: University of Chicago Press, 1978; 3rd paperback edition, 1986), and subsequently by the professedly nonreligionist D. Stone, of the University of Sydney, in his *Popper and after: Four Modern Irrationalists* (Oxford: Pergamon Press, 1982), where Kuhn is described as a greater threat to rationality than Popper, Lakatos, and Feyerabend!

[60] *Grammar*, p. 358.

[61] Ibid., p. 247.

[62] Ibid., p. 145.

[63] Ibid., p. 271.

[64] Ibid., p. 278.

[65] Ibid., p. 279.

[66] Ibid., p. 293.

[67] Ibid., p. 187.

[68] Ibid., p. 181.

[69] In a letter of Dec. 10, 1878, to Fr. R. Whitty, S.J., *Letters and Diaries*, vol. XXVIII, p. 421. Fr. Whitty's reply of Jan. 19, 1879 (ibid.), to a subsequent letter of Newman is expressive of Newman's concern for philosophical orthodoxy and also prophetic in view of the great popularity of transcendental Thomism among Fr. Whitty's latter-day confreres: "My own impression I confess was just what you mention—that the Pope having himself been brought up in the Society's teaching—knowing that some of our Professors in Italy and France were leaving St. Thomas in certain points of *Philosophy*, and feeling that these were important points against the errors of the day—had expressed a wish that our teaching should return to the old lines."

[70] *Grammar*, p. 210.

[71] Ibid., p. 222.

[72] Ibid., p. 385. Newman considered this so characteristic of his thinking that he gave in italics part of the remainder of the quote, which is from his sermon "Mysteries on Nature and Grace", where he argued the epistemologically most pivotal point that "belief in God and belief in His Church stand on the same kind of foundation". See *Discourses Addressed to Mixed Congregations* (London: Longman, Green and Co., 1902), p. 260.

[73] *Grammar*, p. 212.

[74] Ibid., p. 275.

[75] Ibid., p. 252.

[76] Ibid., p. 282.

[77] Ibid., p. 157.

[78] Ibid., p. 151.

[79] Ibid., p. 171.

[80] Ibid., p. 191.

[81] Ibid., p. 300.

[82] *Apologia pro Vita Sua* (Image Book; Garden City, N.Y.: Doubleday, 1956), p. 322.

[83] Ibid., p. 326.

[84] Ibid., p. 320.

[85] *Grammar*, p. 376.

[86] *Apologia*, p. 325.

[87] He did so as Rector of the Catholic University of Ireland. The address is reprinted here as an Appendix for two reasons. One is the rarity of his posthumously published *My Campaign in Ireland. Part I. Catholic University Reports and Other Papers* (printed for private circulation only by A. King & Co., Printers to the University, Aberdeen, 1896) in which it first appeared (pp. 211–14).

The other reason relates to the striking anticipation in it of the substance and tone of his sermon, "The Pope and the Revolution" (*Sermons Preached on Various Occasions* [3rd ed.; London: Burns & Oates, 1870], pp. 263–98), preached on the feast of the Rosary, Oct. 7, 1866. Systematic oversight of this sermon, although easily available, by "liberals" is, of course, understandable as it casts in proper light Newman, who at that time was just beginning his theologically mistaken foot-dragging about the advisability of the definition of papal infallibility (see on this my paper "Newman's Logic and the Logic of the Papacy", *Faith and Reason* 13 [1987], pp. 241–65). Far from being a quasirationalist sowing the seeds of disloyalty in the guise of specious distinctions, he was, as the sermon shows, consumed with a burning loyalty for the person sitting in the chair of Peter. It is doubtful that any Ultramontane has ever stated as touchingly as Newman did in that sermon that we Catholics have the duty "to look at his [the Pope's] formal deeds, and to follow him whither he goes, and never to desert him, however we may be tried, but to defend him at all hazards, and against all comers, as a son would a father, and as a wife a husband, knowing that his cause is the cause of God" (p. 269). The sermon also gives a priceless glimpse of the depth of Newman's Marian devotion, and in particular of his love for the Rosary. About the latter Father Neville, the Oratorian who was most closely associated with Newman during his last years, recalled "his ready reply to a condolence on his loss of the power to say it [the Breviary] being, that the Rosary more than made up for it; that the Rosary was to him the most beautiful of all devotions and that it contained all in itself. . . . From far back, in the long distance of time, memory brings him forward, when not engaged in writing or reading, as most frequently having the Rosary in his hand." Quoted in W. Ward, *The Life of John Henry Cardinal Newman* (London: Longman, Green and Co., 1912), vol. II, p. 533.

[88] *The Spectator*, Apr. 2, 1870, p. 439.

[89] Those twelve lectures constitute volume I of *Certain Difficulties Felt by Anglicans in Catholic Teaching* (London: Longman, Green and Co., 1891). If Newman felt any dislike in writing those lectures it was merely because he did not wish to waste any more time on the Church of England and not because, as often alleged, that he did not fully agree with the devastating thrust of the portrayal there of the Church of England as a mere by-product of political and nationalistic, that is, essentially naturalist, aspirations. Newman would be pained but not surprised by the compromise that the Lambeth Conference of Aug. 1988 adopted on polygamy. He would merely note the preservation of type, which he held high in the *Development*, as evidenced by the courage of John Paul II, who fearlessly denounced polygamy a month later in the presence of an African head of state with four official wives, in addition to some unofficial ones.

[90] In Newman's reply to Pusey's *Eirenicon* in *Certain Difficulties*, vol. II, p. 24.

[91] See *Grammar*, p. 68.

[92] Entry dated Feb. 9, 1860, in *The Philosophical Notebooks of John Henry Newman*, vol. II, p. 78. Tellingly, the context is Newman's reflections on his reading the *Historical Development of Speculative Philosophy from Kant to Hegel* by H. M. Chalybäus, professor of philosophy at the University of Kiel (trans. A. Edersheim; Edinburgh: T. T. Clark, 1854). Half of the pages of Newman's copy of Meiklejohn's translation of Kant's *Critique* were left uncut! See ibid., vol. I, p. 229. The reason behind this was that, as Newman put it, "I do not think I am bound to read them [the German idealists] in spite of what Chalybäus says, for notoriously they have come to no conclusion" (ibid.).

[93] J. Gannon, S.J., "Newman and Metaphysics", *The Irish Ecclesiastical Record* 69 (1947), p. 386. This article, possibly the best on the *Grammar* and on the various problems raised by Newman's philosophy, came to my knowledge only after this paper's conclusion was reached. There is no reference to it in the works of Flanagan and Sillem, or in the editions of the *Grammar* quoted above.

[94] A position of the Archbishop of Canterbury himself. See *The Times*, Aug. 2, 1988, p. 18, col. 8.

[95] *An Essay on the Development of Christian Doctrine* (Image Book; Garden City, N.Y.: Doubleday, 1960), p. 104. Newman is quoted six times in defense of dissent from *Humanae vitae* in *Dissent in and for the Church: Theologians: Theologians and Humanae vitae* by C. E. Curran et al. (New York: Sheed & Ward, 1969). Of the four letters to the editor, published in the Sunday, Sept. 14, 1986, issue of the *New York Times* in connection with the Vatican's declaration that Fr. Curran was no longer a Catholic theologian, two were in support of the Vatican. The writers of the two other letters buttressed their support of Fr. Curran with reference to Newman! A detailed study of the exploitation of Newman by advocates of dissent would pay well the effort.

[96] Quoted from G. B. Smith, *The Life of the Right Honorable William Ewart Gladstone* (New York: G. P. Putnam, 1880), p. 499. Gladstone's words seem to have made no impression on Prof. Owen Chadwick's interpretation of Newman, a chief in his eyes among Roman Catholic modernists and, therefore, an Anglican *malgré lui*.

APPENDIX

John Henry Newman

"CATHEDRA SEMPITERNA"

Deeply do I feel, ever will I protest, for I can appeal to the ample testimony of history to bear me out, that, in questions of right and wrong, there is nothing really strong in the whole world, nothing decisive and operative, but the voice of him, to whom have been committed the keys of the kingdom and the oversight of Christ's flock. The voice of Peter is now, as it ever has been, a real authority, infallible when it teaches, prosperous when it commands, ever taking the lead wisely and distinctly in its own province, adding certainty to what is probable, and persuasion to what is certain. Before it speaks, the most saintly may mistake; and after it has spoken, the most gifted must obey.

Peter is no recluse, no abstracted student, no dreamer about the past, no doter upon the dead and gone, no projector of the visionary. Peter for eighteen hundred years has lived in the world; he has seen all fortunes, he has encountered all adversaries, he has shaped himself for all emergencies. If there ever was a power on earth who had an eye for the times, who has confined himself to the practicable, and has been happy in his anticipations, whose words have been deeds, and whose commands prophecies, such is he in the history of ages, who

No collection of essays on Newman can have a greater décor than an appropriate selection from his writings. In addition to the reasons listed in note 87 (pp. 218–19) above, it is reprinted here as best conveying the thrust of these essays.

sits from generation to generation in the Chair of the Apostles, as the Vicar of Christ and Doctor of His Church.

It was said by an old philosopher, who declined to reply to an emperor's arguments, "It is not safe controverting with the master of twenty legions". What Augustus had in the temporal order, that, and much more, has Peter in the spiritual. When was he ever unequal to the occasion? When has he not risen with the crisis? What dangers have ever daunted him? What sophistry foiled him? What uncertainties misled him? When did ever any power go to war with Peter, material or moral, civilized or savage, and got the better? When did the whole world ever band together against him solitary, and not find him too many for it?

All who take part with Peter are on the winning side. The Apostle of Christ says not in order to unsay; for he has inherited that word which is with power. From the first he has looked through the wide world, of which he has the burden; and according to the need of the day, and the inspirations of his Lord, he has set himself, now to one thing, now to another, but to all in season and to nothing in vain. He came first upon an age of refinement and luxury like our own; and in spite of the persecutor, fertile in the resources of his cruelty, he soon gathered, out of all classes of society, the slave, the soldier, the high-born lady, and the sophist, to form a people for his Master's honour. The savage hordes came down in torrents from the north, hideous even to look upon; and Peter went out with holy water and with benison, and by his very eye he sobered them and backed them in full career. They turned aside and flooded the whole earth, but only to be more surely civilized by him, and to be made ten times more his children even than the older populations they had overwhelmed. Lawless kings arose, sagacious as the Roman, passionate as the Hun, yet in him they found their match, and were shattered, and he lived on. The gates of the earth were opened to the east and west, and men poured out to take possession; and he and his went with them, swept along by zeal and charity, as far as they by enterprise, covetousness, or ambition. Has he failed in his enterprises up to this hour? Did he, in our fathers' day, fail in his struggle with Joseph of Germany and his confederates—with Napoleon, a greater name, and his dependent kings—that, though in another kind of fight, he should fail in ours? What grey hairs are on the head of Judah, whose youth is renewed as the eagle's, whose feet are like the feet of harts, and underneath the Everlasting Arms?

"Thus saith the Lord that created thee, O Jacob, and formed thee, O Israel. Fear not, for I have redeemed thee, and called thee by thy name! Thou art Mine.

"When thou shalt pass through the waters, I will be with thee, and the rivers shall not cover thee.

"When thou shalt walk in the fire, thou shalt not be burned, and the flame shall not kindle against thee.

"For I am the Lord thy God, the Holy One of Israel, thy Saviour.

"Fear not, for I am with thee, I am the first, and I am the last, and besides me there is no God."

* * *

It is not altogether irrelevant to mention here that in January, 1856, Dr. Newman, having occasion to go to Rome on business of very great anxiety, he at once, on alighting from the diligence, went with Father St. John to make a visit of devotion to the shrine of St. Peter, going there the whole way barefoot. The time was the middle of the day, when, as was the case in those years, the streets were very empty, and thus, and screened by his large Roman cloak, he was able to do so unrecognized and unnoticed—nor was it ever known except to Father St. John and another.[1]

His friend Dr. Clifford (the Hon. William J. H. Clifford, late Bishop of Clifton), who with his father Lord Clifford, had travelled with him from Siena, and with whom he dined that day in Rome, knew nothing of this until it was mentioned to him on occasion of his preaching the Cardinal's funeral sermon in 1890.

NOTES

[1] Fr. William P. Neville, his future literary executor, as noted in M. Trevor, *Newman. Light in Winter* (London: Macmillan, 1962), p. 103 (S.L.J.).

INDEX